MODERN DRAMA AND THE
RHETORIC OF THEATER

MODERN DRAMA AND THE RHETORIC OF THEATER

W. B. Worthen

University of California Press
Berkeley · Los Angeles · Oxford

University of California Press
Berkeley and Los Angeles, California

University of California Press, Ltd.
Oxford, England

© 1992 by
The Regents of the University of California

Library of Congress Cataloging-in-Publication Data

Worthen, William B., 1955–
    Modern drama and the rhetoric
of theater / W. B. Worthen.
    p. cm.
    Includes bibliographical references and index.
    ISBN 0-520-07468-8 (cloth)
    1. English drama—20th century—History and
criticism. 2. American drama—20th century—History
and criticism. 3. Theater—Production and direction—
History—20th century. I. Title.
PR736.W64   1992
822'.9109—dc20   91-17677
                                                                  CIP

Printed in the United States of America
9 8 7 6 5 4 3 2 1

The paper used in this publication meets the minimum
requirements of American National Standard for
Information Sciences—Permanence of Paper for Printed
Library Materials, ANSI Z39.48-1984. ∞

*To Denise,
   for the Sabine and the Rio Grande,
   and the life between and beyond them*

Contents

Acknowledgments	ix
Introduction	1

1. Theater and the Scene of Vision — 12
   - Chekhov's Camera: The Rhetoric of Stage Realism — 12
   - Invisible Women: Problem Drama, 1890–1920 — 29

2. Actors and Objects — 54
   - Invisible Actors: O'Neill, the Method, and the Masks of "Character" — 54
   - Visible Scenes: American Realism and the Absent Audience — 70
   - Empty Spaces and the Power of Privacy: Pinter, Shepard, and Bond — 81

3. Scripted Bodies: Poetic Theater — 99
   - Poetic Theater and the Work of Acting — 99
   - The Discipline of Speech: Yeats's Dance Drama — 108
   - The Discipline of Performance: *The Dance of Death* and *Murder in the Cathedral* — 119
   - The Discipline of the Text: Beckett's Theater — 131

4. Political Theater: Staging the Spectator 143
   Transforming the Field of Theater 143
   Breaking the Frame of History: *Hitler Dances* and
      The Churchill Play 158
   History and the Frame of Genre:
      Laughter! and *Poppy* 169
   Framing Gender: *Cloud Nine* and
      Fefu and Her Friends 181

Postscript   Sidi's Image: Theater and the
   Frame of Culture 194
Works Cited 205
Index 221

Acknowledgments

I have been at work on this book for some time, and am happy to have the chance to record my gratitude to the many friends and colleagues who offered help along the way. My sincere thanks to Enoch Brater, Oscar G. Brockett, Stanton B. Garner, Jr., Corinne Jacker, Joan Lidoff, Theresa Kelley, Josephine Lee, Martin Meisel, Gail Kern Paster, Thomas Postlewait, Carol Rosen, and W. O. S. Sutherland for their support, encouragement, advice, and wisdom. Jonathan Freedman and the mountains of Vermont deserve a special word of thanks for so often clearing my mind. I am also grateful to students and colleagues at the Bread Loaf School of English and to my students at Columbia and at Texas for sharpening my thinking about drama and theater. Doris Kretschmer of the University of California Press has shown undue patience with my many concerns, and I am indebted to her, to Pamela MacFarland and Ellen Stein, and to the Press's readers for their attention and care. Audiences at Allegheny College, California State University at Northridge, Columbia University, Duke University, Louisiana State University, the University of Michigan, and Northwestern University graciously allowed me to try out some of these ideas on them. Finally, I could not have written this book without the conversation, confidence, and love of my wife, Denise Sechelski.

I am pleased to thank the John Simon Guggenheim Memorial Foundation for funding the leave of absence that enabled me to complete this work, and the University of Texas Research Institute and the National Endowment for the Humanities for the grants that helped to get it started.

Portions of the third chapter are included in "*Murder in the Cathedral* and the Work of Acting," in *T. S. Eliot: Man and Poet*, ed. Laura Cowan (National Poetry Foundation, 1990); the sections on Yeats are adapted from "The Discipline of the Theatrical Sense: *At the Hawk's Well* and the Rhetoric of the Stage," *Modern Drama* 30 (1987):

90–103, copyright © the University of Toronto. Parts of chapter 4 were adapted from "*Poppy* and the Rhetoric of Political Theater," *Genre* 19 (1986): 173–91, copyright © the University of Oklahoma; and from "*Still playing games:* Ideology and Performance in the Theater of Maria Irene Fornes," in *Feminine Focus: The New Women Playwrights*, ed. Enoch Brater (Oxford University Press, 1989), copyright © Oxford University Press. My thanks to these publishers for granting permission to adapt work I had originally published with them.

Introduction

> It is the spectator, and not life, that art really mirrors.
> —Oscar Wilde, *The Picture of Dorian Gray*

This is a book about modern British and American drama, the sense of theatricality it demands, and the audience it both reflects and creates. Indeed, the burden of the argument here is really *about* this audience, about how modern drama and theater work to frame the audience's experience and to characterize its interpretive activities *as* an audience—to cast the spectators, so to speak, as part of the spectacle.

In the pages that follow I argue that the meanings of modern drama cannot be fully seized without considering how those meanings are produced as theater. For in the theater, drama can speak only through the practices of acting and directing, the construction of the material space of the mise-en-scène, and the arrangement and disposition of the audience. We often think of these activities as free and unconstrained, as based on the unique insights of the theater's practitioners. In practice, though, the theater's ways of producing texts on the stage tend to be highly formal; despite the range of personal "choice" that appears in any production, such choices emerge within the theater's systematic ways of putting the drama into play. Not only are these practices specific to a given moment in history, they also have a manifestly *rhetorical* dimension. The theater works to claim a certain kind of meaning for the drama by claiming—even legitimating—a certain kind of experience for the audience as significant. The rhetoric of theater, that is, frames a relationship between the drama, stage production, and audience interpretation, and it is within that relationship that our experience as an audience takes place.

The rhetoric of theater should be grasped not in terms of a specific production, a given corpus of dramatic texts, or even features of theatrical style, but as what Kenneth Burke calls "a general *body of identifications*" (*Rhetoric* 26).[1] The rhetoric of theater is not present in the dramatic action, nor in individual stage productions, but defines the intersection between the text and the institutions that make it producible—and so, readable—in the practices of the stage. Let me take stage acting as an example of how we might think about this rhetoric. Stage acting relies on a variety of techniques embedded in theatrical training and performance for asserting a fictive character, ways of identifying the dramatic role and its actions *as* a character through a range of specifically theatrical behaviors; this is what we generally call acting *style*.[2] Style in this sense is not just an inert body of vocal and gestural conventions. Instead, style embraces the entire network of disciplines that make acting meaningful in the theater: conventions of movement, bodily carriage, gesture, vocal intonation, facial inflection, language, costuming, and so on. The actor performs an actual, physical activity onstage that signals the fictive actions of a "character." The rhetoric of acting intervenes as the complex of attitudes, assumptions, and habits of interpretation that makes this particular kind of assertion possible, and that invites the audience to read these two behaviors in certain kinds of ways.[3] David Garrick, Henry Irving, and Laurence Olivier each invoked a different behavioral rhetoric, stage

1. Burke's influence on studies of modern drama is well known, and is particularly keen in the work of States and of Donoghue. More recently, Bruce A. McConachie has amplified Burke's connection to stage performance, arguing that in theatrical performance, "Burke's range of identifications includes all the primary means playwrights, directors, designers, and actors use to involve and persuade their audiences of the legitimacy of certain kinds of actions" (46). In this exemplary reading of Burke, McConachie reduces the "hegemonic we" that such rhetoric tries to produce to an identification with or against the actions performed by a given character or characters in the drama, sharply limiting the kinds of identifying processes that we can conceive as part of the theater's rhetoric.
2. For a fine discussion of the relationship between the discipline of the body and theatrical interpretation, see Roach, "Power's Body."
3. Anne Ubersfeld describes the relation between the dramatic fiction and the material reality of the theater in *L'école du spectateur*: the actor "intervient dans la fiction et en ce sens, il réfère à un ailleurs, à une absence"; yet at the same time, "il se livre, sur la scène et devant nous, à une activité concrète en présence d'autres êtres humains, activité qui est de l'ordre de la performance. Ces deux activités sont liées sans qu'on puisse les confondre" (167).

acting that not only conveyed markedly different ideas of action, character, and meaning, but also required different acts of attention from their audiences. Training and technique provide the performer with a paradigm both for interpreting the role (discovering how it is "actable") and for representing it as theater. The rhetoric of acting frames our reading of the actor's performance, and so the kind of "character" we can discover there.

The rhetorical character of acting is relatively plain to see—more plain, certainly, than the activities of the audience. Much of this book will work to expose the similar rhetoricity of *our* performance in the modern theater, to ask how the audience's material and ideological positioning by theatrical performance inflects its interpretive behavior, its ways of seeing the fictions of the drama onstage. The modern theater's history of innovation is directly concerned with producing a certain kind of experience for the audience, and so with producing the audience itself. As Austin E. Quigley suggests, this history describes a movement "away from a nineteenth-century tradition that gave priority to entertaining and instructing audiences" and toward "a modern tradition"

> that gives priority to offering audience members the opportunity to participate in a particular mode of social inquiry. Such participation requires audience members to respond to the challenge of reconsidering their role as audience as a first step in reconsidering the nature of the theatre and the nature of the larger worlds in which they and it participate. (52–53)

Quigley's impressive reading of the interpretive and epistemological horizons offered and subverted by the modern drama, like fine recent studies by Thomas R. Whitaker and Benjamin Bennett, reflects an increasing interest in seeing the audience's performance as part of the meaning of drama.[4] The spectator emerges as a partici-

---

4. See Whitaker, *Fields of Play in Modern Drama*, and Bennett, *Modern Drama and German Classicism* and *Theater as Problem: Modern Drama and Its Place in Literature*. By suggesting that these studies—the most searching studies of modern drama in the past two decades—take a somewhat metaphorical or ideal perspective on theatrical production, I may seem to cavil with work that has done much to spur and inform my reading of modern theatricality, and to which I am in various ways gratefully indebted. I should also note here a more general indebtedness to Bert O. States, *Great Reckonings in Little Rooms*; to the relationship between dramatic action and

pant in a variety of ways, though, and how the spectator's mode of inquiry is channeled depends in large measure on the rhetoric of stage production. Anne Ubersfeld remarks that the spectator is "le sujet d'un *faire,* l'artisan d'un pratique qui s'articule perpétuellement avec les pratiques scéniques" (*L'école* 303). Much as actors represent "characters," individuals are transformed into "spectators" through a specifically theatrical making and doing. Their affective and interpretive behavior is shaped not only by the drama but by the machinery of theatrical representation working on the drama and on them.

Thematic readings of the spectator are corrected to some extent by more symbolic inquiries into the theoretical status of an audience (such as Herbert Blau's luminous study, *The Audience*), and by phenomenological readings of stage production, like Bert O. States's *Great Reckonings in Little Rooms.* The spectator also figures prominently in theater semiotics, which tries to to locate the spectator's perception as a response to the theater's verbal and nonverbal "languages." The rigor implied by the quasi-linguistic methods of theater semiotics has proven elusive, in part because the analogy between stage signification and the working of language is only that—a rich, provocative analogy. The promise of theater semiotics has foundered on the fact that the theater's meanings arise in a congeries of signifying formalities that is too multiplex, indeterminate, and unsystematic in its "lexicon," "grammar," and "syntax" to be readily reduced to the model provided by verbal language.[5] Yet theater semiotics alerts us to an important truth about meaning in the theater: meaning arises not through a given production's direct reference to an external world, but through the production's assertion of a set of available signifiers from the field of stylistic possibilities. Even when a production's style most claims its likeness to life, it is marked by its difference from other stylistic resources that might have been used. In this limited sense, the various rhetorical modes of modern theatrical production function like signs. The meaning of

---

stage activity developed by Bernard Beckerman, *Dynamics of Drama;* and to Michael Goldman's presentation of acting in *The Actor's Freedom.* See also John Peter's discussion of open and closed theatricality in *Vladimir's Carrot.*

5. For a shrewd reading of theater semiotics, see Bennett, *Theater as Problem* 9–13.

a given ensemble of practices and effects is discerned not by reference to the world it represents, but by its difference from other ensembles, other rhetorical modes.

Of course, thematic, symbolic, phenomenological, and semiotic approaches to the audience's share in dramatic performance have charted many of the problems I want to raise here, and I have frequently incorporated their insights in the argument that follows. In considering the theater as a rhetorical arena, however, I attempt to avoid these ways of describing the audience in favor of asking how the theater produces and qualifies the position(s) the audience comes to occupy. Drama in production defines and legitimates a certain range of interpretive behavior and experience as the role the audience performs—this is what I take to be the rhetoric of theater. This book examines some of the rhetorical practices that stage the modern drama in the modern theater and in its audience. I address three ways of organizing the relationship between the drama, its staging, and the audience it creates, which I call the rhetoric of realism, the rhetoric of poetic theater, and the rhetoric of political theater. This taxonomy is not meant to be exhaustive, but to help map three critical modes of theatrical production in the twentieth century, and three modes of audience engagement as well. Each mode locates the meaning of theater in relation to a different aspect of theatrical signification. The rhetoric of realism frames dramatic meaning as a function of the integrated stage *scene*; poetic theater uses the poet's text, the *word*, to determine the contours of the spectacle and the experience of the audience; and contemporary political theater works to dramatize the theatrical subjection of the *spectator* as a part of its political action.

As a performance rhetoric, modern theatrical realism embraces several dramatic genres—experimental naturalism, modern realism, expressionism, the theater of the absurd—that stage the text within its rhetorical priorities: a proscenium stage, often implying a box set; a fourth wall discriminating between stage and audience; objects that both constitute and express character and action; the necessary erasure of the activities of production from the realm of the audience's legitimate interpretation. The rhetoric of realism opposes the visible and integrated scene onstage to the invisible, indeterminable, absent scene of the spectator's interpretation. As Teddy puts it in Harold Pinter's *The Homecoming*, "It's a way of being able to look at the world. It's a question of how far you can operate on things and not in things" (61). The rhetoric of realistic theater ascribes particular qualities, forms of action, and kinds of power to the visible stage and to the invisible audience. This rhetoric, I argue, relates offstage observation to staged activity, naturalizing the behavioral and social stratifications of bourgeois society and transforming them into the relations of "objectivity" that characterize its theatrical style. In the first chapter, "Theater and the Scene of Vision," I describe the origin of this rhetoric in the theory of stage and literary naturalism and suggest how naturalism appropriated the technology of the nineteenth-century theater and gave it a sustaining ideological coherence. I then turn to an important dramatic form at the turn of the century—problem drama, particularly the "fallen woman" play. This drama phrases class and gender problems as problems of visibility. The means (acting/spectating) and the relations (onstage/offstage) of realistic theatricality become, in these plays, the instruments of social control, explicitly duplicating and clarifying the work they perform in the theater itself.

In the second chapter, "Actors and Objects," I redefine the realistic drama's thematic focus on character and environment in terms of stage production, as a function of the relationship between acting and objects on the stage. The formal experimentation of modern drama is often traced by the rhetoric of realism it attempts to displace, and by considering the stage's construction of actors and objects, we can see that the more material the stage becomes, the more consistently it assigns explanatory power to mystified and indecipherable causes: to the romantic interiority of "character" developed by acting in the Stanislavski/Method mode, and to the private freedom of the spectator's consciousness, observing from the offstage environs of the auditorium. The apparent differences between expressionism and documentary realism—between Eugene O'Neill's masked plays and Elmer Rice's *Adding Machine*, on the one hand, and *Street Scene*, *Dead End*, and *Long Day's Journey Into Night*, on the other—turn out to be *only* apparent. By training our attention on acting and objects, I also suggest that the more elusive rhetoric of Pinter and Sam Shepard never really outflanks the priorities of realism or the problematic authority of its offstage spectator. I conclude by considering how Edward Bond's *Saved* provides a kind of alternative; its frustrating and aggressive violence is threatening precisely because it is not readable from the privileged vantage of realism's invisible voyeur.

Poetic theater is usually described in terms of its drama. To see the drama of "poetic drama," though, the text must be seen to direct a theatrical rhetoric as well as a verbal order: as urging the staging of the *word* (rather than the *scene* of realism) as the point of the dramatic event and of the spectators' interpretation. Poetic theater may now seem rather moribund, the toy of an effete and elitist theater, and so it often was. However, in chapter 3, "Scripted Bodies: Poetic Theater," I argue that the poetic theater undertakes a specifically theatrical investigation of the relationship between the text and its staging. The poetic theater examines the provisional authority of the verbal text in relation to the productive practices of the stage, and it has specific affiliations not only with the more vividly "theatrical" experiments of Vsevolod Meyerhold or Antonin Artaud but also with the postmodern textualization of stage space in the spectacles of Robert Wilson, Richard Foreman, and others. W. B. Yeats, W. H. Auden, and T. S. Eliot all worked to devise a radically innovative form of theater by asking how the text might be distributed among the various discourses of stage production. This rhetoric also places the spectator's performance in a different relation to the drama, and to the world beyond it. To escape the disquieting absence of the realistic theater, the spectator in poetic theater accepts a different kind of discipline, the more public discipline devised by the text. Yet, as Yeats and Eliot recognized, this submission to the text's authority can be dehumanizing. For in poetic theater the authority of the text can require the exhaustion, the evacuation, of the performers, both actors and audiences, an implication that reaches its final extreme in Samuel Beckett's theater.

Bertolt Brecht understood that political theater works to dramatize (rather than to conceal) the spectator's performance. Yet Brecht's assimilation and repudiation by the British and American theater in the postwar era often provides the strategy for marginalizing "political theater" on the contemporary stage. In chapter 4, "Political Theater: Staging the Spectator," I describe Brecht's refiguration of the absent spectator of realism and the efforts of the contemporary theater to render the ideological contours of the audience's performance an explicit, self-conscious part of the play. The rhetoric of political theater, that is, explores how our production as spectators can be made to resonate with the dramatic action and with a wider social critique. The contemporary theater stages the spectator in a variety of ways, of which I have chosen three as exemplary: as the subject of history in the plays of Howard Brenton; as an effect of theatrical and social genres in the plays of John Osborne, Peter Barnes, and Peter Nichols; and as a gendered participant in the theater of Caryl Churchill and Maria Irene Fornes. I conclude by setting the rhetoric of European theater itself in a critical context, using Wole Soyinka's *The Lion and the Jewel* to draw out some of the consequences of how we produce ourselves as spectators in the world.

Any argument of this kind will seem to some readers to leave out more than it includes, and I am sympathetic with those who may find the division of modern drama into three rhetorical modes artificial, and the plays used to ramify them idiosyncratic. Other plays might illustrate the rhetoric of modern theater in somewhat different terms, and in practice the rhetorical options I present as distinct usually emerge in blended or hybrid combinations. Here, I have tried to suggest their permeability mainly through the selection of examples: Elizabeth Robins and Edward Bond (usually associated with political theater) are discussed in relation to stage realism, as a way of troubling our sense of its powerful rhetoric, much as Beckett complicates the sense of poetic theater, and Fornes places a political stage in the house of realism. More significant objections might be raised to the Anglo-Irish-American focus of the discussion and to my bias toward scripted drama, which tends to discount more imagistic or nonverbal forms of theater, to bypass film and television, and to overemphasize the innovations of playwrights at the expense of the work of directors. My sense that the rhetoric of theater is deeply implicated in its immediate culture has led me to avoid treating the familiar figures of the European theater at any great length, and the important impact of African, Asian, and Latin American theater as well. This cast of plays from England, Ireland, and the United States points, at a relatively high level of generalization, to a common theatrical and cultural situation, circumscribed here in order to reveal some features of its rhetoric. This selection does tend to homogenize rhetorical and political differences within and without this geographical, linguistic, and dramatic grouping, and I hope at a later date to address some of the differences that I have been able only to point to here.

Of course, film and video have decisively altered our sense of drama and of what is distinctive about modern theater. It might even be argued that the identity of modern stage drama now depends on its shifting or permeable generic boundaries with film and television (see Bennett, *Theater* 255), as well as with other theatrical forms—opera, performance art, improvisational and participatory theater. The rhetoric of these modes of theater is quite different from that of the dramatic stage, though, in large part because they do not claim to reproduce a dramatic text *as* theater. Improvisational theater, for example, discovers the "text" it produces in the performance itself. The libretto of opera, far from governing the production, is shaped by the requirements of the score, which determines many of the features we usually think of as dramatic—the voicing, pace, intensity, and dynamic range of the performance. That is, the drama of opera is framed at least as much by the rhetoric of musical production as by the performative aspects it shares with the dramatic theater.

Film seems to consume its dramatic script, to reproduce it as a unique object rather than as a rhetorical interpretation. Perhaps because it is not live, because the audience is subject not to the charismatic effects of the performance but to the scope of the camera's eye, the rhetoricity of film seems more readily apparent to us. Recent film theory has developed powerful ways of reading film's production of a "spectator," but the apparatus of film production—both the making of films and the milieu of the cinema—differs strikingly from the machinery of the stage. Film subjects its audience through the instrument of the camera, while the rhetoric of theater uses the fiction of the drama to structure an immediate relationship between live individuals, actual deeds, and a material environment. The modern theater depends on various and diffuse practices—including acting and dramatic style, the mise-en-scène, the arrangement of the audience—for staging dramatic texts, practices that have been so readily naturalized to our sense of theater-in-general that their rhetoricity can be difficult to see; *Modern Drama and the Rhetoric of Theater* concentrates fairly exclusively on bringing some features of that rhetoric to light.

Finally, to some extent, the work of directors and companies—

Peter Brook, William Gaskill, Alan Schneider, the Actors Studio, Mabou Mines, Portable Theatre, Monstrous Regiment—is treated selectively or only implicitly here. Theatrical practice intrudes throughout this discussion, though, because the buildings, stages, actors, directors, and audiences that have realized the modern drama in performance form the critical instruments of the rhetoric I want to describe. Rather than underlining the unique genius of the theater's practitioners, my aim in these pages is to ask how their work reveals a common rhetoric of possibility, one that is evoked and often contested in the action of the drama. As a way of lending my abstract or "merely" theoretical account of that rhetoric some ballast, a variety of voices speak here, voices not only of critics and scholars but of journalists, theater reviewers, directors, actors, and playwrights. These voices speak in their own accents, and to their own public, but they can tell us about the work of theater at a given moment in its history, and about its goals, its assumptions, its audiences, its rhetoric. The voices of the theater suffuse the discussion as a way of making the history of this rhetoric palpable, thick.[6]

The rhetoric of realism, of poetic theater, of political theater: these three terms are put forward for their heuristic value, to allow us to isolate aspects of the rhetoric of modern theatricality which in practice are always mixed and intermingled—in a given playwright's, actor's, or director's work, in the course of a single production, and in many of the plays I have chosen for illustration. *Modern Drama and the Rhetoric of Theater* offers neither a history of modern drama nor a thematic reading of major playwrights, though it does concern the development of dramatic and theatrical forms since the turn of the century. As Walter Benjamin commented about another performance medium, "The manner in which human sense perception is organized, the medium in which it is accomplished, is determined not only by nature but by histori-

---

6. For a similar reason, I have not considered the production of the classics on the modern stage. Were I to do so, I would argue that despite our efforts to recover "authentic" period staging practices—an Elizabethan theatricality for staging Shakespearean drama, for instance—those styles would necessarily be informed by our own sense of what meaningful action looks like onstage. Although our sense of the modern open stage owes something to the recovery of Elizabethan stagecraft, any modern production will, I think, inevitably be inflected by the rhetoric of Stanislavski, of Beckett, and of Brecht.

cal circumstances as well" (222). The forms of theatrical production that I discuss here might well work differently at other times, in other places; a friend once told me that when he saw Rice's *Street Scene* in Buenos Aires in the 1970s, the air was charged with the excitement and apprehension of a subversive political event— which is exactly what it was.[7] The scene of modern drama is a rhetorical arena in which texts are staged as theater, and in which individuals are cast as spectators. This book outlines some of the strategies that have made this drama, framed our modes of perception, experience, and activity as spectators in the theater, and so shape the ways we discover the drama, and ourselves, in the discourse of the stage.

7. My thanks to William Hallman for relaying this anecdote.

1

Theater and the Scene of Vision

CHEKHOV'S CAMERA: THE RHETORIC OF STAGE REALISM

Let me recall a brief, brilliant scene from Chekhov's *Three Sisters*. Toward the end of the first act, the Prozorovs and their guests retire from the downstage drawing room to the partly concealed reception room upstage, to celebrate Irina's name-day. Natasha arrives, nervously checks herself in the mirror, and rushes to join the party. The forestage is empty, when two of the omnipresent junior officers suddenly appear. Taking out a camera—still a novelty at the turn of the century—they pose and silence the party, taking one photograph and then another. It is a striking moment. Taking a picture syncopates the action and highlights the stylistic transparency of Chekhov's drama. As the characters withdraw upstage, the play becomes lifelike by becoming random, oblique, untheatrical; the photograph stops the action, fixing it as an image for a second or two in the blue halo of the flash. Bernard Shaw remarked that "drama is no mere setting up of the camera to nature" (Preface 197), and Chekhov's camera both asserts the verisimilitude of his drama and denaturalizes it, exposing that "reality" as a rhetorical effect of the realistic stage.[1]

The history of stage realism is often told as a narrative of technical mastery, in which playwrights from Henrik Ibsen to David Storey find their theatrical expression through the practical innova-

---

1. Hand-held Kodak cameras were, of course, available in Europe at the turn of the century, though their use in the home, and their appearance on the stage, would still have excited comment. Beaumont Newhall's description of Édouard Vuillard's use of the camera to photograph gatherings in his home is suggestive of the scene in *Three Sisters*. A "folding Kodak camera was a fixture in his house, and during social gatherings he liked to put it casually on a piece of furniture, point it at his guests, and ask them to hold still while he made short time exposures." See Newhall 136.

tions of great directors: André Antoine, Constantin Stanislavski, Harley Granville Barker, Elia Kazan, Lindsay Anderson, and so on. This parable presents theatrical change as an evolution in engineering, with playwrights, technicians, and directors collaborating to render the world on stage with increasing fidelity and precision. And yet, as Chekhov points out, stage verisimilitude is an effect of where we sit to receive it. The camera—something of a cliché for realism even in Chekhov's day—can only halt and distort the "life" it would reproduce. Chekhov's camera implies that the effect of the "real" arises not from mimetic fidelity but in our relation to the apparatus that discloses it. The effect of the "real" is something that we produce both before us and within ourselves, a world and an interpretation of it, a reading based, as Émile Zola—that novelist, playwright, and amateur photographer—might have put it, on a systematic "amputation of reality" (287).[2]

I want to begin a different narrative, tracing the rhetorical continuity between the experimental era of Zola's naturalist polemics and the equally experimental work of our own realistic theater a century later. Historically, the rise of modern realism in the theater is usually traced to developments in theater technology dating from the mid-nineteenth century. This complicity between dramatic style and stage technology is informed by a sustaining ideology, what Roland Barthes calls the "ideological unity of the bourgeoisie," a unity that "gave rise to a single mode of writing" (*Writing* 2–3). In *Writing Degree Zero* Barthes traces later divisions in literary form to the breakup of this unified bourgeois consciousness, and we can certainly see a related development in drama as well: the proliferation of such apparently anti-realistic dramatic forms as expressionism, symbolism, Brechtian epic theater, poetic drama, theater of the absurd, "new realism," theater of images, and socialist drama. In the theater, the hegemony of realism is challenged not simply in terms of the style of the drama, but in the terms of stage production as well—different strategies of theatrical production challenge realism's ways of framing a picture of the world and controlling the

---

2. Not surprisingly, perhaps, Zola exempts naturalism from the "amputation" characteristic of earlier modes: "Toutes les formules anciennes, la formule classique, la formule romantique, sont basées sur l'arrangement et sur l'amputation systématiques du vrai."

audience's reading of it. In this regard the theater tells a somewhat different story than Barthes does, in large part because the rhetoric of realistic production has been much more difficult to suspend, even when the drama it stages seems far from the mode of Ibsen, Chekhov, O'Neill, or Storey. Although competing modes of stage production challenge the rhetoric of realism and the audience it produces, they often bear the traces of the "realistic" designs they oppose.

Realism is notoriously elusive, difficult to locate either as a "style" or at a particular moment in history. Here, I treat realistic theater and drama as an arrangement of practices developed as part of a cultural milieu of which we are still a part. To this extent "realism" is always a shorthand for "modern realism," or for "realistic drama and theater since 1850." The date is less important than what it marks—though 1889, the year of the first unaltered production of Ibsen's *A Doll's House* in England, comes to mind—for it points to the joining of literature, technology, and society in a sustaining ideological project. That project is what I mean by "realism," the distinguishing marks of which lie in its character as rhetoric, its ways of using theatrical production—conventions of acting, design, direction—to naturalize a particular relationship between the dramatic fiction and the offstage world of the audience. Unlike earlier modes of theater, realism not only asserts a reality that is natural or unconstructed, it argues that such a reality can only be shown on the stage by effacing the medium—literary style, acting, mise-en-scène—that discloses it. What is most characteristic of realism, that is, is not the verisimilitude it claims as its style (as though Hedda Gabler were more lifelike than Medea or Lady Macbeth simply because she speaks prose and owns a practical stove) but the framing machinery that seems to make such lifelikeness appear. Verisimilitude, instead, arises as an effect of the audience's activity, and it is the rhetorical purpose of realistic theater to assert the perception of verisimilitude as the sign of our proper engagement with the play. The modern realistic stage is a device for claiming and legitimating a certain kind of interpretive activity; its technology and techniques work to frame our ways of reading the stage and the kind of meanings we can find there.

Realism provides a way to hold audiences, performers, and drama in a particular relationship; the stage deploys its dramatic and theatrical style to shape certain forms of audience attention, experience, and interpretation. The formal and stylistic markers of realistic drama in this period are familiar: prosaic dialogue, bourgeois setting and subject matter (or, if the setting is drawn from another class, an implied bourgeois perspective on that class), a conflict between internal psychological motives and external economic or social pressures, a rigorously "causal" plotting, predominance of incident, and so on. These are, in a sense, the features of "realism" that the drama appropriated from the novel in the late nineteenth century, and which similarly assert the drama's unmediated transparency to the offstage reality it presents.

To produce this dramatic effect onstage requires an equally articulate theatrical rhetoric, and before turning to a reading of realistic drama we will need to elaborate this rhetoric more fully. Two points are easily anticipated: the pictorial, "photographic" objectivity claimed for the mise-en-scène, and its ability to govern a behavioristic style of acting.[3] The third moment of this rhetoric—how this complex of dramatic, staging, and acting techniques produces a characteristic experience for its audience—is more difficult to bring into focus, because the realistic theater negates the audience's overt participation in the theater as a necessary part of its proper interpretive activity. Defining *verisimilitude* as a thorough identification of the drama (present) with its performance (transparent), the theater casts its audience as absent from the field of representation. Legitimate theater experience, and so a proper interpretation of the "knowledge" that realistic drama often promises, can occur only when we have been apparently exiled from the field of theater itself.

The realistic stage works to arouse a familiar modern appetite: the desire to view others as theater from a position of unstaged freedom. We might think of realistic rhetoric in the theater as the body of practices that both stimulate and satisfy this appetite for "objectivity." The desire to produce the stage as object, a photographic slice of life free from the mediation of dramatic or theatrical style, becomes visible in the first polemics calling for realistic experimentation in the 1870s and 1880s. As Zola suggests, the rhetoric of

---

3. For a reading of the divergent styles of naturalism and realism in drama and in performance, see Styan vol. 1.

realism claims to duplicate the epistemology of experimental science. Naturalistic playwrights, Zola argues, should imitate "le mouvement d'enquête et d'analyse, qui est le mouvement même du dix-neuvième siècle" (283), by writing ironic, anti-romantic plays illustrating the behavior of characters as the effect of material causes, causes usually located in social pressures or "physiological" urgings. The "science" of theatrical naturalism lies less in the thematics of the drama than in the ideological neutrality it assigns to stage practice, and in the construction of the spectator as a disinterested, "objective" observer. The mise-en-scène appropriates the authority of "science" by assigning a "scientific" transparency to its own instruments, in order to ascribe a similarly scientific objectivity to its audience.

We can see that the machinery of theatrical production is assimilated to notions of scientific objectivity in a variety of ways. Much as the scientist's instruments or the photographer's camera are said to make objective observation possible, so too the technology of the theater is said to determine the "rise" of realistic drama. As Brander Matthews, the first professor of dramatic literature in the United States, found when he surveyed the history of the nineteenth-century theater in 1910, the "real responsibility" for the prosaic style of modern drama "does not lie on Ibsen's shoulders, but on Edison's,—since it was an inevitable consequence of the incandescent bulb" (*A Study* 64). In *The Principles of Playmaking* (1919) Matthews clarifies this history:

> In the course of the middle half of the nineteenth century the actual stage underwent a transformation. It was so amply lighted first by gas and then by electricity, that the actor had no longer to go down to the footlights to let his changing expression be seen. The parallel wings and borders by means of which interiors had been crudely indicated were abolisht and the compact box-set enabled the stage-director to suggest more satisfactorily an actual room. The apron was cut away; and the curtain rose and fell in a picture-frame. The characters of the play were thereafter elements in a picture, which had a characteristic background, and which might be furnisht with the most realistic elaboration. The former intimacy of the actor with the spectators, due to his close proximity, disappeared speedily; and with this intimacy there disappeared also its concomitant, the soliloquy addrest by a character to the audience for the sole purpose of supplying information. The drama immediately became more picto-

rial; it could rely more certainly upon gesture; it could renounce the aid of purely rhetorical oratory; it could dispense with description; and it insisted that the performer should subdue himself to those new conditions and to be on his guard lest he should "get out of the picture." (236–37)

Matthews echoes Zola in treating the representational practices of the realistic theater and drama as the result of evolutionary necessity. Reifying the "fourth wall," displacing the drama from the apron into the recessed box set, integrating characterization with design and costume elements, assimilating acting style to the understated manners of social behavior, and displacing the audience as participant, are all, to Matthews, dictated by the simple fact of their technological possibility. Matthews sees in this technology the origin and cause of realism, but its history is actually bound to the rise of the more spectacular modes of production that dominated other precincts of the nineteenth-century stage: cataclysmic melodrama, Irving's splendid "historical" Shakespeare, the glitter and panache of pantomime and extravaganza.[4] Zola saw naturalism as the result of a positivist literary and social "évolution," both the expression of "l'intelligence contemporaine" and its absent cause, transcending the passing fashions of specific individuals, classes, or institutions (285). Matthews similarly finds the triumph of realism to be implicit in its theatrical environment; although stage technology might sustain a variety of dramatic species, only realism seems fit to survive.

Theatrical realism claims to stage an objective representation by integrating dramatic and performance style into the pictorial consistency of the material scene onstage. The purpose of this consistency is not, in the end, simply mimetic: the aim of realism is to produce an audience, to legitimate its private acts of interpretation *as* objective. How does the rhetoric of realism cast its audience, and render the audience's typical mode of attention—displaced, absent, private viewing—meaningful? The picture frame of the proscenium not only circumscribes a dramatic world, it establishes the characteristic relation between actor, role, and eavesdropping audience through which its meanings are realized.

4. On the limits of technological determinism as a description of naturalism, see Williams, "Social environment" 208.

In *Play-Making* (1912), for example, William Archer describes the dramatist's craft in pictorial terms: the "stage now aims at presenting a complete picture, with the figures not 'a little out of the picture,' but completely in it" (64). Only by visualizing the stage as a pictorial environment, rather than as a stage set, can the playwright find "a safeguard against theatricality" (13). In part because the actor/character cannot emerge from the "picture," the environmental set becomes a decisive factor in the audience's interpretive activity, especially in its reading of "character." In 1911, for instance, David Belasco used the set for the opening scene of *The Return of Peter Grimm* to demonstrate the character's implication in a complex of social, economic, domestic, and even psychological histories:

> The sun comes brightly into the room. Through the window can be seen tulip beds, other flowers, hot houses, and rows of trees. Peter Grimm's botanic gardens supply seeds, plants, shrubbery, and trees to the wholesale trade as well as retail; and the view should suggest the importance and extent of the industry which Peter has inherited and improved. (Marker 71)

A character so fully identified with its productive environment is more completely contained within the stage. "Character" is no longer a medium of theatrical exchange between actor and audience—as it was, say, in Shakespeare's or Garrick's theater, where the making of character was more openly negotiated between actor and audience—but one object among many, part of a dramatic ecology the audience can observe but not enter. The objectivity of the pictorial stage both withdraws it from the audience's influence, and claims to render the drama "absolute," as though it were not implicated in the activities of performance and of observation that fabricate it on the stage.[5]

---

5. Peter Szondi regards the historically specific conditions of the modern theater as an index to essential or universal features of the drama; although we differ markedly on this point, his description of the relationship between drama and audience—with this qualification—is powerful. The "much-maligned 'picture-frame' stage," Szondi says,

> is the only one adequate to the absoluteness of the drama and bears witness to it in each of its features. It is no more connected to the house (by steps, for example) than the Drama is connected (stepwise) to the audience. The stage becomes visible, thus exists, only at the beginning of the play—often, in fact,

The desire to produce the audience in an "objective" relation to dramatic events also requires an increasingly underplayed acting style. Much as the mise-en-scène frames a coherent picture, purged of the traces of the theater, the pictorial stage suppresses a self-evident style of acting as an object of the audience's attention. Realistic acting erases itself from view, renders the actor the vehicle of a fully coherent "character" already present in the dramatic text. The actor's performance is rendered theatrically invisible, and aesthetically palatable, through a thoroughgoing identification between the conventions of "acting" and the manifest codes of social enactment. The increasingly subtle reproduction of domestic behavior informing English acting from Squire Bancroft to Granville Barker is one instance of this development, analogous to the efforts of Antoine's Théâtre Libre, of the Provincetown Players, of the Irish realists, of the Moscow Art Theater, and later of the American Method. This attitude is evident, too, in popular responses to the theater, which often betray this deeply idealized conception of dramatic performance. When the *Times* critic A. B. Walkley asks "What is the very quintessence of acting but the effort to bring about the complete identity" between actor and character, he inscribes in that identity a typical hierarchy of value: "If the actor *is* the part, so that you fail to distinguish one from the other, then he has achieved what he set out to do and he deserves all the praise he gets" (*More Prejudice* 69). In part, this priority reflects the sense that actors' special personality, their public extroversion, and their professional openness to the view of others necessarily violate the essential privacy and inwardness of the self, of authentic experience. In relation to the roles they perform—where "character" is revealed through indirection, unselfconscious disclosure—actors' public self-representation seems nearly patho-

---

only after the first lines have been spoken. Because of this, it seems to be created by the play itself. At the end of the act, when the curtain falls, the stage is again withdrawn from the spectator's view, taken back as if it were part of the play. The footlights which illuminate it create the impression that the play sheds its own light on stage."

Similarly, Szondi continues to describe acting as "subservient to the absoluteness of the Drama. The actor-role relationship should not be visible. Indeed, the actor and the character should unite to create a single personage" (8–9).

logical, and so must be neutralized by a mimetic rhetoric that assigns it an instrumental transparency.[6]

The widespread interest in puppets and marionettes at the turn of the century is also symptomatic of the uneasiness produced by the actors' dizzying self-multiplication. Gordon Craig's experiments, Meyerhold's sculptural plasticity, and Yeats's statuesque acting demonstrate the complicity between "symbolic" or "poetic" and "realistic" acting as strategies for audience implication: both claim to produce an ideal "character" by refining the actor's distracting personal charisma from our view. As Walkley suggests in proposing a marionette production of Thomas Hardy's *Dynasts*, puppet presentation

> would clarify, simplify, attenuate the medium through which the poem reaches the audience. The poet and his public would be in close contact. It is, of course, for many minds, especially for those peculiarly susceptible to poetry, a perpetual grievance against the actors that these living, bustling, solid people get between them and the poet and substitute fact, realism, flesh-and-blood for what these minds prefer to embody only in their imagination.

By using puppets or untrained performers instead of actors, Walkley hopes to dematerialize the actor's troubling opacity, to present the drama to its public through "a 'transparent medium' " (*Pastiche* 174–75, 177).

Realistic theater works to "attenuate the medium" by which the drama reaches its audience as a means of attenuating the audience's complicity in the performance itself. The spectator is cast as an impartial observer, construed outside and beyond both the drama and the theatrical activities—including his or her atten-

---

6. One has a sense of the threatening pathology of actors in this analogy of William Archer's: "Suppose a man imprisoned in a narrow chamber, walled, roofed, and floored with mirrors, some plane, some concave, some convex, some warped in all conceivable ways, wherein every feature of his face, every motion of his limbs should be reflected and re-reflected, until his personality in all sorts of disguises and contortions, should seem to fill all space and stretch away into infinitude. Whose sanity could stand such a strain? Who would not emerge with perceptions clouded and nerves unstrung from a course of this 'self-consciousness torture,' as it might be called?" Archer goes on to note that "it is the inevitable tendency of the actor's art to build round him such a mirror-cell" (*About the Theatre* 219–22). On the pathology of acting in the period, see Worthen, *Idea* 131–53.

dance, participation—that produce it. Staging *drama* that often insists on the pervasive determination of an environment metonymically reduced to the drawing-room box, realistic *theater* suppresses the theatrical environment as both cause and explanation of the drama's meanings or our interpretation of them. "A real subjection is born mechanically from a fictitious relation," Michel Foucault remarks of Jeremy Bentham's panopticon (202). Yet if the panopticon is, like the theater, a "privileged place for experiments on men, and for analysing with complete certainty the transformations that may be obtained from them" (204), it also points to the considerable constraint exerted on the observer, the experimenter, the spectator. Much as it does in the panopticon, the spectator's interpretive freedom in the theater emerges within the substantial control placed on his or her activity by the apparatus that makes observation possible. The warden, after all, is free to gaze on the cells of the inmates only through the window of his own cell-like enclosure. To objectify *others* as public, as controlled by an "environment" which operates as fate, while remaining in a privileged position of observation, beyond representation: like the thematics of realistic drama, the relations that govern the realistic audience have been so fully "detextualized," rendered as a force of nature, that they appear to be merely the condition of theater itself.[7]

Stage technology and acting practice in the late nineteenth century enabled the realistic theater to place the audience before an integrated, freestanding tableau, "leaving the spectator free to draw his own moral from the picture" (Matthews, *Study* 89). The public's freedom of judgment, in the theater and elsewhere, is paradoxically framed by the constraints of the scene in which that freedom is enacted. The rhetoric of realism creates this "freedom" precisely through the denial of its own rhetoricity; this erasure is especially marked in accounts of playwriting, though we can see it in acting and directing as well. It is notable, for instance, that the antithesis to realism—"a picture of life, as it is or as it might be"—is not usually found in the expressionist, *symboliste*, or surreal theater, but in theater that explicitly avows its suasive purpose: political theater, known in this period in terms of its typical dramatic form, the thesis play. Thesis plays fail to produce realistic

---

7. On the detextualization of the body, see Berger.

illusion by acknowledging the rhetorical character both of the drama and of the audience's response. As Archer suggests in *Play-Making*, thesis drama necessarily suffers "artistically from the obtrusive predominance of the theme—that is to say, the abstract element—over the human and concrete factors in the composition. . . . No outside force should appear to control the free rhythm of the action," or of the audience's reading of it (18–19).

Yet in *Play-Making* Archer has written a manual for controlling the dramatic action and its effect on the audience, and the playwriting he prescribes shapes the contours of the audience's freedom and necessity. Archer sees a symbiosis between the world offered by the playwright and the composition of the audience, implicitly acknowledging that the audience's sense of freedom is devised as an effect of the theater. The freedom of the spectator must be read against the substantial ground of necessity, his or her constraint by social opportunity, theatrical manners, and the playwright's clever manipulation of dramatic form and theatrical perspective:

> Again, at one class of theatre, the author of a sporting play is bound to exhibit a horse-race on the stage, or he is held to have shirked his obligatory scene. At another class of theatre, we shall have a scene, perhaps, in a box in the Grand Stand, where some Lady Gay Spanker shall breathlessly depict, from start to finish, the race which is visible to her, but invisible to the audience. At a third class of the theatre, the "specifically dramatic effect" to be extracted from a horse-race is found in a scene in a Black-Country slum, where a group of working-men and women are feverishly awaiting the evening paper which shall bring them the result of the St. Leger, involving for some of them opulence—to the extent, perhaps, of a £5 note—and for others ruin. (238)

Archer's description precisely records the structure of visibility sustaining the production of an audience and its interpretive prerogatives. The lower classes are placed directly before, practically amidst, the spectacle. The theater replicates the spectacle of social life, casting them as an unreflective, tractable crowd, absorbed in sensational events and lacking the interest or ability to penetrate to their cause. The upper-class theater of society drama shifts attention from the race to the response of its well-bred stage audience. While the lower classes are seduced by the superficial hum of events, "society" replicates the world in its own self-absorbed and dizzy futility. In the third example, apparently an instance of the "new drama," the stage claims for its subject the social consequences that result from horse racing. This theater provides the audience with a complex and contradictory role, one that invites both empathetic engagement and a pacifying separation, a summons to action and an actual paralysis. The audience scrutinizes the consequences of gambling and is invited to criticize the social and political organization that permits it. Yet the social process that connects the slum to the track (and, of course, the track to the banks, to real estate interests, to the audience) remains invisible, undramatized, much like the audience's invisible, voyeuristic relation to the stage. These spectators see neither the action of the race nor themselves dramatized but occupy a position of interpretation and judgment. Yet the apparent power of the audience is also neutralized, since that power cannot be put into action: neither the audience's relation to the dramatic subject nor its implication in the theatrical production can be legitimately recognized.

"With Sardou play-making is not merely as much a trade as clock-making; it is the same trade." Although the mechanics of well-made dramaturgy are often mocked, they remain essential to the ideal "impersonality of the drama" in the turn-of-the-century theater (Walkley, *Playhouse* 80, 14). This impersonality is claimed by the mechanical "logic" of the well-made play. The action of such plays turns relentlessly on the revelation of "facts" (secrets, confessions, coincidents, letters, and so on), information which assumes the role of fate for characters and audience alike. Well-made dramaturgy claims to preserve this "impersonality" and, consequently, the freedom of the spectator, by assigning to information itself a transcendent explanatory power. Finding the plotting of Pinero's *The Second Mrs Tanqueray* (1893; unless otherwise noted, plays are dated by first stage production) to be "clear, simple, natural," William Archer explicitly naturalizes Pinero's relentlessly coincidental plot to the process of social life: the "limitations of *Mrs Tanqueray* are really the limitations of the dramatic form" (see 1893 125–39). The explanatory character of this drama is partly epitomized by the functional necessity of the *raisonneur*, who points to a desire for interpretive closure implied in the reciprocity between well-made causality, the information it offers as explanation, and an interpretive situation outside or beyond the action itself. The familiar conventions of well-made plotting constitute a self-propelled dramatic machine. The audience ratifies this dramatic closure by marshaling information into an explanation, one that accounts for and totalizes the process of the dramatic action from which it has been exiled. To Archer, and to his theater, the working of "well-made" conventions has been so fully "transformed into feeling" as to be definitive of the working of ideology more generally: "an ideology which men will not feel to be an ideology," as Georg Lukács once put it ("Sociology" 443).[8]

Realistic production invites empathy and even understanding, but it invites us to practice that understanding only as spectators. June Howard and others have suggested that in naturalistic fiction, the role of the spectator prevents understanding and self-awareness from being translated into action, into the brute behavior so often described by the spectatorial heroes of naturalistic novels (see 106–16). Like the brilliant flash that Jacob Riis used in his pioneer photographs of New York slums, *How the Other Half Lives* (1890), the realistic stage tends to reveal the sordid constraints of social reality while sentimentalizing its characters to a more privileged audience. "Realistic" observation seems finally to deny the working of society at the moment that it is most profoundly active and visible. The politics of the realistic theater, like the rhetoric of realistic theatrical production, are conveyed through the concealment of a specific agency: the mystified social environment of the drama, the behavioristic transparency of acting style, the detheatricalized absence of the audience. Like the camera—its most pervasive metaphor—the realistic theater claims to offer images of an objective reality to an audience of detached observers; like photography, the realistic drama tends to imply how relations of visibility themselves encode other less apparent relations, relations of consciousness, of interpretation, of power.

The realistic stage assigns interpretive power and freedom to a class of patrons identified as absent, largely by imposing a certain

---

8. It should be noted that not everyone was as easily seduced as Archer by the "well-made" structure of feeling in *The Second Mrs Tanqueray*. Shaw remarked that "the only necessary conditions of this situation are that the persons concerned shall be respectable enough to be shocked by it, and that the step-mother shall be an improper person. Mr Pinero has not got above this minimum" (*Our Theatres* 1: 46).

kind of activity on the audience as the sign of its freedom. Meanwhile, it discloses others onstage as the products of an ineffable "environment," through the medium of a mise-en-scène and a histrionic technique that conceals or denies its working, its agency in the spectacle. The rhetoric of realism appears to enable the spectators to escape their own representation as the condition of entertainment, but the "privacy" it produces for the spectators becomes, finally, both a form of privilege and a kind of prison. The rhetorical character of this privacy intrudes again and again in realistic drama, as though the drama were unable to repress its own rhetoricity. Like *Three Sisters*, many plays expose the rhetorical character of stage realism and so dramatize the procedures that constitute "realistic" effects and interpretation; Ibsen's *The Wild Duck* (1885) provides a classic example of this kind of self-reflection. The play is fully within the orbit of realism: the densely material environment both controls characterization and helps to explain the action to the audience; the characters are integrated into their object world; the play urges a thematic concern for inheritance as a figure for the persistence of the past and the confinements of social life; and the play's well-made progression provides the gradual revelation of "facts" with a markedly "explanatory" force. Yet Ibsen strategically questions the confident rhetoric of realism, most directly in the representation of what might be called "well-made" thinking, in that the most benighted, unrealistic form of plotting in the play is practiced by Gregers Werle. Ibsen shows Gregers's disinterested plan to produce a "true marriage" for the Ekdals to be a solipsistic, manipulative fantasy by emphasizing its theatrical quality, particularly when Gregers is disillusioned by the failure of his climactic *scène à faire:* "I was really positive that when I came through that door I'd be met by a transfigured light in both your faces. And what do I see instead but this gloomy, heavy, dismal—" (459). Much as he does when improvising multiple causes for most of the play's effects—the history of blindness in both families, for instance—Ibsen carefully subverts the certainty of "well-made" logic, emptying it of value as an "objective" means to truth or understanding.

Ibsen's most searching investigation of the rhetoric of realism, though, develops through his use of theatrical space, particularly the loft area, that stagey playground whose scattered props and tawdry trees offset the insistent verisimilitude of the studio downstage. Something like chiaroscuro in painting, the obscure garret space—never fully seen by the audience—works to highlight the "reality" of the more visible forestage area, contributing to what Michael Fried has called in another context the "overall impression of self-sufficiency and repleteness that functions as a decisive hallmark of the 'real' " (59). Like Jean Genet's erotic theater, the garret room needs both false and authentic details to be persuasive to Ibsen's characters. To be redeemed from the realm of private fantasy, to function as a reduction of the "reality" that it replaces, displaces, and avoids, the garret needs "real" properties, real trees, a real duck. As an onstage theater, on the other hand, the garret seems to infiltrate and disrupt the realistic insistence that a complex social environment *can* be reduced metonymically to the stage scene through selective behavioral and material identity with the larger world it represents.[9] What seems striking about the loft in this context is not only its fantastic intrusion into verisimilar stage space but the ways in which this theatricalized milieu is entered and interpreted by Gregers and the Ekdals. The spectators onstage are only intermittently able to agree on their reading of the garret space, to join in the single perspective that coerces the theatrical spectators to read as a single public and to view the stage as objective reality. The tragedy, or irony, of *The Wild Duck* is that the garret theater seems not to refer to the world but only to the characters themselves, as when Gregers is shown the wild duck and immediately allegorizes it: "I'm hoping things will go the same with me as with the wild duck."

Ibsen's point here seems twofold. As a spectator, Gregers implies that objective interpretation is impossible, that all schemes claiming objectivity will in fact conceal unacknowledged agendas. To take Gregers as a model would lead us to look for other examples in the play where observation is shown to be a form of self-deluding blindness. Relling's assertion of the "life lie," for ex-

9. On metonymy as reduction, see Burke, *Grammar* 505–07. Bert O. States amplifies Burke's position with reference to the practices of realistic theater, when he remarks: "Metonymy and synecdoche, as we find them on the realistic stage, are devices for reducing states, or qualities, or attributes, or whole entities like societies, to visible things in which they somehow inhere" (65).

ample, might seem to restate Gregers's "claim of the ideal," not to counter it. Relling's ability to interpret and guide the actions of others arises from his adoption of a spectatorial attitude much like Gregers's, perhaps as a way of preserving his own self-image as realistic healer. Werle, too, stages a play—the Ekdal family itself— that is manifestly a form of self-displacement. By providing for Old Ekdal, Gina, and Hedvig, he both assuages his guilt and frees himself from implication in their plight: his power in society is largely signified in the play through his ability to cast the family as a distinct "tableau" while keeping his own relation to the Ekdals in obscurity. And of course Hjalmar Ekdal's profession itself might be taken as an index of Ibsen's skeptical regard for his own theatrical procedures, for photography in *The Wild Duck* is mainly an art of retouching, an art that threatens to lead, in Hedvig's case, to blindness. *The Wild Duck* questions the premise that we can "know" as detached, uninvolved, "experimental" observers; the play offers no position that is not compromised by its procedure for staging others to the view.[10] To fail to attend to the ways that we make the world, to fail to recognize ourselves among the play's gallery of absent authors, is to enter into the delusions afflicting Ibsen's characters and to reproduce the circumstantial contradictions defining our role in the realistic audience.

As Amy Kaplan has remarked in her fine study of American realism, our attitudes toward the form and purposes of realism have undergone an important change since Ibsen's era, perhaps even since the heyday of Tennessee Williams; far from an "objective reflection of social life," realism has become, for us at least, "a fictional conceit, or deceit, packaging and naturalizing an official version of the ordinary" (1). To recognize the ideological work of stage realism, though, requires an inquiry into the specifically theatrical forms of this process, how the rhetoric of realism identifies the drama, its stage production, and the activities of its audience within the stabilizing attitudes of its sustaining culture. This work generally takes a double shape, which Michael Fried,

---

10. Indeed, Ingmar Bergman's 1972 production of the play emphasized just this point, by locating the loft downstage: the Ekdals looked through the loft toward the audience, now placed literally in the sphere of fantasy. See Marker and Marker.

in a telling reading of Thomas Eakins's paintings, suggestively describes:

> The result is a tension or competition between two fundamentally different modes of seeing—one that looks to enter the representational field and to merge its interests with those of the protagonists, inevitably losing sight of the whole in the process of doing so, and another that remains emphatically outside the representation, viewing the painting with something like detachment but also with special concern for "formal" values of a certain sort. (77)

These "conflicting modes of seeing, one excessively intimate and the other excessively detached" (85), are akin to the modes of experience articulated by the realistic theater, which invites sympathy for its Paulas and Hedvigs, but a sympathy that is necessarily performed across a paralyzing distance, a distance that conceals the audience's actual and figural role in the production of the "problems" onstage. The relation between these two kinds of seeing provides the ideological frame of realistic interpretation. In this sense, the realistic theater of disclosure is also a theater of concealment. The question is whether the space of concealment that we inhabit will also be exposed, be shown to be complicit in the making of the world.

The clearest connection between the privilege of privacy and the consequences of public display can be made in relation to one of the most significant dramatic genres of the turn-of-the-century stage, the drama of the "fallen woman." In these plays, the drama of sexual politics depends on the rhetoric of realistic vision; the action negotiates the gendered relationship between privacy and publicity, the power of the spectator and the power of the performer, in ways that clarify the politics of visibility in the realistic theater. This may seem to be a special case, though, and so in chapter 2 I will consider a more familiar aspect of realistic drama, the thematic interplay between character and environment, as a feature of its theatrical rhetoric. To do so, however, will require us to transform the materials of the drama into the activities of theatrical production, to assess the rhetoric of dramatic "character" and "milieu" not as isolated features of dramatic texts but in relation to theatrical acting and the disposition of objects in the environment of the stage. This reading will take us not only across the ground of

American drama and performance in the 1920s, 1930s, and 1940s, but also to the problematic agency of objects and passivity of characters in more recent drama in the realistic mode, in the plays of Pinter, Shepard, and Bond.

INVISIBLE WOMEN: PROBLEM DRAMA,
1890–1920

ALICK: What *is* charm, Maggie?
MAGGIE: Oh, it's—it's a sort of bloom on a woman. If you have it, you don't need to have anything else; and if you don't have it, it doesn't much matter what else you have. Some women, the few, have charm for all; and most have charm for one. But some have charm for none.
—J. M. Barrie, *What Every Woman Knows* (1908)

The rhetoric of realism thematizes the theatrical relationship between the drama, its performance, and the audience. The realistic stage offers an explicitly epistemological drama, both staging new objects of knowledge to the view of its middle-class audience and inspecting the status of knowledge itself, entwined as it is with evasion, blindness, and self-deception. Yet for all their power, the drama's techniques of disclosure bear a disturbing likeness to the structure of theatrical perception in the proscenium house. Knowledge in the drama is both claimed and compromised by the means of its making, as characters insistently deploy the relations of realistic theater—privileged observers, staged objects—as an instrument of understanding and empowerment. In realistic drama, knowledge frequently takes the form of the voyeuristic recognition of subjects unacknowledged by the middle-class audience: the struggles of sexual domination, of poverty, of industrial oppression. By collapsing social, economic, and gender concerns into the dramatic problem of social mobility and visibility, the "woman with a past" presents an important instance of this trope. At the turn of the century, to bring such women into view as anything other than melodramatic villains was widely regarded as a fascinating, risky *coup de théâtre*. As Arthur Wing Pinero's biographer Hamilton Fyfe asked, characterizing much of the contemporary reception of *The Second Mrs Tanqueray*, "Why recognize the existence of women of

Paula's class at all? These subjects are not for public discussion, even by the preacher. We should be kept from all knowledge of such things" (*Arthur Wing Pinero* 145). To bring "women" to the stage is both a stunning and a typical event in the late Victorian period. In many respects the social stigma and attraction of a Marguerite, a Paula Tanqueray, a Mrs. Dane, or Oscar Wilde's Mrs. Erlynne and Mrs. Cheveley are identical to the allure of actresses of the time, the magnetism of Eleonora Duse, Sarah Bernhardt, Elizabeth Robins, Mrs. Patrick Campbell, even of Ellen Terry. Here, I want to ask how the drama of the "woman with a past" represents the rhetoric of realism, how the drama reframes the working of theatrical visibility and interpretation as the structure of social action in the larger world beyond the stage. Staging the "woman with a past" discloses the rhetorical reciprocity between theatrical production and the ordering of society characteristic of the first generation of modern British and American stage realism.

To establish the relationship between class power and theatrical visibility in this drama, I would like first to set the "woman with a past" in the wider context of two plays by John Galsworthy, *The Silver Box* (1906) and *The Skin Game* (1920). *The Silver Box* is often taken as an example of Edwardian social realism, the representation of social ills for the edification and entertainment of the theater-going public. The play opens with Jones, an unemployed groom, being invited into the home of Jack Barthwick, wastrel son of a Liberal M.P. In a moment of drunken exuberance, Jack reveals that the reticule he carries has been lifted from his companion for the evening, a woman of questionable reputation; Jones takes this revelation as his cue to lift a silver cigarette case. When the box is missed, Mrs. Jones—the Barthwicks' char—is automatically suspected. The police raid her flat; she protests her innocence, and is restrained. Jones then confesses his guilt, and when the policeman does not believe him, Jones assaults him. After a struggle, Jones is subdued and taken into custody. The final movement of the play concerns Jones's trial and the Barthwicks' efforts to avoid publicity (because Jones assaulted the policeman, the charges cannot be dropped). In the end, Jones is sentenced to hard labor, and Mrs. Jones is acquitted but left unemployed, without references, adrift.

Galsworthy's immediate concern is evident: to expose the hypocrisy of Barthwick's "equal justice." Like his contemporaries, Galsworthy masks his designs in the guise of impersonality, setting "before the public no cut-and-dried codes, but the phenomena of life and character, selected and combined, *but not distorted,* by the dramatist's outlook" (*Inn* 190). As a detective drama, *The Silver Box* assigns a prominent role to the transformation of information into knowledge, particularly knowledge of the lower classes, who are treated as a kind of public spectacle. In the second act of the play, for example, after Jones has been arrested, Mrs. Barthwick discusses the servant troubles of a neighbor, whose "girl used to have her young man to see her." Such a girl must be dismissed from service, as an example to others. What rankles Mrs. Barthwick, though, is not really the sexual impropriety but what the situation implies, that the serving girl is able to maintain a wholly private sphere of life:

> Servants have too much license. They hang together so terribly you never can tell what they're really thinking; it's as if they were all in a conspiracy to keep you in the dark. Even with Marlow [the trusted family butler], you feel that he never lets you know what's really in his mind. I hate that secretiveness; it destroys all confidence. . . . It goes all through the lower classes. You can *not* tell when they are speaking the truth. (18)

The play works to expose both the Jones and the Barthwick families to our view, but the formal symmetry that relates the moral structure of family life to financial security works to expose a deeply asymmetrical access to privacy and the power it represents. The audience's power is—as Stanislavski recognized—always coercive; privacy in the realistic drama and theater is the sign and the means of privilege. In *The Silver Box*, it is the power to exercise this privilege to stage the lower classes, to force them to dramatize themselves and their native vices, that conveys the Barthwicks' social prestige. Summoning Mrs. Jones to explain the missing box, for instance, the Barthwicks subject her to a relentless interrogation and extract an apparently shocking confession: that she was pregnant with their first child before she and Jones were married. Of course, the words themselves can't be spoken in the polite confines of the Edwardian drawing-room stage:

> BARTHWICK: You mean he—ahem—
> MRS. JONES: Yes, sir; and of course after he lost his place he married me.

> MRS. BARTHWICK: You actually mean to say you—you were—
> BARTHWICK: My dear—
> MRS. BARTHWICK: (*Indignantly*) How disgraceful! (12)

Although Mrs. Barthwick speaks as a conventionally respectable matron, she is in the position to produce the secret information that it is otherwise impolite for her to recognize. Her respectability is based on the proprieties that "protect" her from such acknowledgment, the recognition of women whose sexuality is more openly symptomatic of their oppression. The proprieties that keep such issues unspoken operate at the convenience of the privileged: Mrs. Jones has no alternative but to reply, to expose her past to the view of her betters, onstage and off.

As a figure for the audience of realism, Mrs. Barthwick epitomizes the relationship between visibility, privacy, and class that runs throughout the play and that is finally brought into focus by Jones's climactic trial. While the Barthwicks stage Jones, they are able to control their own entrance onto the public stage, summoning the invisible pressures of "society" to justify their behavior. The Joneses, as the play surely shows, are more completely in that society's control. Despite his "great sympathy with the poor," Barthwick is easily persuaded that his failure to prosecute is "simply not fair to other people. It's putting property at the mercy of anyone who likes to take it," and that the courts take the problem "out of our hands" (24). Barthwick's sentimental liberalism is dramatized as a form of hypocrisy, a refusal to acknowledge that his social responsibilities are enabled by his extraordinary access to the machinery of social representation, a gesture that is literalized in the play's final action:

> MRS. JONES: (*Turning to him with a humble gesture*) Oh! Sir!—
> BARTHWICK *hesitates, then yielding to his nerves, he makes a shamefaced gesture of refusal, and hurries out of Court.* MRS. JONES *stands looking after him.* (32)

Retreating shamefaced from the court, Barthwick leaves Mrs. Jones alone, her unfortunate past, and her unfortunate present, now common property.[11]

---

11. On class in Galsworthy's drama, see Scrimgeour; for a description of the play's attention to verisimilitude in performance, see Kennedy 54–56.

The Silver Box is typical of the social analysis characteristic of the realistic theater, the theater's tendency at once to stage the social other while protecting the audience from the consequences of such contact, much as Mrs. Barthwick averted her eyes when "one of those unemployed came up and spoke to me" (18). The play's vision of social order is signaled by the power that an unseen, unpublicized, socially privileged audience has to control its own presentation, and to enforce the representation of others. In its depiction of privacy as power, *The Silver Box* exposes the detachment of realistic drama—"the selfless character which soaks it with inevitability," that so attracted Galsworthy—as an instance of the wider social economy surrounding and defining theatrical representation (*Inn* 192).

Sitting in the dark, beyond the dramatic action, the audience exerts an obscure pressure on the realistic stage's claim to objectivity. In *The Silver Box*, a woman's "past" provides an instance of the unspeakable, and so provides an occasion for the Barthwicks to dramatize their own status by making her speak. Regarding the "woman with a past" solely as a figure for Victorian-Edwardian sexual anxiety markedly oversimplifies her subversive and overdetermined position in the structure of social precedence, an instability not assignable simply to the issues of sexual freedom and the "double standard." Galsworthy's late play *The Skin Game* (1920) is particularly suggestive of this figure's general implication in the class dynamics of performance, not least because it at first seems unconcerned with the "woman question." The play dramatizes the social disintegration of an English country village. The Hillcrists, an established landed family, have been forced to sell some property to the Hornblowers, industrialists "representative of the newly rich, pushfully aggressive, brutally energetic manufacturing class," in the words of an early critic. From the outset, the play establishes an unstable and ironic relationship between the two families, for "caste feeling finds its antagonist not in morality but in vulgarity" (Coats 139). As a gentleman—"a man who keeps his form and doesn't let life scupper him out of his standards" (352)—Hillcrist sells property to Hornblower with the understanding that his tenants will remain undisturbed, an understanding that Hornblower violates in order to put the property to more productive use: digging claypits and building a pottery. The predictable conflict between the gracious gentry and the rapacious manufacturer then develops a fascinating twist. Although Hornblower may be crude and grudging at times, his works will "supply thousands of people" (356), and the play exposes the Hillcrists' treatment of him as unmannerly, dishonest, and dishonorable. When Hillcrist complains that Hornblower's works would spoil the views from his home, Hornblower is justly amazed: "How the man talks! Why! Ye'd think he owned the sky, because his fathers built him a house with a pretty view, where he's nothing to do but live. It's sheer want of something to do that gives ye your fine sentiments, Hillcrist" (357). Hillcrist's spectatorial distance from the community—he could relocate the dispossessed tenants to his own property, after all—enables him to conceive his social responsibility in moral generalities, as empathy rather than as action. As Hornblower points out, "You county folk are fair awful hypocrites. Ye talk about good form and all that sort o' thing. It's just the comfortable doctrine of the man in the saddle; sentimental varnish" (358).

Galsworthy gives the play its decisive turn, however, at the close of act 1, when the "past" of Hornblower's daughter-in-law Chloe suddenly intrudes and provides the organizing focus for the play. Chloe bears the actress-like marks of illicit entry into respectable society—"Lots of women powder and touch up their lips nowadays," Hillcrist's daughter Jill says of her (361)—and raises Hornblower's suspicions when she joins with Mrs. Hillcrist to bring about a compromise between the two families; he reminds them that "ladies should keep to their own business" (370). In fact, though, Mrs. Hillcrist is keeping to her business, the ordering of gender in the closed society of the provincial town. Chloe, it emerges, has been a "highly recommended" figure in London life. As Mrs. Hillcrist describes her, blackmailing Hornblower, "When cases are arranged, Mr. Hornblower, the man who is to be divorced often visits an hotel with a strange woman. I am extremely sorry to say that your daughter-in-law, before her marriage, was in the habit of being employed as such a woman" (379–80). Chloe's "past" completely alters the battle for status and power between the two families. Although Hillcrist recoils at first from the blackmail, the claims of property eventually overcome his "standards." Hornblower, once energetically scornful of landed propriety, is finally crushed by it. He sells the Hillcrists back their property at a ruinous loss, but the secret gets out nonetheless. His family's reputation in the village is ruined, his son's marriage is destroyed, and when Chloe throws herself into the gravel pit his grandchild is miscarried.

The "woman with a past" clarifies the social relations informing the open struggle for property: the sweet science of social manners is in fact a bare-knuckle brawl, a skin game of class power. The prizes are material, but the fight is waged in the ideological register of reputation, privilege, and honor, the register that assigns a stigmatizing priority to Chloe's illicit past. As in *The Silver Box*, "knowledge" has ruined Hornblower and his family, but in *The Skin Game*, that illicit past also reveals what might be called the natural history of class conflict and implicitly relates it to the structure of realistic theatricality. Early in the play, Hornblower recalls Shaw's Andrew Undershaft, boasting that although he has "no ancestors" and "no past," his industry will assure him the "future" (356). The fact that Hornblower's family and future can be ruined by the Hillcrists' manipulative code of "honour," implies that the "comfortable doctrine of the man in the saddle" not only pervades this society but orders the function of its history as well. The play opposes men and women, new and old, future and past, bourgeois and aristocrat, industry and agriculture. By giving Chloe's past the power to destroy Hornblower as neither his rapaciousness nor his vulgarity could, the Hillcrists (and Galsworthy) insert Hornblower into a history that subjects him to the proprieties of the landed classes.

Describing the realistic playwright's relation to the world he dramatizes, Galsworthy suggests that the "dramatist's license, in fact, ends with his design."

> In conception alone he is free. He may take what character or group of characters he chooses, see them with what eyes, knit them with what idea, within the limits of his temperament; but once taken, seen, and knitted, he is bound to treat them like a gentleman, with the tenderest consideration of their mainsprings. (*Inn* 196)

Although *The Skin Game* works to expose the hypocrisy of the Hillcrists' gentility, Galsworthy tends to "treat them like a gentleman," to realize their code of empowerment in the play's framing structure of visibility. The play forces the Hillcrists to betray their own aristocratic ideals, but they nonetheless do finally succeed in contaminating and destroying the Hornblowers. As a representation of the operation of knowledge in class and social relations, the "woman with a past" locates the power of the voyeur, the spectator's power to subject or destroy the other by making it a figure on the public stage.

To be offstage in this drama is hardly to be powerless: the ability to stage others while remaining private and unseen becomes both a sign and an instrument of privilege. In this sense, realistic drama thematizes the relations of visibility governing its theater as the social environment of the world it shows on the stage. The drama, the theater, and their society naturalize the working of realistic vision as a feature of the environment, as constitutive of reality itself. Galsworthy's plays refract theatrical representation as a feature of social class; Pinero's *The Second Mrs Tanqueray* draws our attention more directly to how the means of the realistic stage—acting, imitation—define the representation of gender both in the theater and in society at large. The play is a celebrated example of the genre. Aubrey Tanqueray, a widower, marries Paula Jarman, a well-known companion to the gentlemen of the social elite. When his daughter Ellean decides to return home from the convent where she was raised, a competition for Aubrey's attentions arises between Ellean and her stepmother. Fortunately, Ellean takes a European tour with a respectable neighbor, leaving Aubrey and Paula to sort out their new relationship. But Ellean returns with a suitor, who turns out to be one of Paula's former lovers: Paula, recognizing that there is no place for her in this society, commits suicide. In the view shared by Bernard Shaw and Martin Meisel, the play both piques and placates its audience by providing for the final denunciation and execution of Paula under the guise of an avowed desire for "tolerance." More recently, Austin E. Quigley has argued that Cayley Drummle's observation of the action—he calls himself "a spectator in life; nothing more than a man at a play, in fact . . . an old-fashioned playgoer" (*Tanqueray* 87)—masks his pivotal role as "the agent of condemnation," whose "sentimentality and forgiveness" (responses analogous to those the play invites from its audience) "perpetuate rather than revise the very standards to which Paula's youthful behaviour might pose a challenge" (Quigley 85).[12] The figure of the spectator

---

12. Shaw, *Our Theatres in the Nineties* 1: 45–46; and Meisel, *Shaw and the Nineteenth-Century Theater* 141–59. Quigley argues that the audience whose

works to confirm the complicity of "tolerance" in the dramatic necessity of Paula's suicide.

Paula's visibility to spectators like Drummle and the larger audience of which he is a part is not merely the sign of a sexual double standard, in that Paula and her kind play a significant role in the reproduction of the social order itself. Even at the outset, Paula clearly has a kind of currency among the male characters in the play, all of whom know her and may know her intimately; she is particularly close to Drummle, who serves as her confidant. To say that the way of the world—the "name we give our little parish of St James's" (86)—works through the occlusion of this woman is only half the story, for tolerance provides a screen for Paula's commodification, valuation, and exchange. Initially, the play poses Paula as unique in her ability to elide the boundary between St. James's and her own marginal status, momentarily obscured by her cultivated performance. Unlike crass Mabel Hervey—herself recently married into the aristocracy—Paula easily enters the gestural realm of Aubrey's class. The play works to establish, despite obvious differences in manner and character, the similarity between Paula and Mabel, and to urge that Paula too is "a lady who would have been, perhaps had been, described in the reports of the Police or the Divorce Court as an actress.... Her affections, emotions, impulses, her very existence—a burlesque!" (80–81). Mabel's evident vulgarity seems to confirm Drummle's portrait, but his remarks are equally applicable to Paula, for the language of the theater trails her throughout the play as well. The brilliance with which Paula enacts the manners and customs of the St. James's parish renders her

---

views are represented by Drummle "is thus challenged and undercut by the action of a play that undermines the very perspective the audience is encouraged to adopt.... The play lacks, as the well-made play must, a convincing advocate of alternative values; but *the action of the play itself* becomes an advocate of alternative values, an action that outruns, and demonstrates the limitations of, the benevolent perspective of its *raisonneur*" (89). This salutary effort to theorize the play's theatrical operation is, in this detail, perhaps at odds with Pinero's conception of Drummle. Writing to George Alexander in April 1893, Pinero expressed doubts about the casting of the part: "Read over the first act and note how bright and chirpy Drummle ought to be. In a very serious play a ray of brightness is invaluable" (Pinero, *Collected Letters* 143).

much more problematic to the society of the play and to the patrons of the St. James's Theatre where the play was first performed. Arriving late and alone at Aubrey's rooms, for instance, Paula dreams about her married future:

> It was perfect. I saw you at the end of a very long table, opposite me, and we exchanged sly glances now and again over the flowers. We were host and hostess, Aubrey, and had been married about five years. . . . And on each side of us was the nicest set imaginable—you know, dearest, the sort of men and women that can't be imitated.
> (89)

Ready to penetrate Aubrey's society through imitation, Paula nevertheless hopes that the traces of her origins will be erased by her performance: "I seemed to know by the look on their faces that none of our guests had ever heard anything—anything—anything peculiar about the fascinating hostess." It is, of course, precisely her ability to "imitate" this class that makes her valuable, even attractive, and at the same time vulnerable to devaluation, "anybody's, in less gentle society I should say everybody's, property," as Drummle blithely remarks of Mabel (80). For "imitation" debases the currency of social status, and finally marks Paula's illegitimacy.

Drummle's reference to Mabel Hervey as an "actress" is a common euphemism, but nonetheless points to the kinship between Paula and the stage. Both the public display required by their profession and the wider, nondomestic sphere of their experience tended to class actresses among public "women" rather than domestic "ladies." Tracy C. Davis argues that the routine violation of "conventions of dress, make-up, gesture, and association that distinguished 'respectable women' from the demi-monde" tended to associate actresses with prostitutes in the public imagination, and were often conventionalized in Victorian pornography (314).[13] Paula's valuation is that of the realistic theater, which regards the world that can be staged as degraded. Paula shares her public

---

13. Shaw recognized that the actress's professional development required "a latitude in her social relations which, though perfectly consistent with a much higher degree of self-respect than is at all common among ordinary respectable ladies, involves a good deal of knowledge which is forbidden to 'pure' women," and he characteristically urged the actress to be proud that she "is essentially a work-woman and not a lady" (*Our Theatres* 3: 277).

status with "women" of all kinds—street prostitutes, actresses, even suffrage speakers—a kinship that exiles her from the inimitable world of much of the St. James's Theatre audience. As Wilde's Lord Goring (*An Ideal Husband*, St. James's Theatre, 1895) remarks of a similar woman, "Well, she wore far too much rouge last night, and not quite enough clothes. That is always a sign of despair in a woman" (423).

Once married, in fact, Paula's enactment of the snooty conventions of respectability works to mark her difference from those she copies, rather than her similarity to them. In a key scene, when Aubrey's old friend Mrs. Cortelyon presents herself apologetically to Paula for an introduction, it is Paula's masterful performance of injured respectability that betrays her, signifying her inadmissibility into the inner circle.

> PAULA: Why, because it is two months since we came to Highercoombe, and I don't remember your having called.
> MRS CORTELYON: Your memory is now terribly accurate. No, I've not been away from home, and it is to explain my neglect that I am here, rather unceremoniously, this morning.
> PAULA: Oh, to explain—quite so. (*with mock solicitude*) Ah, you've been very ill; I ought to have seen that before.
> MRS CORTELYON: Ill!
> PAULA: You look dreadfully pulled down. We poor women show illness so plainly in our faces don't we? (100–101)

This powerful scene conveys Paula's anger, her desperation to forge a respectable home life, and her fear that she is being undermined by Mrs. Cortelyon, who offers to escort Ellean on the European tour. And yet the effect of the scene is to stress Paula's misplaying of the proprieties of respectability. Playing the role of "Mrs. Tanqueray," Paula's performance can only be an imitation, dramatizing the "termagant aspect of poor Paula at the expense of her more sympathetic, her equally natural and genuine, qualities," as Pinero wrote to Mrs. Patrick Campbell (*Collected Letters* 147). Even Pinero finds Paula's performative aspect vulgar; it is hardly surprising that Clement Scott saw Pinero's "natural and genuine" heroine as "a woman so vulgar, so shrewish, so unlovable, so destitute of taste that she sets the sensitive teeth on edge.... She is simply vulgar and ill-bred" (qtd. in Booth 2: 338–39).

Such performances dramatize the function of "imitation" in this society. Regenia Gagnier has argued that Wilde's drama tends to present this society as "a society of spectacle only," in which the pervasiveness of imitation signals the deeply fetishized nature of upper-bourgeois social enactment (113). *The Second Mrs Tanqueray,* on the other hand, treats acting in a more limited way, not as a generalized social behavior, but as a practice, a profession, required of an oppressed female class for the entertainment and stimulation of male patrons. The play treats Paula as a better class of prostitute than Mabel Hervey, but when Paula uses acting to pursue her own ends rather than to make her a partner fit for public display, she is classed among the vulgar interlopers, as a version of Mabel rather than as the seductive "Mrs. Jarman." Entering this society as an actress enters the stage, Paula can only perform as an ephemeral player:

> Oh, I know I'm "going off". I hate paint and dye and those messes, but, by and by, I shall drift the way of the others; I shan't be able to help myself. And then, some day—perhaps very suddenly, under a queer, fantastic light at night or in the glare of the morning—that horrid, irresistible truth that physical repulsion forces on men and women will come to you, and you'll sicken at me.... You'll see me then, at last, with other people's eyes; you'll see me just as your daughter does now, as all wholesome folks see women like me. And I shall have no weapon to fight with—not one serviceable little bit of prettiness left me to defend myself with! (129)

To Pinero's audience, this speech seemed representative "not of Paula's case alone, but of every case like hers, and in a modified degree its truth comes home to all who wantonly break the laws which the experience of the world has made for men and women." Indeed, we may be too cavalier in believing that Paula's suicide provided a comforting denouement for a hypocritical Victorian public. Hamilton Fyfe, for one, thought that suicide "ought only to be permitted in fiction to characters which we may justly regard as heroic. It ought not to be allowed to dignify weak characters which have no heroic elements about them. It is in no sense an expiation; it is merely a way of escape, and a way which very few of the Paulas ... take, however much they may talk about it" (*Arthur Wing Pinero* 144, 147). Seen "with other people's eyes," Paula's performance is devalued as mere "acting." The privileged audience reserves full humanity only for itself.

In his day, "Pinero's power, Pinero's insight into human nature," were widely recognized; like many of his contemporaries, J. T. Grein praised Pinero's women as "amazingly womanly. It is not I who say that, but I have it from women who have studied Pinero's work as closely as any critic."[14] Yet Shaw argued that there is "no cheaper subject for the character draughtsman than the ill-tempered sensual woman seen from the point of view of the conventional man," the point of view inscribed in the social perspective of realistic objectivity (*Our Theatres* 1: 45). Shaw rightly suggests that Pinero's conventional morality duplicates the rhetoric of realistic theater, the ideological "point of view" engrained in the social and theatrical apparatus that represents Paula Tanqueray. To become visible through "imitation," as both Paula and the actress do, is at once to become an eroticized "public" woman, a token of masculine desire easily replaced by another of her kind. The Cayley Drummles remain invisible in this economy, just offstage in the audience of old-fashioned playgoers: as the incest motif implies, Paula is redundant, expendable to the inimitable society she enters. Lecturing at Harvard in 1886, the American playwright Bronson Howard outlined the conditions of dramatic survival for characters like Paula: "In England and America, the death of a pure woman on the stage is not 'satisfactory,' except when the play rises to the dignity of tragedy. The death, in an ordinary play, of a woman who is not pure, as in the case of 'Frou-Frou,' is perfectly satisfactory, for the reason that it is inevitable. . . . and so an audience looks with complacent tears on the death of an erring woman" (27–28). In the theater, the audience both produces Paula and executes her, reproducing its role in the commerce of sexuality in society at large. In this sense, the "intellectual virility" that Archer demanded from the new English drama is, in 1893, already thoroughly present in the structure of realistic representation (*1893* 144). As the staging of Paula Tanqueray shows, the woman mentioned only impolitely in the drawing room serves as erotic currency onstage and off, dramatizing the implication of realistic vi-

---

14. Grein, *Dramatic Criticism 1900–1901* 279; Grein, *Dramatic Criticism* 267.

sion in the structures of power, distinction, and "virility" that maintain this theater and this society.

Shaw was convinced that "fine art is the subtlest, the most seductive, the most effective instrument of moral propaganda in the world, excepting only the example of personal conduct; and I waive even this exception in favor of the art of the stage, because it works by exhibiting examples of personal conduct made intelligible and moving to crowds of unobservant unreflecting people to whom real life means nothing" (Preface 185). Nonetheless, Shaw's intention to rectify the conventional sentimentality of *The Second Mrs Tanqueray* in his play *Mrs Warren's Profession* (written 1893-94) is to some extent undone by his own invocation of the rhetoric of realism, the strategies at hand for "exhibiting" woman on the stage. Shaw's ironic play takes the attitudes sustaining Pinero's dramaturgy as its subject, staging "Mrs. Jarman's Profession" as an emblem of capitalist exploitation and using Vivie Warren's romantic disillusionment to suggest the possibility of social change. Since all "progress is initiated by challenging current conceptions," it is not surprising that Shaw confronts the ideological structure of Pinero's drama. Insofar as progress is "executed by supplanting existing institutions," though, we may ask whether Shaw's retelling of the romance of the "fallen woman" as a parable of capitalism succeeds in supplanting the institutions that represent and objectify "realistic" society in the theater (Preface 194).

As in Pinero and Galsworthy, staging the unspeakable woman provides Shaw with his chief means of criticizing the forms and currents of social power. And, once again, while the knowledge of such women is the prerogative of the wealthy and proper, disacknowledging them is the most common way of exercising that power. The necessity to claim understanding and to disavow knowledge of Mrs. Warren's profession can be keenly felt in the play's critical reception. Although J. T. Grein thought that "most of the women, and a good many of the men [in the audience of the 1902 Stage Society production] . . . did not at first know, and finally merely guessed, what was the woman's trade," the play's moral stance (it may "in some awaken a curiosity which had better been left in slumber") and the model of maturity it offered were deeply troubling. Grein criticized both the play's propriety for the stage—"there was a majority of women to listen to that which could only be understood by a minority of men"—and Shaw's violation of the dramatic conventions that should provide an interpretive guide for the audience. Shaw, that is, confuses the genre's moral structure and directly challenges its paradigmatic characters, "a mother really utterly degraded, but here and there whitewashed with sentimental effusions, and a daughter so un-English in her knowledge of the world, so cold of heart, and 'beyond human power' in reasoning that we end by hating both." Casting "a cold-blooded, almost sexless daughter as the sympathetic element," Shaw transforms the sentimental rite of passage central to this drama into an intellectual experience. The characterization of Vivie seems to violate the proprieties of social inclusion that assimilate young women into adult society: "By all means let us initiate our daughters before they cross the threshold of womanhood into the duties and functions of life which are vital in matrimony and maternity. But there is a boundary line, and its transgression means peril—the peril of destroying ideals" (1900–1901 293–96).

Shaw, of course, found a gentlemanly code of oppression in such "ideals," arguing that "Mrs Warren's Profession is a play for women; that it was written for women; that it has been performed and produced mainly through the determination of women that it should be performed and produced" (Preface 200). As a realistic staging of "woman," however, Shaw's play remains to a large extent complicit in strategies of realistic visibility and the society it constitutes. For Shaw replaces Cayley Drummle's eroticized "property" with a similarly idealized "woman," or, more accurately, a man in woman's costume. Shaw's play so fully subordinates the gender economy of prostitution to the parable of capital that its ability to examine gender *as* a commodity on the social market is forestalled. The histrionic sign of the new woman's freedom in the play seems to be her ability to act like a man—smoke a cigar, have a firm handshake, and so on. "I am a man's creation as you see": Vivie's characterization might be said to anticipate the playing of Caryl Churchill's Betty in *Cloud Nine* (1979), in which the male actor's portrayal of a woman effectively erases the feminine from the categories of patriarchal reality.[15] By providing his heroine

---

15. As Catherine Wiley points out, Vivie's "superiority lies not in her repudiation of the false and debilitating femininity other women suffer

with a veneer of "masculine" behavior, and by characterizing her romantic attachment to Frank as childish, Shaw effectively removes Vivie from the political continuum represented by Mrs. Warren and so refuses to examine how the ordering of gender and the commodification of sexuality inform the economic order that the play subjects to open attack. In this sense, Shaw both criticizes Vivie's isolation—she knows "nothing but mathematics" at the play's outset, and is *"absorbed in its figures"* at the close (217, 287)— and depends on it to preserve the asymmetry between illegitimacy and respectability, between illicit knowledge and the power demonstrated by its denial. As he would do later in Man and Superman (1905), Shaw assigns an environmental cause to sexual practice, and so removes the construction of gender and sexuality from the dialectical process of his drama. If the economy creates only Mrs. Warren's profession, it remains possible to bracket her activity off from the practice of respectable femininity, a discrimination between "real" and "ideal" social institutions that the play generally takes as illusory. Maintaining an isolating barrier between Vivie's intellectualized energy and the sexuality she shares with Mrs. Warren, Shaw duplicates the divisions between pure and impure women that sustain the theater of Pinero.

"Woman's great art is to lie low, and let the imagination of the male endow her with depths" (Shaw, *Our Theatres* 1: 202). The rhetoric of realism finds it difficult to treat the "woman question" because its strategies of staging woman are themselves representative of the social machinery the plays attempt to criticize. To transform the politics of this theater, Elizabeth Robins's *Votes for Women!* (1907) attempts to open its rhetoric to question. This transformation is a difficult one, as Robins suggests in a collection of essays on the suffrage movement. "Let us remember it was only

---

under, but in her belief that she is no different than a man"; as a result, she is "thus as devoid of identity as her mother, Paula Tanqueray, and Mrs. Dane, since she looks like a woman yet is not one; and Shaw's answer to the woman question is unveiled as no answer at all" (121). Gail Finney makes a similar comment of Shaw's *Candida*, remarking that for Shaw "androgyny is an ideal, but for all his attempts to present men and women as equal and alike, as in *Candida*, he succeeds only in perpetuating sexual stereotypes that underline the differences between the sexes" (226).

yesterday that women in any number began to write for the public prints":

> But in taking up the pen, what did this new recruit conceive to be her task? To proclaim her own or other women's actual thoughts and feelings? Far from it. Her task, as she naturally and even inevitably conceived it, was to imitate as nearly as possible the method, but above all the point of view, of man.
> She wrote her stories as she fashioned her gowns and formed her manners, and for the same reasons; in literature following meekly in the steps of the forgotten Master, the first tribal story-teller, inventor of that chimera, "the man's woman." *(Way Stations 5)*

It is a mark of Robins's intimacy with the conventions of the "new drama" that *Votes for Women!* does, in fact, "imitate as nearly as possible the method" of problem dramaturgy, as its contemporaries recognized: the play's heroine is "a new figure in the long procession of 'women with a past.' "[16] In the play, a young orphan, Jean Dunbarton, is to be married to a charismatic Conservative member of Parliament, Geoffrey Stonor, who claims to be sympathetic to the suffrage cause. In the opening scene, however, she meets Vida Levering, a vivacious and inspiring social activist in the mold of Christabel Pankhurst. Moreover, she learns from a respectable older woman the secret of Vida's past—sometime earlier, pregnant and deserted, Vida had an abortion. Act 2 takes place at a suffrage rally, where it becomes apparent to Jean that Stonor was the man involved. In the final act, Vida negotiates a deal with Stonor: Vida will convince Jean that she has surrendered her claims to Stonor, so that Jean will marry him, and Stonor will sign an agreement to support women's suffrage in Parliament.

Votes for Women! skilfully and pointedly develops the standard gambits of problem drama, particularly the illicit erotic past of the heroine. Like Paula Tanqueray, Vida continually demonstrates a fluency in the social manners definitive of good breeding, as well as a penchant for violating those proprieties. Unlike Paula, how-

---

16. Qtd. in Marcus 315. Marcus's chapter on *Votes for Women!* provides an extensive documentation of Robins's involvement in, and sponsorship of, the suffrage movement. Robins used the profits from *Votes for Women!* to buy a farm in Sussex, which she used to shelter suffragettes both before and after their prison sentences, and to house women in medical school; see also Peters 309.

ever, Vida Levering is interested not in penetrating society, to attain the status of the "inimitable" upper classes, but in reorganizing the social and political order that defines the place of women. Politics is notoriously difficult to stage in realistic theater, which tends to identify political subject matter with tendentiousness of purpose, with "thesis drama." Sexual politics can be spoken about only indirectly, as when someone alludes to Vida's secret "past" as an excuse for her poor standing in society. To mention abortion onstage would have been to bait the censor and lose, much as Shaw had done merely in referring to Mrs. Warren's "profession." Yet as Robins and others recognized, abortion provided a powerful device for politicizing women's social subjection in dramatic terms, and for epitomizing the ideological coercion that keeps the oppressed silent and their suffering unspoken. The unspeakable operation transforms a man's "indiscretion" into a woman's criminal misconduct, presenting her concealment now in terms not of the euphemistic manners of polite society but of the explicit code of the law. In *Votes for Women!* the woman's past is not at issue; it is the man's crime, and its hold on his future, that spurs the drama.[17]

While Paula's past destroys her future, Vida's past authorizes and validates her political activity. Reversing the paradigm of her friend Henry James's *The Bostonians,* in which the child suffrage-orator Verena Tarrant is moved by otherworldly inspiration, Robins locates Vida's developing mastery of platform oratory in the au-

---

17. In Harley Granville Barker's *Waste* (1907) abortion also comes to haunt a man poised at the brink of political success. Barker avoided the word "abortion" but could not escape the censorship; *Waste* was given two private performances in 1907 but not produced publicly until 1936. Robins had better luck with the censor, even though she coyly used the word in another context, and left it to the audience to get the point: "He called them [people without a political stance] 'wretches who never lived,' Dante did, because they'd never felt the pangs of partizanship. And so they wander homeless on the skirts of limbo among the abortions and off-scourings of Creation" (60). On *Waste* and the ensuing censorship controversy, see Kennedy 85–98, and Hynes, *The Edwardian Turn of Mind* 222. On staging *Votes,* see Kennedy 57–61. Thomas Postlewait notes the romantic attraction between Archer and Robins, and suggests that a variety of circumstances—their delay in producing Ibsen's *Little Eyolf* onstage, Robins's seclusion, inaccuracies in later memoirs—may point to the possibility that Robins was pregnant and gave birth to a child in 1895 (118–19).

thoritative testament of her own experience. In *Votes for Women!*, women's suffrage is a principal topic of discussion among the characters, and it is not surprising that women who "want to act independently of men" leave themselves open to vicious reclassification by those men: they are seen as "unsexed creatures" (47). Typically, though, the unsexing that transforms ladies into women seems to put them directly in the center of the erotic marketplace. *Votes for Women!* and *The Silver Box* shared the London stage for three weeks in the spring of 1907, and they share similar attitudes toward publicity, gender, and class. The woman of the street is always public property, for sale, and "ladies" who enter the public sphere are seen as risking their sanctioned feminine privacy. As an actress known for her pioneering work in bringing Ibsen's plays to the English stage, Robins's professional life was daily concerned with the fierce test of publicity, which directly pointed up her status both as woman and as commodity. In *Ancilla's Share*, Robins remarks that a "double cause is at the roots of man's long disrespect for the actress—the professional ground, which she shared with the actor, and the ground she occupied alone. . . . To say 'a public man' is to convey the idea of one arrived at eminence, usually at office; at honours, if not honour. To say 'a public woman' is, or was recently, to say a woman of the streets" (76). In *Votes for Women!* Vida retains the marks of the actress, transformed into a sign of power, part of her ability to define herself before the masculine social spectator. An agitator for improved shelters for indigent women, Vida occasionally disguises herself as a working woman, much as Robins would later disguise herself in the uniform of the Salvation Army to conduct research among the poor for novels and political tracts (Marcus 338). This "acting" becomes the instrument of her social awareness, an activity that reveals the working of gender oppression lurking within the institutions of society.

In her novel *The Convert*, an adaptation of *Votes*, Robins elaborates Vida's response to taking the public stage:

> Vida glanced at the men. Their eyes were certainly fixed on the two ladies in a curious, direct fashion, not exactly impudent, but still in a way no policeman had ever looked at either of them before. A coolly watchful, slightly contemptuous stare, interrupted by one man turning to say something to the other, at which both grinned. Vida was conscious of wishing that she had come in her usual clothes—above

all, that Janet had not raked out that "jumble sale" object she had perched on her head. (74)

The realistic theater literalizes the thematics of visibility informing social relations at large. Vida discovers in *Votes* that far from being a sign of "unsexed" status, a woman's independence seems to register her availability, and vulnerability: "I put on an old gown and a tawdry hat. . . . You'll never know how many things are hidden from a woman in good clothes. The bold, free look of a man at a woman he believes to be destitute—you must *feel* that look on you before you can understand—a good half of history" (50). To become a "woman" in this society is necessarily to risk the protection, enslaving though it is, of class, position, and sanctioned femininity. For a lady to step into the part of woman is, for women of Vida's class at least, to step from the auditorium onto the stage, and so to step into the perspective from which "realism" becomes visibly the encoding of masculine power, as many suffragettes in the period discovered.

"For a man to lay down laws as to what is and is not 'womanly' and 'seemly,' appears to me, theoretically, a piece of impertinent Helmerism," William Archer remarked of *A Doll's House;* yet the rhetoric of realism enacts just such a patriarchal law (1894 69).[18] Robins uses Vida's performance to reveal the strategies that subject women both psychologically and politically. And although the play generally duplicates the action of the problem play, it contains one remarkable departure, the central rally scene in Trafalgar Square, where Vida addresses the audience onstage and in the auditorium, a scene particularly noted by its contemporaries for its lifelike quality. Archer recalled it as one of "the most admirable and enthralling scenes I ever saw on any stage. . . . Throughout a whole act it held us spellbound, while the story of the play stood still, and we forgot its existence." Predictably, though, Archer finds the scene's didactic quality intrusive: "It was only within a few minutes of the end,

---

18. Max Beerbohm is, perhaps, most revealing here, for in reducing the play's use of well-made conventions to a "syllogism"—" 'I was seduced. I had not the vote. Therefore all women ought to have the vote' "—he at once exposes Robins's reliance on the well-made convention and dismisses her attempt to validate feminine experience as justification for political action (463); see also MacCarthy 34–35.

when the story was dragged in neck and crop, that the reality of the thing vanished, and the interest with it" (*Play-Making* 20). In a drama demonstrating the need of women to discover the disabling gaze of the absent masculine spectator, the central scene—and the most directly political one—interrupts the invisible barrier between stage and auditorium and elaborates a continuity between the drama, its performance, and the spectator's observation. Vida's performance transforms the audience's silent, concealed observation into a kind of *gest*, an ostensibly "private" act now realized in terms of its public consequences. For Vida not only takes the stage, she stages her audience as well, dramatizing the politics encoded in the realistic theater's claim to a neutral, objective mimesis. Speaking to the audience, Vida dramatizes the relationship that the theater conceals, the role of the private masculine spectator in producing the angry, resistant public woman.

Robins's strategy here points up the necessity for a critical realism to dramatize the implication of the spectator in the subjection of the figures of the stage. Much recent work theorizing the representation of women onstage has argued that the theater, like film, like reading, works as ideology by positioning its spectator, by addressing and so constituting its audience. Catherine Belsey's remarks on realistic texts might be applied to realistic performance as well, for the realistic theater similarly represents "a world of consistent subjects who are the origin of meaning, knowledge and action" onstage, and offers "the reader [spectator], as the position from which the text [spectacle] is most readily intelligible, the position of subject as the origin both of understanding and of action in accordance with that understanding" (51–52). To adapt Belsey's phrasing, however, invites us to consider the different means available to texts and to performances for positioning and articulating these subjects, and also to ask how reading provides an inadequate model for describing the spectator's subjection to ideology in the theater. A provocative opportunity is provided by Susan Glaspell's now-classic short story *A Jury of Her Peers* and its original stage version, *Trifles* (1916). Both the story and the play concern a similar sequence of events: a county attorney, Sheriff Peters and his wife, and a neighboring couple, Lewis and Martha Hale, are called to an abandoned Nebraska farmhouse to investigate the strangulation of John Wright. While the three men search the house, Mrs. Peters and Mrs. Hale are confined to the kitchen, where they discover and conceal the clues that would explain the crime and condemn Wright's wife, Minnie, as a murderer. As the two women reconstruct the narrative of Minnie's life, they are continually drawn to the significant "little things" of Minnie's kitchen world, rather than to the "evidence" sought by the men, evidence which leaves the woman's story untold: the state of the kitchen, a sudden imprecision in Minnie's quilting, her patched and worn clothing (25). As Annette Kolodny suggests, Glaspell presents a reading of "woman" as a text invisible to the men (who judge Minnie, and repeatedly evaluate and qualify Mrs. Hale and Mrs. Peters), who finally fail to interpret either the scene, the crime, or "the women's imaginative universe, that universe within which their acts are signs" (58).

Both *Jury* and *Trifles* reverse the "woman with a past" paradigm, for Minnie's criminality arises not through her contact with public life but through her subjection to an oppressive—normal— domesticity. The signal narrative strategy of *Jury* requires the reader to criticize the relationship between gender and interpretive authority, for the narrative exposes the operation of patriarchal ideology both in the story and in the reader's interpretive activity as well. From the outset, *Jury* identifies the narrative point of view with that of Mrs. Hale, and even her husband's recounting of his discovery of the crime is placed within her narrative voice: "Lewis often wandered along and got things mixed up in a story. She hoped he would tell this straight and plain, and not say unnecessary things that would make it harder for Minnie Foster" (8). To readers, Mrs. Hale's voice colors the typically realistic interdependence of environment, character, event, and narrative reconstruction, most explicitly when the objects in the kitchen are presented for our inspection:

> Everyone in the kitchen looked at the rocker. It came into Mrs. Hale's mind that this chair didn't look in the least like Minnie Foster—the Minnie Foster of twenty years before. It was a dingy red, with wooden rungs up the back, and the middle rung gone; the chair sagged to one side. (10–11)

In *Jury*, objects emerge as evidence only within codes of narration already inscribed as feminine, as illegitimate or trivial alongside the masculine strategies of detection practiced by the authorities. This pattern is enforced as Mrs. Hale interprets the environment through reference to her own trifling experiences; looking at Minnie's flour, "She thought of the flour in her kitchen at home—half sifted, half not sifted. She had been interrupted, and had left things half done. What had interrupted Minnie Foster?" (19). To read the short story, then, we must abandon these interpretive prejudices and learn to read within Mrs. Hale's perspective. *Jury* requires the reconstruction of the "immasculated" reader (male or female) within the female narrative voice.[19] To read Minnie, and so to read the narrative of *A Jury of Her Peers*, is to engage reading as a political activity, one in which intelligibility and interpretation are shown to arise from the constructions of gendered behavior. Only women can read with women's eyes, but *Jury* positions its readers to recognize and record their anger by being schooled in the act of resistant reading.

Staging such a narrative obviously entails a critical refiguring of this process, the replacement of the narrative voice by the mise-en-scène, and of the reader by the spectator. Although Glaspell copied much of the short story's dialogue from the earlier *Trifles*, the interpretive and political activities required of the spectator are markedly different from those required of the story's reader. While the narrative voice of the story simultaneously constructs and interprets the material world, the theater presents only the stark "loaded locale" of the stage room, the realistic box where "everything is in view, lying in wait" (States 68).

The kitchen in the now abandoned farmhouse of John Wright, a gloomy kitchen, plainly left without having been put in order—unwashed pans under the sink, a loaf of bread outside the bread-box, a dish-towel on the table—other signs of incompleted work. (5)

In *Jury*, the objects are made to signify through Mrs. Hale's reading of them. She identifies with Minnie—and reveals Minnie to the reader—by reading the "text" of her kitchen. Not to read with Mrs. Hale is to retain a spectatorial distance and condescension identi-

---

19. As Patrocinio P. Schweickart suggests, invoking Judith Fetterley's sense that cultural forms "immasculate" the subject, a feminist model of reading might imply a strategy of "connection" rather than mastery, a relationship between reader and narrative voice arguably structured in the reading of Glaspell's story (41, 52–53). On reading *Jury*, see Fetterley.

fied with the men in the story: a "kind of *sneaking*" attitude, "locking her up in town and coming out here to get her own house to turn against her" (*Jury* 23). In the theater, though, the objects of the stage room are shorn of this narrative voice, the voice that requires the audience's assent and that shapes its reformation as readers. In *Trifles*, Mrs. Hale and Mrs. Peters come to the same conclusions they reach in *Jury* and deceive the authorities in the same way. Yet while in reading the story our insertion within a woman's resistant perspective is critical to an informed reading of events, in the realistic theater our relationship with Mrs. Hale and Mrs. Peters can only be an accessory one: however much we pretend to see through their eyes, we really see only with our own.

It might be argued, of course, that as spectators we are free to adopt the point of view of the characters onstage, and *Trifles* certainly urges the audience to believe that the women are correct in their reading of events. At the same time, though, the play consistently presents the "freedom" and "objectivity" of a spectator's observation as false, irresponsible, and uninformed, not really empowered to resolve the "truth" that realistic dramaturgy promises and withholds. In both story and play, the role of spectator is a damning one: Mrs. Hale convicts herself for her years of detached observation, for the assumption of a spectatorial distance that has allowed Minnie's suffering to go unseen. *Jury* requires our transformation as readers and leads us to "see" Minnie by rejecting the unseeing "spectating" performed by the men. *Trifles*, while inviting a sympathetic evaluation of Minnie Wright, stages the narrative within a framework that exposes but maintains the subject/object, male/female dichotomies that the story brilliantly elides in the process of reading. The figuration of reading as a gendered activity in *Jury* works through our identification with Mrs. Hale's perspective, a kind of reading that is explicitly interested, biased, engaged. Readers of *Jury*, men and women, cross the boundary into a feminist reading practice. The audience of *Trifles* can observe this activity and sympathize with it, but only from a distance, the explicitly "masculine" distance with which the realistic theater insistently "others" its objects. *Jury* and *Trifles* expose the spectator, revealing *his* objectivity as a gendered means of social control, and as a form of blindness as well. The politics of *Jury* asks us to forsake the blindness of the spectator by teaching us to engage in a political practice of reading. *Trifles* also invites us to forsake this blindness, but it has yet to imagine an alternative to the dichotomies of realistic theatricality, a new way of seeing.

Read in contrast to *Jury*, *Trifles* forces us to recognize the constraints imposed on the realistic spectator's freedom of interpretation, the extent to which it is precisely the freedom *not* to see. *Trifles* also suggests the difficulty of exposing the politics of realistic theatricality, and of engaging in a social critique with a theatrical apparatus so fully implicated in the production of social reality itself. Despite a powerful and distinguished tradition extending from Gerhart Hauptmann and Zola to Sarah Daniels, David Storey, Edgar White, August Wilson, and others, realistic methods have a compromised implication in the social ills they often appear to criticize. In the end, the thematics of observation provide an important figure for the realistic theater's inability to transcend its own conditions of representation, its reliance on a species of "objectivity" that mystifies the audience it would—and often does, indirectly—subject to inquiry.

2

Actors and Objects

INVISIBLE ACTORS: O'NEILL, THE METHOD, AND THE MASKS OF "CHARACTER"

> None of us can help the things life has done to us. They're done before you realize it, and once they're done they make you do other things until at last everything comes between you and what you'd like to be, and you've lost your true self forever.
> —Eugene O'Neill, *Long Day's Journey Into Night*

The realistic location of character in a sustaining, possibly determining stage world inextricably entwines character and environment at the moment it dialecticizes them. This thematic interdependence is both the hallmark of modern realistic drama since Ibsen and Strindberg and the main problem of realistic theatrical production: to preserve and express the romantic interiority of "character" in a stage medium that compromises it, exhausts it, or simply has no means of speaking it. As we have seen, realistic drama and theater are traced by a concern to relate visibility to objectification, and privacy to empowerment, strategies of representation complicit in broader social attitudes toward the purpose and scope of identity and action. The drama is concerned with character and environment, but the theater expresses this concern in its own materials—actors and objects. Much as the drama identifies the privacy of character in the romantic language of an evanescent "self," so the stage is driven to discover a practice for making this self articulate in performance. It is hard for us, perhaps, to see realistic acting as rhetorical, in large measure because the charismatic force of bodily display tends to overpower our sense that acting is a mode of interpreting and of signifying, as well as a mode of being and performing. Realistic drama particularly requires a performance rhetoric that makes its thematic emphasis on privacy and interiority legible, and legible in ways consistent with the mastering integration of the mise-en-scène. As acting responds to the problems of realistic characterization, so scene design, the reproduction of theatrical space as a fictive locale, evokes the dramatic "environment" through the work of stage practice. The realistic mise-en-scène is traced by the impossibility of finding an authentic privacy for the performer and providing it with authoritative expression in a material, detheatricalized environment. The dialectic between dramatic character and its environment, and between acting and its material stage, is also replicated by the audience of realism. For the theater constructs its audience by inverting this relationship: the audience's untheatricalized freedom before the spectacle is assured by suppressing the determining role of *its* environment, the theatrical milieu that shapes the process of its performance.

In this chapter, I want to consider how realistic acting and staging are complicit in the production of two zones of indeterminacy, of "privacy" characteristic of the rhetoric of realism: the dramatic "character" and the interpreting "spectator." This will first involve a reading of the theory of realistic acting and the elaboration of this theory offered by Eugene O'Neill's masked drama. I then turn to the use of material space, the rhetoric of the stage set in American expressionist plays (Elmer Rice's *The Adding Machine*) and realist theater (Rice's *Street Scene*, Sidney Kingsley's *Dead End*) of the 1920s and 1930s. Finally, I argue that the plays of Harold Pinter and Sam Shepard, despite their brilliantly disorienting surfaces, tend to confirm the priorities of this rhetoric, a rhetoric that is more directly confronted in the plays of Edward Bond.

To approach the thematics of character and environment in realistic drama through their articulation as the actors and objects of the realistic theater is to ask how the drama operates with and through the machinery of its stage. The realistic drama's obsession with the disclosure of elusive or unconscious motives is made challenging as an acting problem by the necessity of avoiding explicitly "theatrical" means of realizing them—the passionate arias of melodramatic acting or the explosive rant of the heroic mode. Yet the realistic claim to verisimilitude ultimately requires much more than underplayed acting. At its most extreme, it requires the performers to refrain from acting, to become identical with and thereby transparent to "character," in much the way that the practical properties and furnishings become transparent to the objects they signify in the drama. Yet the way that the realistic actor would finally come to disappear has more to do with the discovery of a private zone of untheatrical space, a privacy that enables and complicates the actor's submission to the mise-en-scène and that reciprocates the privacy assigned to the offstage audience. The difficulty of producing oneself as a public object, a task that the realistic actor shares with James Tyrone, Willy Loman, and other realistic characters, makes the discovery of this privileged interiority the chief dramatic and theatrical problem of the realistic mode. In Philip Fisher's remarkable phrase, the problem of realistic acting is a version of the problem confronted by the characters the actor plays, the necessary and difficult act of "disappearing in public" (155).

How does acting in the realistic mode of Stanislavski and the American Method textualize the actor's behavior, the character's behavior, and the behavior of the spectator who observes?[1] The familiar history of Stanislavski in America is both vexed and a trifle tedious: the constant revision of the "system" by Stanislavski and his disciples; the endless bickering between Lee Strasberg, Stella Adler, and others over its Americanization; the limitations of Method style when applied to drama outside the repertoire of modern realistic drama—surely these controversies have lost their teeth. I don't, of course, mean to dismiss the important differences between Stanislavski and Moscow Art Theater progeny like Vsevolod Meyerhold, Richard Boleslavsky, and Eugene Vakhtangov, or to

---

1. Joseph R. Roach has suggested that the Method's preeminence in American acting owes something to its paradigmatic function in Thomas Kuhn's sense. Recalling that paradigmatic texts are "sufficiently powerful to deflect a group of practitioners away from competing theories and methods of investigation" and that "they are open-ended enough to create a whole new set of problems" for the newly defined group of practitioners, Roach proposes considering *An Actor Prepares* as such a text: "When one views Constantin Stanislavski's *An Actor Prepares* (1936) in this light, with its American proponents of Method Acting serving as the redefined group of practitioners and *emotion memory* providing the puzzling anomaly, one can see why Kuhn's description of communities of scientific knowledge might provide an illuminating analogy for the history of acting theory" (*The Player's Passion* 14). For an overview of the Method in America, see Gray; for the classic account of its influence on the Group Theater, see Clurman. On Stanislavski's conception of acting, see Worthen, *Idea* 143–53.

homogenize the variety of approaches to Stanislavskian realism developed from the 1930s through the 1960s. But think for a moment of the terms we use to describe, and to prescribe, craftsmanship in acting: the necessity of acting in response to the "given circumstances"; mental and physical concentration and relaxation; the analysis of a scene into behavioral "objectives," even "beats" of desire; how actors work in the moment and "live truthfully under the imaginary circumstances of the play" (Bruder et al. 5). As a shorthand for the Method, these notions have come to permeate our conception of acting, at the very least of a certain kind of acting, and we may find it difficult to denaturalize them from our sense of theater itself, to see them in history as the product of a specifically modern, "realistic" innovation. Robert Lewis, for example, defending the Method from its detractors and from its own excesses, argues that the Method applies "to *every kind of acting*—good acting—and not narrowly to realistic acting as such" (xii). Lewis is echoed by Charles Marowitz, who praises Stanislavskian performance by finding in its outlines a universal technique of the stage: "Each time an actor is performing with credibility and without recourse to cliché, motivated from within and unshakably involved in his role, he is practising the Method and affirming the precepts of Constantin Stanislavsky. . . . Because the Method is not an invention or a modern discovery, it is simply an articulation of truths which have existed for centuries" (*Method* 36–37). Institutionalized in the training of drama schools, in college and university theater programs, and in the practice of the professional stage, the ethical orientation and many of the specific practices associated with the Method have become so pervasive as to describe a kind of basic equipment for acting. More important, the Method describes what it is we look for as an audience when we look for dramatic "character" in the realistic theater, and how we look for it as well.

Like all modes of stage production, the Method prescribes a body of techniques for producing a significant relation between the actor's stage performance and the fiction of dramatic character, relations that imply a certain range of interpretive activity for the spectator as well. The work of Stanislavski and his inheritors was instrumental in defining the form and process of realistic performance, and it is not surprising to find the Method traced by a familiar rhetoric. Like realistic drama and its theater, the Method insists on the transparency of its means of signification, on the repression of the actor's work as a legitimate object of the audience's attention, on an economy of meaning identified exclusively with the fictive drama the performers produce, on the exclusion of the spectators from the spectacle. The principal feature of Method characterization is that "character" is withdrawn from the audience, produced as an object ideally removed from the interference of the observing public. The actor turns his or her attention away from the audience in order to objectify the performance and to subject "character" to the scenic integration of the dramatic setting and of the ensemble of performers/characters. This integration of performers into the setting rapidly becomes a goal of realistic performance, and Stanislavski provides its classic formulation: an actor must seek the "public solitude" necessary to confront "the abnormal circumstance of an actor's creative work," the fact that "it must be done in public" (278). Much like realistic characters, actors in this mode perform for an audience that cannot be acknowledged, for to recognize the audience would be to render the performance theatrical, to be cast in an oddly inauthentic, spectatorial role, *indicating* a performance that is not fully inhabited. As the authors of a recent handbook remind us, this "realistic" attitude toward the audience has been fully naturalized as the condition of theater in our era: "Audiences are intelligent and highly suggestible; theatregoers come to the theatre to immerse themselves in illusion. The more attention you call to any theatrical artifice, the less the audience will accept it, because you are calling attention to the artificial nature of the theatre as a whole" (Bruder et al. 8).

The Method's strategies for interpreting textual features and for representing them as significant behavior are part of the assertion of an objective relationship between the audience and the stage: "character" is represented as an organic and distinct object in the field of the spectator's attention to the drama. The actor takes his cue from the director, who unifies the play's action in terms of a "super-objective" or "spine," phrasing as an abstract theme the activity to be accomplished by the performance as a whole. The actor finds his own "objectives" as a way of producing character in relation to, and as a vehicle for, these thematic goals. As Lorrie Hull describes in her textbook of the Strasberg Method:

> He asks questions such as: What is the theme of the play? (What is the play about?) Does his character have a main action (spine) or driving force? How might a character's main action be expressed in each of the character's scenes? (148)

Such determinations—theme, spine, main action, driving force—clearly arise from the kind of questions that are trained on the text, a paradigm for the production of "character" specific to realistic theatricality. Stanislavskian performance pursues a "life in art," a life that is necessarily progressive or processual. By conceiving the action as directed toward a single motivational "objective," Method performance integrates and subordinates characterization to the static harmonies of the scenic milieu and the dramatic theme.

Determined by its spine of objectives, character in Method performance becomes an object to be plotted, much in the manner of Hedda Gabler's pistols or Blanche Dubois's luggage. We can more readily see the critical consequences of the Method in the light of a more explicitly "literary" interpretive practice. Francis Fergusson's landmark study *The Idea of a Theater* is a case in point, for Fergusson readily combines a Method approach to script reading with a New Critic's sense of the organic text. First published in 1949 at the height of the Method's impact, *The Idea of a Theater* presents as its central heuristic the conception of "analogies of action" latent within a play's language, characterization, and scenic structure. In their repetitive combinations, these analogies articulate the play's organic dramatic form, for each component works to realize the play's spine of action and meaning. The spine

> is to be used to indicate the direction which an analysis of a play should take. It points to the object which the dramatist is trying to show us, and we must in some sense grasp that if we are to understand his complex art: plotting, characterization, versification, thought, and their coherence. For this purpose practical rules may be devised, notably that of the Moscow Art Theater. They say that the action of a character or a play must be indicated by an infinitive phrase, e.g., in the play *Oedipus*, "to find the culprit." This device does not amount to a definition but it leads the performer to the particular action which the author intended. (230)

The actor's performance is determined by a single thematic, one that claims its origin in the dramatic action or in authorial intention. And much as Stanislavski does, Fergusson—who was trained in the Method by Richard Boleslavksy and Maria Ouspenskaya at the American Laboratory Theater—locates these objectives in the demands of the text itself, rather than in the critical procedures used to discover them, the infinitive phrases, the analogical correlations of a character's immediate activities with thematic abstractions, and so on. "Character," like the objects of the set, becomes a vehicle for the production of a single, integrated "meaning," a theme or spine achieved within the controlling perspective of the absent spectator's vision.

To discover such objectives, the actor requires an analytical technique, one that necessarily inflects the kind of "meaning" that can be produced through it. The actor frames objectives by segmenting the script in terms of a motivational subtext. Character is represented as an effect of a coherent series of "beats" of desire that seem to motivate and substantiate the spoken text and the visible deeds of the stage. The beat identifies actor and character in the typical terms of the Method, posing an undecidable difference between the present experience of the actor and the represented emotion of the character as the sign of effective performance; in good acting, actor and character are affectively fused. The actor's engagement with "real" experience while presenting a fictive character marks the farthest extension of realistic rhetoric into the practice of acting; in the Method, to "signify" or "indicate" the character is to fail, to interpose a sense of the performer's activity between the audience, its reading of the character's behavior, and its interpretation of psychological attitudes and motivations. The presence of the actor's real experience asserts the absence of technique, seems to render the actor transparent to a character whose feelings seem grounded in live reality rather than being produced as artifice. Like the scenic rhetoric of which it is a part, realistic acting conceals its rhetoric behind the "reality" of the objects it stages: real doors, real emotions.

Actor training reveals the continued effect of Stanislavski in the series of complex activities designed to improve and to monitor the actor's sensitivity to authentic expression.[2] To develop this respon-

2. Training in this mode might proceed from simple exercises like the breakfast drink ("The student creates his usual breakfast drink [commonly

siveness, actors work not only on sense memory and sensitivity exercises but also on taking cues from unspecified, preverbal, or unverbalized "impulses" rather than from preconceived "meanings" that may seem latent in the words of the text (as, for example, in Sanford Meisner's well-known exercise in which the actors improvise a given situation using only a single word or phrase, repeated again and again). By learning to act on impulse ("I wanted to eliminate all that 'head' work, to take away all the mental manipulation and get to where the impulses come from"), the actor's attention is diverted from the audience, and from the technique he or she is obliged to use to lend the drama a voice (Meisner and Longwell 36). The sense that successful acting happens when the actor is able to react through the text is revealing of our convictions about what is most powerfully "real"—for actors and for audiences—about realistic theater. Resisting "head work" assures that the character will be experienced as something prior to language, as a spontaneous, reactive, "free" subject.

Let me try to suggest in larger terms how acting inspired by the Method characterizes the actor's performance, enabling us to read (and so to write) the script of "character." Like the actor, character is withdrawn into a distinct, frontally oriented and visible space of representation; it is integrated to the verisimilar codes that organize that space as a scene; it is a discrete whole, a subject proceeding toward an "objective" through a series of consequential activities; it exists and can be known, but only through reaction, indirection; it cannot be staged or theatricalized and remain true to itself; it is free. And, finally, its course is marked not so much by the explicit verbal text as by the subtext of will and desire. The Method's reliance on subtext offers something of a logocentric view of the relationship between the dramatic text and the actor's portrayal of character. The actor's task is to look beneath the distortions of the verbal text, to

---

orange juice or coffee]. All of the objects in the exercise are created imaginarily.") and sunshine ("The student creates the feeling of exposure to the sun. The instructor will be able to see if the senses are working when the student is not reproducing a motor activity."), through more complex exercises like private moments, animal exercises, combinations of animal exercises with human characteristics, all designed to train sensitivity to circumstances of emotional production (see Hull 45).

find or to invent the subtextual spine of beats that will provide the text with actable life. The Method attempts to authenticate the realistic character's presence on the stage by recovering "speech" from its belatedness to "writing," by locating the traces of speech prior to the words of the play. Much as the Method trains its performers to register subtextual experience faithfully before proceeding to work with texts, so their performance tends to locate character in an ultimately private and indeterminate zone of unverbalized motivation, in what David Richard Jones calls "modernist internality": "With the vanishing of soliloquy and tirade, conscious articulation of subtextual psychology has become a sine qua non of impersonation. The written drama has never had less rhetoric of feeling, but acting has never had more" (76). Character, like the acting that produces it, develops through the operation of desire toward a particular objective through a spine of activity. At the same time it continually disappears, becomes speechless behind the mask—of the text, of acting—that falsifies it even as it brings it to the stage.

Although we may also find ourselves through other kinds of performance, there is little point in trying to repudiate Method notions of acting and character: acting imbued with these values of "truth," interior fidelity, subtextual vitality, and character coherence may reflect our own most immediate sense of who we are, or want to be, in the theater. The rhetoric of the Method is at once a mode of representation and a mode of suasion, a means for producing onstage and for reproducing in us a sense of being and judgment, a sense of what *is*. Such acting is, in an important sense, ideology as behavior. "Character" can only be recognized from a transcendent or voyeuristic perspective, by an audience that is also speechless, not subject to staging. Realistic performance asserts a material world that intercedes between two zones of privacy where the self is held to be complete and fulfilled: in the palpable but unknown interiority of the actor/character, and in the unconstrained freedom of the invisible observer. The determinism of the dramatic environment comes to seem almost illusory, as the rhetoric of realism assigns its most consequential authority to these mysterious realms of privacy within and beyond it.[3]

---

3. Herbert Blau has recently described the Method as presenting "what looked like overtures of intimacy" that nonetheless kept "the audience at a

Actors and Objects   63

When we think of the plays that popularized and were popularized by the Method, the first that come to mind are understandably connected with New York's Group Theater—like Clifford Odets's *Awake and Sing!* (1935)—or with its members after the Method had become recognized—Elia Kazan's production of *A Streetcar Named Desire* (1947), for instance. Such plays are now so closely associated with the style of the Method, though, that they obscure its rhetoric, how its strategies for producing character as acting develop an interpretive relationship between the audience, the performer, and the play. The Method's insistent emphasis on character interiority, a subversive indeterminacy lurking beneath its confident location of the actor in the given circumstances of the stage, is explored more provocatively in experimental and even expressionistic plays that subject the rhetoric of realistic enactment to distortion. I am thinking here in part of the European tradition represented by the plays of Ernst Toller, Georg Kaiser, August Strindberg, and Frank Wedekind, and of its American counterpart in plays like *The Hairy Ape* (1922), Rice's *The Adding Machine* (1923), or Sophie Treadwell's *Machinal* (1928). I also have in mind Eugene O'Neill's recalcitrant drama of the late 1920s, particularly *The Great God Brown* (1926) and *Strange Interlude* (1928). These are bizarre and unwieldy plays, manifestly part of the same dramatic project as *The Iceman Cometh* (1946) and *Long Day's Journey Into Night* (written 1939-40), yet at the same time dwarfed by those later plays. The economy of characterization that O'Neill discovered late in his career can make *Brown* and *Interlude* seem even more inflated in retrospect, deserving of O'Neill's reputation for banal pretension, the feeling that "his masks, asides, soliloquies, choruses, split characters and the like are really substitutes for dramatic writing . . . provoked not by a new vision but rather by a need to disguise the banality of the original material" (Brustein 327). The strongest impression left by O'Neill's drama, though, is not so much that the "masks, asides, soliloquies, choruses, split characters and the like"—to say nothing of the melan-

---

distance. Putting aside the paradoxical stylization of a technique concealing itself, the process was focused in the apparent offering of a 'private moment' (named and nurtured by Lee Strasberg, this was the inversion of 'public solitude'), which was not only private but secret, giving no access" (*The Audience* 256).

choly Caribbean dirges, the little formless fears, the tom-toms, pipe dreams, and foghorns—are superfluous, but that they are part of O'Neill's deepest and most consistent dramatic project: the exfoliation of an unconscious, intensely private, and interior self in the public action of the theater. O'Neill's drama is sometimes grandiose, gratuitous, and overwritten, and it never really escapes (perhaps O'Neill never wanted to escape) the highly charged seductions of melodrama.[4] But O'Neill's experimentation with the stage's resources represents a specifically *theatrical* inquiry into the status of realism. O'Neill's masked plays undertake a critical review of the rhetoric of realistic "character" and how it is produced and interpreted in the theater, notions that have become canonized both by the practice of the Method and by O'Neill's late plays.

The Great God Brown and *Strange Interlude* take the disclosure of character as their theme and present the drama in terms that both recall and question the rhetoric of realistic acting. At the moment that the Method is devising means for producing the actor as transparent to character, O'Neill works in what seems to be another direction entirely, toward a drama that formalizes and discriminates the relationship between actor and role through the use of masks. O'Neill's masked plays of the 1920s represent a theory of realistic performance, a use of masks to explore both realistic character and the dialectic within which realistic acting and dramatic characterization are defined.[5] "Looked at from even the most practical standpoint of the practicing playwright, the mask *is* dramatic in itself, *has always* been dramatic in itself, *is* a proven weapon of attack," O'Neill wrote in 1932, after nearly a decade of experimentation ("Memoranda" 117). Yet despite his (and others') imitations of Greek drama, O'Neill's plays seem to have less in common with the iconic masking of the classical theater or with the whirligig

---

4. O'Neill himself recognized, and possibly oversimplified, the impact of his father James's career in *The Count of Monte Cristo* on his own sense of theater: "My early experience with the theater through my father . . . really made me revolt against it. As a boy I saw so much of the old, ranting, artificial, romantic stage stuff that I always had a sort of contempt for the theater" (qtd. in Sheaffer 205).

5. O'Neill's work with masks is part of a widespread interest in masks in the American theater in the 1920s, a vogue that preoccupied, among others, O'Neill's friends and partners Robert Edmond Jones and Kenneth Macgowan. See Smith 64–66.

disguise of *commedia dell' arte* and its derivatives in the Renaissance than might be supposed.[6] O'Neill's masks interrupt the realistic identification between actor and character, the actor's psychological and somatic commitment to identity with the role, in order to expose the rhetoric of this integration. A dialectic emerges between the character's mask of public behavior and the actor's face, which is made to signify internal, inexpressed, or inexpressible attitudes. As O'Neill suggested when recommending the use of masks in future productions of *The Hairy Ape*—"From the opening of the fourth scene, where Yank begins to think he enters into a masked world; even the familiar faces of his mates in the forecastle have become strange and alien"—the mask articulates a deep conviction regarding public life: "One's outer life passes in a solitude haunted by the masks of others" ("Memoranda" 119, 117). The mask expresses the character's painful objectification, the degree to which spectators imprison the self at the moment they seem to recognize it. When, as often happens in these plays, a character is unmasked, the actor's face asserts a more privileged interiority, a "subtextual" realm of feeling and action, a kind of "public solitude" threatened by its disclosure in the world.

This use of masking would seem, like the Method, to fetishize the interiority of experience, to render it as a mystified source of authority and transcendence. And the insistent dualism of O'Neill's masks does seem to align the interior "self" of the characters with presence and truth, a presence and truth that can be known only to the spectator in the privacy of the auditorium, but usually not in the public world shared with the other characters: "Play of masks—removable—the man who really is and the mask he wears before

---

6. Michael Goldman has remarked on the relationship between a dramatic role and a series of maskings, and on acting itself as a process of "showing how a character *acts*—that is, how he moves in and out of his repertory of roles; how he changes his disguise to meet every moment of the play, responding to changes in his situation and in the characters around him, revealing one thing and hiding another" (*The Actor's Freedom* 92). Goldman provides a useful heuristic both for readers and for performers of the drama, but this description of roles as masks has more in common with the exuberant roleplaying of Hamlet or Viola than with the earnest and tortuous dualism of O'Neill's characters. On masks, see also 49–50, where Goldman compares masks with the iconic aspect of dramatic roles.

the world" (Floyd 41). This dualism seems to oversimplify the scrupulous identification required by Method performance and by the complexity of the major roles in the realistic dramatic repertoire: Rosmer, Astrov, Larry Slade, and so on. Yet O'Neill believed that in *The Great God Brown* masks pursued a more invasive vision of character, not "the bromidic, hypocritical & defensive double-personality of people in their personal relationships—a thing I never would have needed masks to convey" (*Selected Letters* 246). As in the theater of Ibsen or Strindberg, the inner character can be expressed only indirectly, for when the masks are removed the characters are unrecognizable to one another (except for Dion and Cybel, who are recognizable only when they are unmasked). Such revelation is forbidding in O'Neill's play, for the unmasked characters are fearsome to behold, as if both the act of self-disclosure and the act of witnessing it were equally appalling. Early in the play, for instance, Dion removes his mask, revealing "*his face, which is radiant with a great pure love for her and a great sympathy and tenderness.*" Margaret, "*who has been staring at him with terror,*" puts on "*her mask to ward off his face*" and cries out, "Dion! Don't! I can't bear it! You're like a ghost! You're dead! Oh, my God! Help! Help!" (343–44). The appetite for masks in O'Neill is the same appetite embodied in the Method's promise of spontaneity, a desire to locate a palpable yet indeterminate, untheatrical "self" onstage, within the artifice of the actor's performance.

"Perhaps I have sometimes been off the track, possibly my use of masks and asides is artifice and bombast," O'Neill later confessed (*Selected Letters* 440). Yet the most bombastic conception of the play—that masks can be transferred between characters—is also its richest. Allowing the actors to address their masks, this device literalizes the practice of acting, in that the actors duplicate in their own performances the objectifying gaze of the spectator, as though the self were always constrained by an audience, projected, imagined, internal, or invisible. In a critical scene, staid Billy Brown addresses Dion Anthony's mask before assuming it, and assuming a role in Dion's life as well:

> Then you—the I in you—*I* will live with Margaret happily ever after. (*More tauntingly*) She will have children by me! (*He seems to hear some mocking denial from the mask. He bends toward it*) What? (*Then with a sneer*) Anyway, that doesn't matter! Your children already love me

more than they ever loved you! And Margaret loves me more! You think you've won don't you—that I've got to vanish into you in order to live? Not yet, my friend! Never! (359).

The Great God Brown populates the privacy of "character," for if "one's inner life passes in a solitude hounded by the masks of oneself," then there is no spectatorial vantage from which to view the self or the world it engages ("Memoranda" 117). "Character" in this drama never escapes its subjection to and falsification by the coercion of the spectator, by the spectators in the audience, those on the stage, and those haunting the theater of the self.

As "an attempt at the new masked psychological drama which I have discussed before, without masks," *Strange Interlude* follows from the premise of *The Great God Brown* ("Memoranda" 119). Yet although O'Neill initially conceived the roles in *Strange Interlude* as masklike, he focused the play's action more exclusively on the subtextual dimension of theatrical speech: "Method—Start with soliloquy—perhaps have the whole play nothing but a thinking aloud . . . speech breaking through thought as a random process of concealment, speech inconsequential or imperfectly expressing the thought behind" (Floyd 74). At first glance, the "asides" seem much like the actor's face in *The Great God Brown,* a technique for presenting a character's interior, private, and spectatorial commentary on the artifice of public behavior. But the asides quickly open a *mise-en-abîme,* implying an endless regress of self-deceit. This duplicity becomes particularly evident at moments of confession, such as when Leeds seems to recognize his reasons for preventing Gordon from marrying Nina before going off to the war:

> Yes. That's exactly it. She knows in some queer way. And she acts toward me exactly as if she thought I had deliberately destroyed her happiness, that I had hoped for Gordon's death and been secretly overjoyed when the news came! (*His voice is shaking with emotion*) And there you have it, Charlie—the whole absurd mess! (*Thinking with a strident accusation*)
> And it's true, you contemptible...!
> (*Then miserably defending himself*)
> No!...I acted unselfishly...for her sake! (493)

The device is often clumsy, particularly so if we read—as Brooks Atkinson did, reviewing the play for the *New York Times*—"the nickel-weekly jargon that Mr. O'Neill offers as thinking" as an authoritative subtext, an uncompromised access to the "true" motives of the characters. Yet O'Neill's engagement with "character" is even more disturbing, for in *Strange Interlude* there is no recourse to depth, privacy, or interiority that is not already theatricalized, a shallow stage for the masks of oneself.

The prose of realistic dialogue asserts its verisimilitude by insisting on its unliterary banality. The drama—in Ibsen, Strindberg, Chekhov, O'Neill—often arises through the necessity of wanting to say more than such language allows. The need to carve out a subtext beneath the lines, or to reach beyond the envelope of style for the evocative, but potentially bombastic, melodramatic, or excessive phrase is always implicit in the discourse of realistic style, giving rise as much to O'Neill's masks as to Ibsen's "vine leaves" and "castles in the air." The sense of a world of entrapment from which the self provides only an illusory point of private repair is O'Neill's most characteristic contribution to the realistic drama: for O'Neill, hell is not only other people but the masks of oneself that each of us contains. The elaborate theatrical mechanism of O'Neill's masked drama may too often misfire, but this revision of realistic characterization persists in O'Neill's later drama as well, where the theatricalization of interiority marks O'Neill's most challenging response to the rhetoric of realistic characterization.

Critics have frequently noted the metadramatic aspect of *Long Day's Journey Into Night,* the sense in which the family of Tyrones is a family of actors, each performing for others and indeed performing for the internal audience of an evanescent "self."[7] The play presents us with a rich sense of the interdependencies and deceptions of family life, and the characters' contradictory acknowledgments and evasions seem to lend them a typically realistic mystery. The absence of an intrusive expressionism shouldn't blind us to the play's manifest conventions of disclosure, as when Mary comments on Edmund's illness:

> I know he'll be all right in a few days if he takes care of himself. (*As if she wanted to dismiss the subject but can't.*) But it does seem a shame he should have to be sick right now. (16)

7. See, for example, Chothia 188–89, and Bogard xviii.

As in *Strange Interlude,* O'Neill stages "character" through the dialectic of self-deception, or failed self-deception, in which Mary's hope that Edmund will improve declares her belief that he won't, in which her concern for her son only partly masks her fear for herself. Like many plays in this mode, *Long Day's Journey Into Night* is structured around a series of confessions, a self-staging to an audience of observers, and these confessions often have the calculated quality of performance. Such confessions seem both to cast others as spectators, consumers of the lies of self-disclosure, and to be performed for an internal, equally critical audience as well. Jamie's hatred of Edmund, Tyrone's bitter disappointment in his career, Mary's regret for her idyllic childhood seem both actual and "enacted," inscribed as fictions at the moment they declare the privilege of truth.[8]

The rhetoric of realistic characterization—in drama and in the practice of acting—claims a romantic interiority as an authorizing ground of dramatic explanation. The progress of the dramatic action is explained as a function of the psychology and development of the characters, motives that can finally be seized only from a similarly privileged point of absence and privacy offstage. Many plays in this mode, those of Ibsen and Chekhov as well as those of American realists like O'Neill, Arthur Miller, and Tennessee Williams, stage this self as self-delusion, a fiction or evasion, as a commodity for others' consumption that masks an inner emptiness. Like realistic fiction, which claims to position the reader in the plenitude and presence of the bourgeois subject who is often both its fictive subject and narrator, realistic theater seems to assign to the voyeuristic audience the ability to complete the drama, to relate events to interpretation, to discover the meaning of the drama in the reconstitution of its spine.

To practice this kind of interpretation, the audience of realistic theater must accept its construction by this rhetoric, assent in particular to the occlusion of its own manifestly theatrical relation to the

---

8. In his brilliant study, *Modern Drama and German Classicism: Renaissance from Lessing to Brecht,* Benjamin Bennett traces the drama of divided consciousness—internally divided within character and divided between the stage and audience—to the achievement of German classicism. On the relationship between self-division and theatrical observation, see 291, and chapter 8.

events on the stage, a relation often exposed in the drama as illegitimate, duplicitous, merely "theatrical." O'Neill's drama points out that the consumers of the "truth" of character consume only performances, not selves, masks of disguise and disclosure manufactured to seem believable, much like the characters staged by Method performance. The peculiarities of realistic discourse in the theater prevent the drama from representing "consistent subjects who are the origin of meaning" (Belsey 51–52). All its subjects are, at least, duplicitous, actor-characters, and O'Neill's drama often assigns a similar undecidability to the characters' internal stages, where they find themselves peopled by a cast of others. The rhetoric of the Method, with its premium on the authenticity of impulse, works to assert a consistent subject, while the drama works to undermine its credibility. The realistic theater stages an asymmetrical relation between the spectacle on the stage and its silent consumers, for the audience's claim to integrate character and action stands apart from the dialectics of the dramatic performance it observes.

VISIBLE SCENES: AMERICAN REALISM AND THE ABSENT AUDIENCE

I have stressed here the psychological aspect of realistic "character" and its production as acting. The interpretive perspective urged by this drama is clarified in plays of a more sociological orientation, in which the objects of stage design become metonymic figures for a world of material and metaphysical constraint. The anxiety of psychological realism is that the self may be only an act. The sociological mode lives on the fear that the world is only a theater, that there is no escape, no point of vantage from which others—or the environmental forces of economy, society, history—can be viewed: that it is not possible, in other words, to be a spectator after all. O'Neill's expressionism is tightly trained on psychological processes, but expressionism generally opens a wider vista on the relationship between character and a social environment. Gerald Rabkin is right to find a "monodramatic" impulse in expressionist drama, in which "all technical devices, all characters and situations combine to reveal the psychological workings of the mind of the hero, or as the case may be, the antihero" (131). Yet for all its solipsistic focus on the experience of its central character, as a stage practice expressionist drama depends on the interpretive relations engrained in the realistic mode it appears to challenge. Even though it represents the externalized affect of a given character, the material stage of expressionist theater is itself a constraint, a world seen from the dystopic perspective of its victims rather than from the "objective" perspective of its privileged audiences. In performance, expressionistic plays tend to literalize the relations of realism, as characters are enclosed in a mechanistic and alien material world onstage, still searching for an elusive realm of private experience.

Elmer Rice's *The Adding Machine* (1923), for example, provides a kind of negative image of the realistic drama it swerves to avoid. The play's scenographic devices are familiar examples of the allegorical dimension of the expressionistic mode: the giant adding machine; the *ballet mécanique* of the Zeros, Ones, Twos, Threes, Fours, Fives, and Sixes; Zero's trial; the meeting with Shrdlu and Daisy Devore beyond the grave. In part, the play satirizes its central character, the organization man whose failure of imagination and will makes him an eternal slave. Even when he meets Daisy in the Elysian fields, after all, Zero maintains the moral standards of suburban society ("Anyway, they wouldn't stand for this—the way we been going on"), and the play closes with Lieutenant Charles injecting Zero back into worldly existence for another incarnation: "You can't change the rules—nobody can—they've got it all fixed. It's a rotten system—but what are you going to do about it?" (99, 105). Lukács argues that the "much-heightened sense of the significance of milieu" enables the modern "drama of individualism" to become problematic, and so dramatic in its characteristic fashion ("Sociology" 434); Zero's nullity becomes dignified in exact proportion to the extraordinary power embodied in the scenic environment necessary to express and control him. And as in realistic drama, both the mechanistic mise-en-scène and the language of the text work to mask a possibly unrecognized, perhaps barely representable subtext of desire. This aspect of language is most evident in the play's brilliant second scene, where Daisy and Zero check an endless series of figures. The public language of accounting dissolves (for the audience) to reveal a private and incommunicable discourse:

DAISY: Six dollars. Three fifteen. Two twenty-five. Sixty-five cents. A dollar twenty. You talk to me as if I was dirt.

ZERO: I wonder if I could kill the wife without anybody findin' out. In bed some night. With a pillow.
DAISY: I used to think you was stuck on me. (72)

Although Rice thought *The Adding Machine* to be "the very antithesis of Ibsenism," it is, like most expressionist theater, substantiated by the realistic rhetoric it repudiates (*Living Theatre* 124). Rice described the difference between realism and expressionism to Dudley Digges, the first Mr. Zero, in the conventional terms of dramatic style: "In the realistic play, we look at the character from the outside. We see him in terms of action and of actuality. But in the expressionistic play we subordinate and even discard objective reality and seek to express the character in terms of his own inner life" (*Minority Report* 198–99). The "objective reality" that expressionism appears to discard is, in fact, simply—in the party scene, the trial—re-presented from the perspective of its victim. As in the realistic theater, the material world of the expressionist stage both constrains the character and becomes the character, in much the way that realistic heroes often find the signs of the degraded world they oppose etched within themselves.[9] For this reason, it's not surprising to find that Rice's sense of Zero restates the realistic dialectic between external pressure and a private zone of interior contradiction:

> For I conceive Zero as a complex being. A bundle of inconsistencies and contradictions, of impulses and fears, of desires and inhibitions. His conduct in a general sense is determined by hereditary influences, childhood environment, education and the social inheritance, but more particularly it is influenced by the state of his digestion, the weather, his internal secretions and the multitudinous sensory stimuli of light and sound, touch and temperature, taste, motion and pain. (qtd. in Murphy 150–51).

Plays like Sophie Treadwell's *Machinal* (1928), John Howard Lawson's *Roger Bloomer* (1923), and *The Adding Machine* suggest the problem posed by expressionism: namely, that as a *style* it superficially departs from a realistic ideology that it reifies in the rhetoric of its stage production. The expressionistic mapping of the dynamics of character onto the scenic materials of the stage presents a

---

9. See Williams, *Modern Tragedy* 98.

world governed by alienated, abstract forces that the characters in the plays are barely capable of recognizing. As Raymond Williams argues, the increasingly threatening and hostile realistic environment becomes (often in plays written by the same authors and produced by the same companies) transformed into a realization of the characters' responses to that environment, staging the characters' responses to the world as the dramatic world itself (*Drama* 339–40). In a sense, Rice's career is emblematic of Williams's observation, for in turning from the expressionistic mode of *The Adding Machine* and *The Subway* (1929) to the scenic realism of his most famous play, *Street Scene* (1929), Rice reveals the complicity between these two modes of production, a complicity based primarily on the determining power located in the *scene*. Moreso than the expressionistic theater, drama in the sociological mode uses the object world of the stage design to control the audience's interpretive perspective on the action. Much as the mechanistic quality of expressionistic staging reduces the characters to machines, in the sociological drama the extent to which stage objects become agents of the action transforms the characters into things.

To view the lower classes as objects is one of the originary aspects of realistic theater; as Martin Meisel observes, even Zola's "public places, inhabited by functioning representations of all classes and occupations, suggest a sociological rather than a psychological perspective, and ultimately an alternative to bourgeois drama" (*Realizations* 374). The supposed neutrality of this environmental absence of perspective is enforced in *Street Scene* through the rhetorical arrangement of stage space. The *New York Times* reviewer commented on Rice's (and designer Jo Mielziner's) "lithographic New York environment" and saw it as the hallmark of a play apparently without "a point of view," without a perspective on the "traits of our slummy life." The title claims the play's slice of life for its subject, a working-class scene modeled on a brownstone front on New York's West 65th Street. Mielziner found the play "a work of strong, almost journalistic realism," and his celebrated set seemed to spill its contents directly onto the foreshortened playing area (*Designing* 148). The space, defined by the edge of a street running parallel to the proscenium downstage and the facade of the brownstone occupying the entire upstage wall, is one of maximum frontality. Directing the play, Rice orchestrated a variety of dramatically inconsequential activities to enhance the apparently random and lifelike process of the action, down to laying a concrete sidewalk on the stage and using prerecorded street noises throughout the performance to create an auditory as well as a visual environment. But it was Mielziner's set that became the play's protagonist, brooding over the drama, integrating the scattered and inconsequential lives of the characters.

As in plays like *The Silver Box*, the condition of such characters is to be visible, revealed to us on this occasion because of the summer heat and the size and poor ventilation of their apartments. The brownstone becomes a kind of vitalistic center of the action, and the characters become its furniture, a point emphasized toward the end of act 2, when two objects are about to be brought from the building: the corpse of Mrs. Maurrant and the belongings of the evicted Hildebrand family. The objectification of the characters is implied as well in the position that the play's environment assigned to its audience:

> What distinguishes "Street Scene" from a host of synthetic forerunners is Mr. Rice's remarkable sense of character. Here are not merely the automatons of the giddy city streets, but the people—the intellectual Jew who runs on endlessly about the capitalistic classes, the Italian musician who dreams of the flowery land from which he came, the office girl who wants to move out to Queens, the pleasant woman who is quietly sacrificing her life to a sick mother, the ruffian taxicab driver, the flirt, the school teacher, all brought into focus with telling strokes of character-portrayal. (Rev. of *Street Scene*)

Life "on the grimier edge of the middle class" is replete with social and ethnic types—the cranky Jewish intellectual, the happy-go-lucky Italian, the stoic Swedish janitor, and so on—whose verisimilitude is a function of the reviewer's voyeuristic point of vantage outside the social, economic, and ethnic conditions they inhabit. Rice echoes the review when he discusses his own audience and implies that the class differential between stage and audience is necessary for the scene to seem an image of social reality. No grimy social others here. The "cross section of the New York theatregoing public" that Rice sought was predictably an educated, professional-class audience of "college students, office workers, hospital nurses, lawyers, shopkeepers, a sprinkling of actors and of personal friends" (*Living Theatre* 219). Not surprisingly, the least stereotypical characters in the play are those who reflect this audience: Rose (who has a job in a real-estate office) and Sam (who is planning to go to law school). These characters are granted the richest interior life, the most complex motivation, the least obtrusive ethnic tics; their longing for escape is the most urgently felt, and their opportunities for mobility are the most keenly realized.

The object-like quality of the characters can be read in the context of Mielziner's massive set. The set creates and specifies an immediately recognizable locale, but it also functions dialectically, to signify an absence, an unattainable elsewhere that seems to have been forced out of the picture by the weight of the material world. Rice recalled critics like St. John Ervine complaining of "a garbage can, an actual and veritable garbage can," onstage; such effects helped to compose a concrete locale to sustain and substantiate the action (*Minority Report* 256). The totality of Rice and Mielziner's scenic integration also seems to render the characters' desire for something else—Mrs. Maurrant's indefinite longing for something better, imperfectly realized in her tawdry affair with the sleazy milk collector; the romance of Rose and Sam—powerful, poignant, and impossible. The materiality of the set, in this sense, seems oddly to express not the drama's openness to the unscripted world offstage but its closure to the world beyond this street. This feeling of closure underlies the play's sketchy politics as well—"And if you was to elect a Socialist president tomorra, it would be the same thing" (129)—and reifies them in its plot structure. Although the events of the day appear to the characters as points in a disconnected yet unremitting repetition of the same, the play insists that the audience regard the action as part of a natural cycle of change and renewal. *Street Scene* closes, after all, with the arrival of new tenants and with a new round of gossip developing among the inhabitants of 25 West 65th.[10] *Street Scene* requires and projects an audience of

10. As a television producer suggested to Rice in 1954, explaining why *Street Scene* could not be considered as a vehicle for a weekly television series, the play requires an asymmetry between stage and audience at odds with Madison Avenue's sense of good advertising: "Foremost among these objections is the squalor of the setting, the lower class social level of all the chief characters, and the utterly depressing circumstances which they all find themselves in," circumstances opposed to how the "American consuming public" is presented "by the Advertising Industry today . . . middle class, not lower class; happy in general, not miserable and frustrated; and optimistic, not depressed" (*Living Theatre* 223).

others, whose freedom—to dream, to judge, to depart, not to be seen—exactly reverses the determined scenic milieu that stands for reality on the stage.

The scenic rhetoric of realistic theater insists on the explanatory power of the stage milieu and on the inaccessibility of the "self"—of some characters at least—that the scene claims to control. In something like Mielziner's celebrated design for Arthur Miller's *Death of a Salesman* (1949; the working title was *The Inside of His Head*), the world of realism falls open to enable contact between two zones of privacy, a one-way transaction illuminating the actor-characters onstage for an unstaged and concealed audience. Willy Loman's expressionistic timebends do not, after all, open him more fully to the understanding of his family, who remain, as the characters in realistic drama generally do, isolated from one another, trapped within themselves, their language, and the walls that surround them. This sense that scenic or sociological realism locates two complementary realms of interiority, of freedom, while dramatizing an intervening realm of economic and material necessity can be felt throughout the drama of the 1930s, particularly in plays like *Street Scene* and Maxwell Anderson's *Winterset* (1935; the set, also designed by Mielziner, was dominated by the enormous pier of the Brooklyn Bridge), in which the set operates like the outsized machinery of expressionist theater to dwarf, control, and objectify the characters as cogs in the urban machine. When there is escape from such scenes, it often appears as escape into an unknown and unknowable elsewhere, a figure for the unreality of the characters' desire to depart the scene: the *Liebstod* of Anderson's Mio and Miriamne, Rice's Elysian Fields, the "certain place where it's moonlight and roses" that draws Moe and Hennie at the end of *Awake and Sing!*

The rhetoric of realism is torn between the assertion of an environmental causality—assimilated to the economy by Odets, to social pressure by Galsworthy, to the double standard by Pinero, to gender and class oppression by Robins and Shaw—and the necessity to retain the freedom of its characters, a freedom that seems increasingly internalized and impalpable. This dialectic between visible constraint and an unknown inner freedom apparently inverts the circumstances of the absent audience of realism but actually duplicates them: our "freedom" exists similarly in the form of consciousness, while our actions are hedged by the manifest proprieties of our attendance in the theater. This tension is expressed in the Method's reliance on "given circumstances" vivified by the actor's "emotion memory," and in the dramatic function assigned to privileged moments of privacy or withdrawal from society in the drama.

These concerns can also be seen in the working of the visible mise-en-scène itself, in a play like Sidney Kingsley's *Dead End* (1935). The play is set on a New York street that dead ends into the filthy East River, and provided the occasion for one of Norman Bel Geddes's most intricate and splendid sets. More than the familiar brownstone of *Street Scene,* Geddes's design strikingly evoked the dialectic between engagement and detachment characteristic of realistic vision. Instead of the frontally oriented brownstone, *Dead End* presented the audience with a deeper, more urgent perspective. The entire front of the stage was transformed into an East River pier, extending the width of the proscenium and jutting several feet beyond the curtain line into the orchestra pit. A narrow street, running between a dilapidated tenement (audience left) and a huge coal hopper (downstage corner, audience right), angled upstage to the audience's right, disappearing in a dark horizon. As one reviewer noted, "So real it all seemed that I, sitting there in mid-river, found myself paddling to keep afloat" (Gabriel). On the audience's left, downstage and roughly parallel to the proscenium, a narrow and fenced path led to a swanky apartment offstage; a small gate faced the street, beside a raised and fenced terrace: *"The wall is of rich, heavy masonry, guarded at the top by a row of pikes. Beyond the pikes, shutting off the view of the squalid street below, is a thick edging of lush green shrubbery"* (453). The upstage side of the terrace abutted the side wall of the tenement, freshly painted and adorned with a large trelliswork. The dreary front of the building faced the litter-strewn street, and other tenements could be seen on adjacent blocks, replete with broken windows, washlines, and dirty mattresses airing on the fire escapes. As Brooks Atkinson remarked in his review, Geddes "reared up a setting that pushes the thought of the author's drama ruthlessly into the audience's face. Not only in its accuracy of detail but in its perspective and its power his setting is a practical masterpiece."

Onstage, the drama and its scenic environment brought two

urban landscapes into an uneasy proximity: "What you have seen and heard in New York, wondering and apprehensive" (Atkinson) was brought up against East Side privilege, symbolized less by the unseen apartment or the green and growing terrace than by the small gate downstage, painted a dazzling white against the gloom and darkness of the set. The dramatic action is divided between showing the life of the slum's inhabitants and the conflict that erupts when they are confronted by their immediate spectators, the wealthy inhabitants of the apartment building. The scenic environment is similarly duplicitous, both receding into the city topography and aggressively threatening its audience. Geddes emphasized this perspective with a variety of devices—miniature laundry hanging on "distant" clotheslines, raking the street upward toward the back of the set—and then filled in the environment it governed with a famous array of realistic effects: street litter, recorded sounds of street noise and lapping waves on the pier, boys climbing dripping wet from the "river" in the orchestra (really a net below stage level, where they were sprayed with mineral oil), actors without stage makeup.[11] Perspective constitutes its fictive scene by displacing the audience from it. Like the wealthy, slightly unreal inhabitants of the unseen apartment, we are screened from a reality we enter only empathetically. The little gate signals *our* access to, and protection from, the life of the street as well.

"The street has imaginative, as well as actual, perspective," Edith Isaacs remarked for *Theatre Arts Monthly*, and within that perspective the environment utterly controls the characters' lives: "Before a word is spoken, you recognize that this place of darkness and dirt is captain of their soul and master of their fate" (891). The

---

11. Geddes used an RCA recording crew to make recordings of waves lapping against a pier, the sound of boys diving into the river, vehicle sounds, dogs barking (various kinds and duration), babies crying, and so on, which were broadcast from speakers located at various points in the set both before the curtain rose and during the play itself. On the complexity of the design and placement of speakers (river sounds emanated from a speaker near the front of the stage), see Sobel. Various articles were published noting that no special stage makeup was used for the performance; women wore cosmetics in character, and the men appeared without makeup. One article also notes that the boys were dirtied with cork instead of real dirt, and that they were sprayed with mineral oil before climbing out of the "river" onto the stage; see " 'Dead End' Cast Shuns Make-Up."

scene urges a cyclic social evolution in much the manner of *Street Scene*, with which it was inevitably compared. The boys who hang out on the pier eventually get into trouble with the wealthy apartment residents; their future is embodied by the gangster Babyface Martin, once a child here himself, who comments, "Da kids aroun' here don' change" (471). The stage's receding perspective, however, was offset by its aggressive confrontation of the audience, reaching out into the auditorium to force a kind of complicity between the viewer and the scene. The forestage acting area was dominated by the gang, and one of the boys' principal activities throughout the play was diving off the pier into the "river" in the orchestra pit.

Despite its melodramatic plot and sentimental characterization, *Dead End* seemed to strike a certain apprehension in its audiences, reflected not so much as a response to the play's dramatic action as to its characterization of the gang. The rumor that the boys were really not actors at all is a testament in part to the polish of their performance and in part to Kingsley's dialogue. This is, after all, a play in which boys talk about diving "bareass" into the river (460); they taunt one another with "Sissy, sissy, sucks his mamma's titty!"; one boy shouts "Frig you! . . . Ah, I'll sock yuh inna tit" to his friend's older sister (465); and they "cockalize" victims like Milty and the rich boy Philip. Such performance emphasized the verisimilitude of the scenic milieu by puncturing familiar stage conventions: the boys were neither winsome waifs, nor sentimental stage hooligans. "It seems to me no group of children could be so perfect in their portrayal of the various roles or be so filthy in body and mind unless they were accustomed to such an environment," complained one reviewer, and *Variety* warned—or hoped—that "the script will have to be tempered somewhat to keep the law out."[12] Geddes's design shaped Kingsley's sharpest assault on the audience's sensibilities, by thrusting the "realistic" behavior of desanctified stage children appropriately through the proscenium, practically into the audience's lap.

Like Method acting, like realistic dramatic action, the design of *Dead End* locates the privileged perspective of the spectator as a

12. Rev. of *Dead End*, *Brooklyn Citizen* 29 October 1935; Rev. of *Dead End*, *Variety* 30 October 1935.

zone of privacy and illusionistic completion; breaking the proscenium, it dramatizes the relationship between that privacy and social empowerment. Appropriately enough, the subject of architecture becomes critical to the play's thematic design, extending and clarifying the function of stage space in its theatrical organization. The romantic plot in the play involves another neighborhood character, an unemployed architect named Gimpty, who cannot hope to make the money to support the woman he loves and must watch her sail out of his life on a yacht, knowing that she loves him but will not live in poverty. Gimpty sits watchfully on the edge of the scene throughout the play, observing events while he sketches designs for an urban scenario that will never be built, a city of dreams. He comments on the relationship between environment and character in the play:

> New York with its famous skyline . . . its Empire State, the biggest God-damned building in the world. The biggest tombstone in the world! They wanted to build a monument to the times. Well, there it is, bigger than the pyramids and just as many tenants. . . . I wonder when they'll let us build houses for men to live in? (491)

Kingsley's echo of Ibsen's Master Builder Solness is important here. Solness, climbing the dizzying tower toward his castles in the air, undertakes a vertiginous assault on the uncanny, unknowable interiority of realistic character, and an assault on the reliability of the material stage world to express it. Architecture, in *The Master Builder,* figures one of Ibsen's characteristic projects of self-creation, whose awkward place in the rhetoric of realism marks their descendance from an earlier, more expansive romantic dramaturgy.[13] Gimpty, on the other hand, is unemployed, unable to build the world where he might stalk that romantic self. In the scene, but not part of it, Gimpty's drawings precisely register the dialectic of engagement and detachment typical of realistic observation, reified here in the design of the set itself. As the play's title implies, *Dead End* stages a world of material limitation, in which characters are unable to climb where they build, and an unchanging future is visible in the static present. Only the audience remains disencumbered, floating in an unimaginable freedom.

13. See Goldman, "The Ghost of Joy."

EMPTY SPACES AND THE POWER OF PRIVACY: PINTER, SHEPARD, AND BOND

In productions like *Street Scene* or *Dead End*—and, of course, in the less spectacular settings of plays from O'Neill's *Iceman* to Edward Albee's *Who's Afraid of Virginia Woolf?* (1962)—the realistic theater reaches an inescapable impasse, one engrained within the rhetoric of realism itself. As the scene becomes increasingly concrete, "character" itself may seem to become a kind of object, unless it is withdrawn from the scene altogether, into a shadowy interior realm of masks, motives, and desire. Projected as a point of observation, freedom, and completion outside the stage, the audience comes to reflect this sense of character as an unrepresentable absence at the heart of the play. Yet when we think of the drama of an undiscoverable interiority of character resisting an inscrutable, vaguely oppressive milieu we may not now be thinking of Ibsen but instead of the drama of the absurd, of plays like *Waiting for Godot* (1953), *The Chairs* (1952), *The Empire Builders* (1959), or *The Birthday Party* (1958).

Martin Esslin remarked in *The Theatre of the Absurd* that "it is not merely the subject-matter that defines what is here called the Theatre of the Absurd"; it is a "sense of the senselessness of life, of the inevitable devaluation of ideals, purity, and purpose," conveyed by openly abandoning "rational devices and discursive thought" in order to "achieve a unity between . . . basic assumptions and the form in which these are expressed" (5–6). Esslin was certainly right to sense the absurd's interest in altering the "logic" of realistic drama and modern theatrical experience. But though such plays openly dispense with verisimilitude, they often remain dependent upon realistic priorities: a stage world of material constraint, identified with an internally consistent dramatic "scene"; characters influenced by, yet resisting, a stubbornly mysterious environment; an audience of offstage observers who seem—at times, at least—to be identified with the threatening authority of the milieu itself. This is not to say that absurdist theater could not prove baffling and recalcitrant. Nonetheless, a generation of audiences and critics rapidly discovered that the absurd could be read as a version of the quotidian world outside the theater, its plot troped by the preexisting text of reality, refined to its "existential" essentials. Are plays like *Rhinoc-*

eros (1960) or *The Firebugs* (1960) about the Communists or the Fascists? Is Godot God? Don't Pinter's plays describe the modern failure to communicate? Although playwrights, performers, scholars, critics, and audiences rapidly became impatient with such questions, they are the kind of question that the theater of the absurd initially seemed to invite. In the theater, the drama of the absurd first made sense as a departure from verisimilitude within the rhetorical ordering of stage realism.[14]

Film and television, too, have readily appropriated the rhetoric of realistic production, not a surprising development given the way that the camera can be used to project a single, absent subject. And, of course, a large and significant body of drama effectively develops from the realistic tradition—think of the plays of August Wilson, Beth Henley, Brian Friel, David Storey, Marsha Norman, or Neil Simon, for example. On the contemporary stage, the rhetoric of realistic production has been invaded not so much by the symbolism and expressionism so complicit in defining the project of realism at the turn of the century as by aggressively antirealistic modes like absurd theater, happenings, the theater of Brechtian alienation, poor theater, and indeed by conceptions of pace, temporality, and dramatic organization reintroduced to the stage from video and film. The bizarre and unexpected turns of plot, unusual mises-en-scène, or oblique and refractory language characteristic of David Mamet, Harold Pinter, Sam Shepard, Maria Irene Fornes, and other playwrights like them often seem to signal an effort to reshape the project of realistic theatricality. In many respects, though, this drama capitulates to the categories of meaning and interpretation found in earlier realistic modes, especially the classic dialectic between character and environment, still visible in the drama, in production practice, and in the figuration of an audience. In the contem-

---

14. Timothy J. Wiles rightly remarks that the formal and thematic innovations of the theater of the absurd are largely "literary" in inspiration, development, and effect, rather than deriving from specifically performance innovation (117–18). In much later plays—Beckett's *Catastrophe* (1982), Pinter's *One for the Road* (1984) and *Mountain Language* (1988)—theater of the absurd develops a more searching critique of the structure of realistic representation in the theater, as the formal complicity between absurd theatricality and the theatricality of state-sponsored torture directly criticizes the modes of interpretive authority practiced by the offstage spectator, the powerfully absent subject both of realism and of its derivative stages.

porary theater, a determining offstage order no longer needs to saturate the visible space of the stage with objects in order to be realized. Even in a world of scattered and disheveled things, we can see that "Something is taking its course" (Beckett, *Endgame* 13).

As we have seen, realistic theater emphasizes the integration of the stage scene, a scene which governs interiorized "characters," the apparent intervention of a material "world," and a similarly interiorized interpretive practice identified with the absent "audience." Although much contemporary drama seems to frustrate these priorities by compromising the intelligibility of the material world onstage, in fact it tends to confirm the illusory or irrelevant status of that world in relation to the drama's privileged points of explanation—the mysterious "character" it holds and expresses, and the mystified privacy of the offstage spectator. Pinter's drama is a case in point, in part because its relation to realism seems at first confrontational. Pinter's plays are explicitly dependent on the codes of realism: think of the replay of the past in *Betrayal* (1978) or *Old Times* (1971), or of Ruth's role as the "woman with a past" in *The Homecoming* (1965). In the theater, Pinter's plays require the scenic "objectivity" of the realistic mode, and it is apparently against the grain of realistic expectation that this drama is achieved. Pinter's early drama of rooms locates the domestic scene of realism within a menacing offstage milieu whose relation to the scene onstage is inscrutable and threatening. Pinter's rooms seem to have become unmoored, no longer to disclose upon a readable offstage social environment, something like the disconnected street of *Street Scene*. They give on to a world that sends strange signals down the dumb waiter in *The Dumb Waiter* (1960), or sends disturbing visitors like Goldberg and McCann in *The Birthday Party*, or Riley in *The Room* (1960). Paradoxically, though, this dislocation seems to dematerialize the stage world and to forge a more explicit complementarity between the privacy of the character and the privacy of the spectator.

The stage displays its objects, but they fail to cohere, to claim a self-evident and natural relation to the characters and to a larger dramatic world, a coherence that can confidently be seized within an external perspective. As Mick says to Davies in *The Caretaker* (1960), surveying the junk-filled room, "It depends how you regard this room. I mean it depends whether you regard this room as furnished or unfurnished. See what I mean?" (71). In contrast to an earlier realism, the objects onstage seem abstracted from an informing context that would supply them with apparently immanent meanings; we decide what they mean and how they are related to one another, in a world which is said to be "open to any number of different interpretations" (73). The audience is dislodged from an interpretive perspective that exceeds the action, is forced to read the stage as the characters do. Like the characters, we discover that the scene's "meaning" is not implicit within the scene itself, waiting to be disclosed to an objective eye offstage. To cling to this perspective is usually the sign of desperation or defeat in Pinter's plays, as it is for Teddy in *The Homecoming:*

> It's a way of being able to look at the world. It's a question of how far you can operate on things and not in things. I mean it's a question of your capacity to ally the two, to relate the two, to balance the two. To see, to be able to *see!* I'm the one who can see. (61–62)

To "operate on things and not in things" is, in *The Homecoming*, precisely to fail to see the play. Yet the nostalgia for this mythological authority points to ways in which Pinter's theater relies on the paradigms of the realistic stage. The sense that Pinter's characters subject both language and the environment to their own immediate needs seems both to extend and to challenge the romantic impulse of Ibsen's or Chekhov's drama, where "character" is confined by a material world incapable of expressing it fully, a world that seems mute and degraded in relation to a barely visible inner vitality. Pinter's presentation of character is only superficially more decentered and depthless than, say, the characterization of Rosmer or Solness, for character and objects are dialecticized in Pinter's theater not because they are unlike, but because they are so like one another. In Pinter's plays, character seems largely provisional and instrumental, a function of action and interpretation whose "identity" is explicitly constituted in the play only by its use, and so by of our reading of it. In this regard, Teddy is right to feel that the characters can be known only as things that "move about," as "objects"; where he goes wrong is in assuming that he can occupy a position outside the scene, where his perspective will work on these shifty things, transforming them into *fixed* objects. To present "character" as an object—even as a changing one—is to recapitulate that aspect of realism that locates character in a world by rendering others as "things," reserving (as Teddy does) the privileges of humanity, of subjectivity, for the self offstage. The real problem of Pinter's theater is that it seems increasingly difficult to find that offstage vantage.

Pinter's theater both suspends and retains the authority of the spectator over the objectified others onstage; the plotting of Pinter's plays similarly frustrates but preserves the longing for a totalizing narrative. Confessions are usually deployed in realistic drama to provide the audience with information about the action and the characters' motives, but in Pinter's drama confessions are emptied of this authority. Lenny's monologues in *The Homecoming*, for instance, are so strongly colored by their instrumentality in the present moment as to become indistinguishable from fiction. As a result, when Sam finally blurts out the "truth"—"MacGregor had Jessie in the back of my cab as I drove them along" (78)—the anticipated *scène à faire* signally fails to resolve or to explain the action. In the relationship between Jessie and Mac resumed by Ruth, in the brilliantly illuminated tableau of the slumping man and two women in *Old Times*, in the syncopated reverse sequence of *Betrayal*, Pinter recalls the "retrospective" method of Ibsen. Yet if the "past" is refused as an "objective" point of reference and explanation, becoming instead an instrumental fiction in the present action, this, too, seems only to literalize the problematic undecidability of the past in realism itself. Even in Ibsen or O'Neill, the past must be kept open, susceptible to negotiation, if the romantic interiority of "character" is to remain an open dramatic possibility. That is, despite some apparent innovation, the status of the past in Pinter points to the realistic theater's need to preserve character as a figure for the absent audience's similar privileges of privacy. As Ruth puts it in *Old Times*, "There are things I remember which may never have happened but as I recall them so they take place" (32). It might be argued that realism's complementary zones of privacy—character, audience—are aligned to some extent here, as the mysteries of motivation and of interpretation are both assigned to an absent and indecipherable "self."[15] In this sense, Pinter's theater

15. The sense that Pinter's actors should avoid "filling" the silences, and so "filling" the characters with a readable subtext is now familiar. See Hall 16, and Van Laan.

might more fairly be described as parasitic upon realism than as radically reorienting it.

Beckett is surely the most original playwright of the postwar era, but Pinter's strategies for representing a "realistic" surface shorn of the interpretive coordinates of earlier modes may well be more immediately influential. Sam Shepard's theater is similar in this regard, for although it is more spectacular and extroverted, Shepard's stage is also traced by a nostalgic recasting of the rhetoric of realism. The arabesques of character in Shepard's plays are traced on the forms and traditions of American drama: the Westerns hovering behind *Tooth of Crime* (1972) and *True West* (1980); *Buried Child*'s (1978) Milleresque gothic; the social realism of *Curse of the Starving Class* (1978). This generic backdrop provides the horizon of thematic expectation from which Shepard's characterization departs, much as the consumer trash that clutters Shepard's verbal and object world departs from the "natural" social and material environment of domestic realism. The object world of Shepard's theater is a world of commodities, interchangeable items in the discourse of consumer culture, much as the lexicon of plays like *Tooth of Crime*—the languages of drugs, crime, rock music, and cars—is subject to shifting uses, values, and meanings, and so to different kinds of implication in the world onstage. Character also has this status in Shepard's drama—think of Kent and Salem in *La Turista* (1967)—and often seems more like a mode of transaction or of temporary possession than of identity. Character exists where it is consumed, practiced, or reproduced: the Old Man in *Fool for Love* (1983) represents himself in two families; in *True West,* Austin and Lee exchange occupations; in *Curse of the Starving Class* Wesley returns wearing Weston's clothes ("And every time I put one thing on it seemed like a part of him was growing on me. I could feel him taking over me" 196); Vince assumes his inheritance in *Buried Child* and also assumes Dodge's place on the sofa. Crow's enactment of Hoss in *Tooth of Crime* is the type of such possession:

> Very razor. Polished. A gleam to the movements. Weighs out in the eighties from first to third. Keen on the left side even though he's born on the right. Maybe forced his hand to change. Butched some instincts down. Work them through his high range. Cut at the gait. Heel-toe action rhythms of New Orleans. Can't suss that particular. That's well covered. Meshing patterns. Easy mistakes here. Suss the

bounce. (CROW *tries to copy* HOSS's *walk. He goes back and forth across the stage practising different styles until he gets the exact one. It's important that he gets inside the feeling of* HOSS's *walk and not just the outer form.*)
(228)

While Pinter's characters are ruthlessly improvisational, avoiding the implication of a "center" or "depth" that would enable them to be seized by an audience of spectators, the rhetoric of character in Shepard's drama works through a recollection of this depth or presence: the blank indeterminacy of Pinter's characters is, in Shepard's plays, produced as an absence, a lack. The characters compete not to convince others but to inhabit a space, a role, an occupation, a family, the fiction of a self.

Much as acting in Pinter's plays does, producing character in Shepard's drama requires the performer to swerve from the rhetoric of Method performance. Pinter's characters seem improvisational, while acting in Shepard's plays requires the performer to assert the authority and presence of a "self," but a self emptied of identity. Although Shepard's plays are often compared with Arthur Miller's or Tennessee Williams's, the acting they require differs from the "studio realism" appropriate to the American classics in the pace, violence, and volatility with which a given "spine" can be discarded and replaced.[16] As Shepard warns the actors of *Angel City* in his prefatory note to the play (1976), character is subject to continual renegotiation:

> Instead of the idea of a "whole character" with logical motives behind his behavior which the actor submerges himself into, he should consider instead a fractured whole with bits and pieces of character flying off the central theme. In other words, more in terms of collage construction or jazz improvisation. ("Note" 6)

The collage of characterization in Shepard's plays requires the performer to project the role, and the self that appears to inhabit it, as though it were capable of instant deformation, multiplication, or exchange. Although this characterization seems to liberate both actor and audience from coherent realistic psychology, in fact Shepard's characterization is usually dominated by a "theme," a principle of wholeness realized in the bits and pieces of discontinuous

---

16. On "studio realism," see Zinman.

performance. Shepard's characters have the "post-auratic" fascination of advertising images: their jagged performances outline an illusion of completeness in order to pique a nostalgic appetite for wholeness—whole characters, whole selves—while at the same time deferring that satisfaction.[17]

Much as Shepard invokes a longing for the presence of "character" in the realistic mode, so beyond the scene onstage seems to lurk a weirdly disorienting but nonetheless influential order, a milieu that recalls the offstage social environment of realistic drama. Shepard has commented on his early interest in *Waiting for Godot*, and the action of Shepard's plays often implies an "absurd" sense of the stage as an arbitrary, possibly malevolent environment (see Chubb). The spare stage space of Beckett's theater encourages the audience to read the action as existential parable; Shepard's stage tends to locate its objects more concretely in a bizarre and threatening society. The action of a Shepard play often transpires against a dimly seen world of chance encounters, transactions, deals, and contracts, governed by a vague and unstated order, like the mysterious "code" of *Tooth of Crime* or Taylor's business world in *Curse of the Starving Class*:

> You may not realize it, but there's corporations behind me! Executive management! People of influence. . . . Everything's going forward! Everything's going ahead without you! The wheels are in motion. There's nothing you can do to turn it back. The only thing you can do is cooperate. To play ball. To become part of us. (178–79)

The metonymy of realistic staging urges the audience to read the box-set drawing room as a point where the economic, social, and personal realms intersect; like the box set itself, this drama claims to render those realms visible, understandable, open. In Shepard's drama, the stage continues to imply this metonymy, but the randomness of action and characterization conforms to a fear that the world is ultimately inscrutable, a loss of confidence in the ordering of the world onstage and off.

The object world of Shepard's plays seems not to act upon the characters, nor to provide instruments for their expression, for the objects of Shepard's plays frequently don't work, are destroyed in

---

17. See Wilcox 561. For a useful and incisive overview of Shepard, see Blau, "The American Dream."

the course of the action, or multiply beyond use like the toasters in *True West*. At one point in *Curse of the Starving Class*, we see Wesley building a door, a pot of artichokes boiling away on the stove, a pile of laundry on the kitchen table, while Emma sits making large charts out of cardboard, wearing jodhpurs and riding boots (see 160). Emma works intently, but the objects onstage are assimilated to several independent designs or projects, as though no "spine" of activity could hold them together. In *True West*, the golf clubs, typewriter, toasters, even the amplified howling of coyotes are liberated from their usual function, and so from their ability to register a world in which those functions are given and expected: they become weapons in the conflict between Lee and Austin. And yet, in another sense, the objects and the projects in which they figure—fixing the door, the 4-H project, writing a screenplay— seem to betray the same longing traced in Shepard's characterization. The codes of behavior and action and even the physical disposition of objects that structure the world may not finally be readable as a consistent reality, actual or fictive, like the West that eludes the characters in *True West*. But making that world remains *as* a project, and demands to be read as a sign of the desire for that world.

Shepard's is a drama of defamiliarization, and so works within the rhetoric of realism that it depends on. Edward Bond's drama is more vigorously a drama of alienation, in which the estrangement of the materials of dramatic and theatrical production develops a political critique of that rhetoric. In many respects Bond's career as a playwright recapitulates earlier debates about the use of "realism" in political art. Bond's drama is reminiscent of the Balzacian richness and variety that stand at the heart of Lukács's vision of realism, a panoply of characters and situations that makes no pretense to a naturalistic "milieu theory, a view of inherited characteristics fetishized to the point of mythology," but instead claims to penetrate "the laws governing objective reality . . . to uncover the deeper, hidden, mediated, not immediately perceptible network of relationships that go to make up society." Abandoning the pretense of objectivity, the "creative realist" (and here Shaw may come to mind as much as Lukács's heroes) works to shape a "living dialectic of appearance and essence" ("Realism" 36–39). In general, though, Bond's stance toward the rhetoric of the mise-en-scène owes more to the "experimental" realism of Brecht, an attitude well described by Fredric Jameson:

> The spirit of realism designates an active, curious, experimental, subversive—in a word, *scientific*—attitude towards social institutions and the material world; and the "realistic" work of art is therefore one which encourages and disseminates this attitude, yet not merely in a flat or mimetic way or along the lines of imitation alone. Indeed, the "realistic" work of art is one in which "realistic" and experimental attitudes are tried out, not only between its characters and their fictive realities, but also between the audience and the work itself, and—not least significant—between the writer and his own materials and techniques. ("Reflections" 205)

This account of Brecht forecasts much in Bond's work as well, particularly its position in the culture of the contemporary theater, its attitude toward that theater and toward the relationship between the stage and the audience. And although Bond has frequently adapted the style of Brecht's drama, his theater pursues Brecht's more urgent assault on the practices of the stage, particularly the rhetoric implicit in realistic production, and its construction of a "realistic" social audience.

Bond's theater generally avoids the scenic integration characteristic of realism: the space of a Bond play is usually open and spare, like the unlocalized space of Brecht's theater, but without Brecht's theatricalizing technology, the placards, film screens, turntables, and so on. It is not surprising that Bond avoids the scenic clutter of realism, and the informing ideology of social stability it has historically implied.[18] In the absence of Brecht's scenographic markers and the thematic pointing of alienation effects, and given the existential neutrality conventionally claimed by the open stage in the post-absurd era (as common, now, in productions of *King Lear* or *Heartbreak House* as in productions of *Godot*), Bond's repudi-

---

18. In "Us, Our Drama and the National Theatre," Bond describes his sense of the politics of realism: "The bourgeois theatre set most of its scenes in small domestic rooms, with an occasional picnic or a visit to the law courts. It thought it understood the world and believed that nothing in it needed to be changed very much. Things merely needed to be adjusted from time to time with the right word of advice, the right letter or the right sympathy" (8).

ation of scenic integration makes the stage space of his theater unusually difficult to read. This is particularly true of plays like *Saved* (1965), where Bond is recognizably working within the realm of a sociological realism, but a realism in which the material and social environment might seem almost entirely to have disappeared. How can we read the openness of the scene in Bond's theater not as the vaguely hostile and indifferent emptiness of the absurd, but as an attempt to disentangle realistic representation from the oppressive social practices that form "the physical, institutional, legal, domestic environment—in a word the social environment" ("Activists" 89)?

Despite Lukács, Bond is oddly the inheritor of one strain of realistic theatricality deriving from Zola and the naturalists: the desire to analyze and expose the working of society through a "scientific" or "rational" art.[19] For this reason, Bond works to set his "scenes in public places, where history is formed, classes clash and whole societies move" ("Us" 8). Bond invites his audience to read the open stage as resisting the integration of the material mise-en-scène and of a single mastering perspective on the action, a unifying principle beyond the frame of the stage. Bond's open stage works to resist realistic notions of environmental causality. He divides the stage space and interrupts linear narrative to break down the integrating force of the realistic scene, to build "alienation into the play's structure." Not surprisingly, he follows Brecht's lead in characterization as well, "showing characters in their various social roles and in various social situations . . . rather than developing a character from its *geist*" ("On Brecht" 34).

Objects, too, in Bond's theater, gain meaning not through assimilation to a pervasive scene or to the internalized motivation of a given character, but from their use in a specific situation, as Bond suggests in *The Pope's Wedding* (1962), where he calls for a dark, bare stage, littered with a few objects to indicate location: "The objects are very real, but there must be no attempt to create the

19. As Terry Eagleton notes in an exemplary reading of Bond's nondramatic writings, Bond's representation of violence in society, and so of society itself, is torn between an implicitly naturalistic "biological" account of the causes of violence and more explicitly Marxist "cultural" explanations (132).

illusion of a 'real scene' " (227).[20] Shown, like the characters, in various roles and situations, the objects onstage develop a public history, one that this theater asks us to learn to read. A table, for instance, may seem beautiful from a distance, but when we look more closely we discover that "It's chipped and scoured. The table was made for a ballroom or a minister's office but now it's a carpenter's workbench. We're not deceived by the elegant proportions or antique design. We look and see a workbench. We learn to know what things are by their texture. Texture is evidence of truth." Bond uses the term "texture" to locate both characters and objects in history. For texture also "concerns what someone does," and "when the character is treated as part of the play's texture it's placed in its social context. Instead of being abstract and spiritual it becomes political and is seen to be a matter of class." Inviting us to read actors and objects as moments in a public history, Bond hopes to alter our habits of interpretation, the ways we read ourselves and the physical world we create. He hopes, finally, to provide "an image of the world where the audience act" ("Activists" 133, 132, 143).

Bond's use of objects in stage space represents an important dramatic concern: to open the relations between classes, between objects and people, stage and audience, to view, rather than collapsing them into the realistic assertion of homogeneity before a single point of observation. This relational aspect of Bond's drama undermines the authority and power assigned to privacy by realistic theater: the privacy of the spectator beyond the action, the similar privacy accorded to the privileged classes in society, and the privacy of realistic versions of character. And much as Bond refigures the role of objects onstage, so he calls for a different kind of enactment from his performers as a means of refusing the rhetoric of realistic characterization. Bond hardly dispenses with "character" in the psychological sense. To make acting and character "public," Bond treats them as part of the material "pictoriality" of his stage, asking his actors to apply "a concept, an interpretation" to the role.

20. On Bond's use of properties, and for this insight about *The Pope's Wedding*, I am indebted to Peter Holland's fine article. For an economic reading of the characters' relationships with one another in *Saved* (discussed below), see 28–29.

Actors and Objects 93

This "concept" differs from Shepard's "theme" precisely because it *is* an interpretation, concerned less with the character's self than with relating "the character to the social event." As Bond discovered directing *The Woman* (1978), the "open space demands a new sort of acting":

> At the first run-through of *The Woman* at the NT [National Theatre] I was astonished at the way acting forced the play into the ground, buried it in irrelevant subjectivity. Much of the acting still belonged to the nineteenth century. The company were acting emotions, hugging feelings to themselves, gazing at themselves, speaking to themselves even when they shouted. They were private performers on a public stage, still part of the bourgeois theatre. ("Us" 8–9)

"This," Bond goes on to say, "is the decadence method acting has been reduced to." Bond's stage doesn't provide an integrated scenic environment, one that would frame circles of attention radiating out from Stanislavskian actor/characters. Instead, Bond's theater stages a select set of things—Shakespeare's letter at the opening of *Bingo* (1973), for example—that work to externalize "character" in relation to its object world, in what Bond has come to call "public soliloquy," such as the one Terry delivers to the boardroom table in *The Worlds* (1979). For the table's history is social history, both prompting and organizing individual reflection: "How often do we use a table like that? When we're married? They lay us on something smaller when we're dead. They [the board of directors] use it every day" (66). This apostrophe to furniture recalls Gayev's salutation to the bookcase in *The Cherry Orchard*, but rather than prompting a personal display of feeling, the table enables Terry to seize on the difference that privilege makes even in the simplest objects and activities of daily life. Terry comes to this recognition in public, while teaching the audience to read the table's "texture" and his own implication in the texture of social life as well. As Bond remarked in "Notes on Acting *The Woman*," "If we try to act this play in a Chekhovian way we get bad Chekhovian acting because the play is always struggling against our performance. We have to release the play into its natural freedom. That means that each character in the play wants to tell us his story. He does not want to relive it" (127).

Although Bond generally maintains the realistic boundary of the proscenium, his drama works to retrain habits of attention learned in the realistic theater.[21] As we have seen, the work of the spectator in the realistic theater is refracted in realistic drama in a number of ways: in the power accorded to the privacy of the "self," in the privileges that sustain privacy in social and class relations, in the characters' haunting fear of being staged to the view of others. Bond's drama qualifies privacy differently, and requires us to locate it on a different spectrum of personal and social relations. The third scene of *Bingo*, the scene between Shakespeare and the gibbeted girl, is a case in point. The girl's suffering prompts one of Shakespeare's most "poetic" speeches in the play, one of the few points at which Bond satisfies the audience's desire to hear the character speak as we might imagine Shakespeare to have spoken, that is, like a Shakespearean dramatic character: "Then a swan flew by me up the river. On a straight line just over the water. A woman in a white dress running along an empty street." To speak "Shakespearean" poetry Shakespeare must look away from the girl at hand. He attributes a transcendent humanity to the girl only by ignoring her immediacy, as he had done, of course, in failing to protect her earlier in the play: "(*He goes to the gibbet. The* OLD WOMAN *watches him.*) Still perfect. Still beautiful." Shakespeare, sensitive even here to the violence of the society in which he lives, nonetheless protects himself from the consequences of his own vision even as he composes it as poetry. Poetry, that private speech of a "Shakespeare" we know only through his public plays, arises to prevent vision, to hedge Shakespeare from a world partly of his own making. As the Old Woman reminds us, "Her's ugly. Her face is all a-twist. They put her legs in a sack count a she's dirty. . . . She smell. She smell" (27–28).

This sense of the privilege of privacy informs the action of Bond's most conventionally realistic play, *Saved*. Bond set the play in South London because he had the sense "that it's physically flatter—there are those miles and miles of long straight streets that always look the same. I used to call it the brick desert, and this feeling of being in

---

21. "Alienation isn't the removal of an emotion, it is the adding of a commentary," and Bond describes several exercises for producing alienated emotion in the theater, public soliloquies of the kind that Terry delivers in *The Worlds*. See Hay and Roberts, *Edward Bond: A Companion* 49.

a desert of bricks seemed to be absolutely right for the play" ("Drama" 7–8). The brick desert shows openly what more orderly streets tend to conceal, "the hidden debris of waste and destruction that are already involved in a prolonged act of communal violence" ("Author's Note" 17). Onstage, the play vividly marks the difference between the visibility of its lower-class characters, and the privacy of the theater audience, for privacy of any kind seems impossible in the desert of *Saved*. Sexual encounters—real or imagined—take place in the open: Harry intrudes on Len and Pam in scene 1, and thinks he has intruded on Len and Mary in scene 9; Len listens from his room to the sounds of Fred and Pam in hers. In scene 4 (perhaps the most trying scene for the audience), the baby's offstage wailing forces each of the characters to work to create a little private space—to eat, watch television, talk—by shutting out the baby, and one another. In *Saved*, there is no escape from others, not in the park, not fishing, not even in jail. Yet the lack of privacy does not imply sociability, as though contact with others naturally resulted in community. Throughout the play, Len's dogged, even annoying efforts to forge a connection with other characters—helping Mary with the groceries, trying to interest Pam in the baby—dramatize the difficulty of making social relationships in *Saved*. The society of the play is compressed yet atomized, as though the characters' unremitting openness to view signaled their vulnerability in a world in which privacy is distributed along class and economic lines, in a way reminiscent of the world of Galsworthy's Mrs. Barthwick, for whom the privacy of the "lower classes" can only be seen as a threatening "secretiveness." Len's desire for a refuge—a "fair little place" to build a family (31)—can only be a kind of fantasy, imagined in the brief seclusion of the rowboat isolated at the center of the stage. And, of course, even this dream comes abruptly to an end when Fred pulls the rowboat to shore and flirts with Pam.

It's one thing to dramatize "character" as public; it's another to catalogue the social consequences that arise from the systematic objectification of "character" along class lines, the deprivation of the resources that would make the privileges of privacy—essential to the realistic audience's sense of humanity—accessible. This deprivation extends from the sphere of the social environment to the sphere of "character" as well, and poses challenging problems for the enactment of Bond's dramatic roles. Malcolm Hay and Philip

Roberts remark that "English-trained actors sometimes experience difficulty in working with Bond's text," looking for ways to justify their performances in psychological terms (*A Study* 62). Bond partly prevents this kind of justification by downplaying the importance of an emotional subtext, by emphasizing the prosaic directness of the characters' speech, and by forcing the actors to conceive character as part of the dramatic scene rather than as its cause. In *Saved*, characterization more directly confronts the privilege of the "self" as a social phenomenon.

This point may be difficult to grasp, but we can glimpse it by comparing one of Lenny's oblique narratives in *The Homecoming* ("One night, not too long ago, one night down by the docks, I was standing alone under an arch" [30]) with Fred's instruction to Len about how to bait his fishing hook. Although Lenny's speech does not disclose his "motives"—as it might if the scene were written by Miller or Williams—it does create the *impression* of motivation, a pressure arising in the private interiority of character. This impression stems, in part at least, from Lenny's transformation of the immediate situation into a narrative of violence and domination. Spoken under the living-room arch to a woman of ambiguous intentions, Lenny's narrative works to replace the present scene, to provide a reading of it, a plot for it; Lenny becomes dramatic at just the moment that he resists and rewrites the material world. Fred's language, on the other hand, is tied immediately to the world of objects: "Now yer thread yer 'ook through this bit. Push it up on yer gut. Leave it.—Give us that bit. Ta. Yer thread yer other bit on the 'ook, but yer leave a fair bit 'angin' off like that, why, t' wriggle in the water. Then yer push yer top bit down off the gut and camerflarge yer shank. Got it?" (59). In *Saved*, language is unable to replace material reality, to become the instrument of the characters' representation and transformation of themselves and their situation. Bond's characters relate to words as they do to objects, as a given, material dimension of an inescapable social horizon: "No 'ome. No friends. Baby dead. Gone. Fred gone" (123). As a result, "character" emerges in different terms, through a rigorously externalized convention of dramatic speech that prevents the audience as well as the performers from locating the substance of the action exclusively in the characters' motives. It's not that the self has been extinguished in these characters, but rather that its possibility is withheld from the audience as a privileged point of reference and explanation.

Saved challenges the realistic audience's habits of reading the stage most directly in scene 6, the baby-stoning scene. The baby is a figure for the play's adults, vulnerable, speechless, battered, ignored, and treated with a mixture of sentiment and loathing. The violence they enact on it replicates the treatment they receive. They, too, after all, are regarded as having no humanity, "no feelin's," "Like animals" (77). What is most resistant about this scene is not the violence itself; observing scenes of lower-class urban violence has a long history in the modern theater. Instead, the scene challenges us by refusing to cast us as "realistic" spectators, whose distance contains within it an enabling interpretive power. Herbert Kretzmer, reviewing the play, found it to be "peopled by characters who, almost without exception, are foul-mouthed, dirty-minded, illiterate, and barely to be judged on any recognizable human level at all. . . . it cannot be allowed, even in the name of freedom of speech, to do so without aim, purpose, or meaning." *The Times* similarly found the play to do "nothing to lay bare the motives for violence," violating the expectations of "domestic naturalism." Preventing the audience from identifying with the characters, from valorizing their actions through the ascription of private motives, or from locating the cause of their acts in a determining environment, Bond presents the chilling violence of the scene in a way that disables the interpretive strategies of the realistic mode. The violence on the stage comes at us with the immediacy it has outside the protective distance of the theater, in a way that is more real than realism ever allows.

This aimlessness is achieved in *Saved* in ways symptomatic of the play's wider assault on its privileged audience. The motiveless violence practiced on the infant seems to reciprocate the similarly aimless, pervasive violence that the play's invisible social order practices on its characters. "Power has its principle not so much in a person as in a certain concerted distribution of bodies, surfaces, lights, gazes; in an arrangement whose internal mechanisms produce the relation in which individuals are caught up" (Foucault 202). The play's refusal of realistic causality might be read as an effort to disrupt the forms of theatrical interpretation, habits of reading the social other that extend beyond the bounds of the theater. These habits are also evident in sympathetic readings of the play, which tend to reify the audience's social superiority as interpretive authority. Martin Esslin remarks that "Bond succeeds in making his audience see deeply into the minds, and comprehend the motives, of human beings who are not only practically unable to talk but also incapable of understanding their own motives," concluding that "by illuminating their speechlessness and letting us see into their tormented souls, which are even more tormented by being unable to express their anguish, Bond shows us that these people too are full human beings, capable of the noblest emotions and actions" ("Introduction" xiv–xv). To see *Saved* from this perspective, though, is implicitly to remain within the absent social "environment" that *Saved* attempts to criticize, a notion of the environment that conceals oppression in the guise of an inactive empathy. How can we know that the characters *are* "tormented," or that their deeds are not a rich and perfect, fully articulate act of expression?

Bond removes the signals that would enable the audience to repair confidently to this position of interpretive "freedom" and empowerment, the privacy of the spectator that the play repeatedly withholds from its characters. The play is rigorous on this point. *Saved* equally resists the impulse of *The Homecoming*, to position its audience in a kind of interpretive alignment with the characters: Bond refuses the notion that the audience can share the perspective of this oppressed class, in the theater or elsewhere. This may, finally, be the point of the play's brilliant final scene, which takes place entirely in silence. Bond claims that the play "ends in a silent social stalemate, but if the spectator thinks this is pessimistic that is because he has not learned to clutch at straws" (Appendix 309). At its close, the play withdraws the usual materials of interpretation, especially the dramatic speech that discloses the characters and their motives to us. Instead, we are given a lower-class family in a more typical and actual social relation, one that epitomizes the play's final attitude toward its theatrical and social audience: silent, withdrawn, observable but not speaking to us. As in plays like *Street Scene* or *Dead End*, the play reifies the proscenium as an instance of the more insistent boundaries of class. Although *Saved* invites us to view, it refuses to identify our reading of the scene as insight, as privileged vision.

3

Scripted Bodies: Poetic Theater

POETIC THEATER AND THE WORK OF ACTING

> The working-man who went to the music-hall and saw Marie Lloyd and joined in the chorus was himself performing part of the work of acting; he was engaged in that collaboration of the audience with the artist which is necessary in all art and most obviously in dramatic art.
> —"London Letter," *Dial* (December 1922)

> The working man who went to the music-hall and saw Marie Lloyd and joined in the chorus was himself performing part of the act . . .
> —"In Memoriam: Marie Lloyd," *The Criterion* (January 1923)

Announcing a commitment to a popular, collaborative, even entertaining form of theater, T. S. Eliot's famous obituary for Marie Lloyd provides a useful point of repair from the austerities often associated with "poetic drama." Eliot seems to have tinkered with his *Dial* "London Letter" when preparing it for publication the following month in *The Criterion*, introducing a number of small changes in wording and emphasis. In both texts, Eliot mourns the loss of Marie Lloyd and marks in the passing of this "expressive figure" the decline of music hall and the more general demise of theater as a social institution. And both versions similarly describe the theater's function in society: through performance, the theater provides a form of expression for the audience it serves. Having given "artistic expression and dignity" to the life of the lower classes, the music hall emblematizes the waning of a truly popular art of theater. The middle classes, with no "independent virtues as a class," have nothing to express through the sociable arts of the stage; their characteristic mode is the solitary and "listless apathy" of the cinema spectator. It is at this point—characterizing the audience—that Eliot seems to have hesitated. Is the working man who joins in the chorus constituted by the event, as a "part of the act," or does he create and determine the meaning of the event, perform "the work of acting"? The revision in phrasing is subtle, but it traces the dialectic that the rhetoric of realistic theater claims as an identity: the difference between the fictive "action" of the drama, and the present activity of performance. The spectator of cinema can "receive, without giving," but the theater both provides a role for the audience as "part of the act" and provides the means to render it significant, dramatic. Like the music hall, theater enables the spectators to identify themselves in and through "the work of acting."

Eliot's remarks on music hall may at first appear tangential to the project of a modern poetic theater. Its working-class affiliations, its physical virtuosity and stagey vivacity, and the ephemeral quality of its verbal "texts" all seem to lie far beyond the languid artifice of verse drama. Yet to consider the rhetoric of modern poetic drama is to return to the complicity between performer and audience that attracted Eliot to the popular stage. For the rhetoric of a poetic drama imagines the possibility of a poetic *theater* and invites us to rethink our understanding of poetic drama in relation to its stage production. The terms themselves are distracting. I do not mean "poetry *in* the theater," the kind of rhythmic recitation associated with the performance of Yeats's early plays, nor—a greater evasion—the so-called "poetry *of* the theater" popularized by Cocteau and others, the imagistic, visual "poetry" of the mise-en-scène. A poetic theater implies the text's direct intervention in the rhetorical ordering of realism, reclaiming the text's authority over the physical "languages" that construct the drama as theater. The plays of Yeats, Eliot, Auden, and Beckett are, in this sense, strategic attempts to theorize the possible relation between the dramatic text and the discourses of its production onstage. As such, the theory of a poetic theater has implications for our understanding of modern theatricality that range beyond the confining sense of a precious "poetic drama."

Modern poetic drama usually opens from a repudiation of the prosaic drama of daily life associated with Ibsen and Chekhov, and its rhetoric as theater emerges most clearly in this contrast. While the rhetoric of realism emphasizes the visual coherence of the stage *scene,* poetic theater claims to replicate the verbal order of the absent text, the authority of the *word,* in the array of its staging. The defining moment of realism is the erasure of the productive activity of the theater, of the "work of acting" as a legitimate "part of the act." Speaking, acting, movement, gesture, costume, and design are all employed to assimilate the dramatic text to the scenic ensemble, the stage picture. The rhetoric of poetic theater challenges stage realism, but only incidentally on verbal grounds. For how the verbal order of the drama is staged *as* poetry depends on how it is identified with and through the activities that stage it: as characterizing acting, elocution, lyrical song, and so on. Poetic drama begins its assault on realism when it resituates the text in the mise-en-scène, refiguring the authority of the word in the theatrical relationship between the drama, the spectacle, and the audience.

Only when the verbal formalities of the text are deployed in such a way as to govern the productive discourses of the stage does a poetic theater become possible, a theater in which the linguistic complexity of the text is visible throughout the spectacle. I don't mean, of course, to deny the "poetic" complexity of language in verse drama, but I do mean to suggest that when produced as theater, it may be indistinguishable from the complexity of prose, since the "poetry" emerges in performance only as an effect of its production, in the way that it is communicated through speech and acting. This definitional problem has been repeatedly recognized by the practitioners of poetic theater themselves. As Eliot suggests, the difference between a poetic theater and verse drama has to do with the theater's ability to stage the text:

> A verse play is not a play done into verse, but a different kind of play: in a way more realistic than "naturalistic drama," because, instead of clothing nature in poetry, it should remove the surface of things, expose the underneath, or the inside, of the natural surface appearance. It may allow the characters to behave inconsistently, but only with respect to a deeper consistency.

Poetic drama exposes a "deeper consistency," not only through its verbal design, but also in the way it presses the performance to evade the scenic priorities of stage realism; the stage can "use any device to show their real feelings and volitions, instead of just what, in actual life, they would normally profess to be conscious of" (Introduction). Indeed, Eliot's later plays, like the later plays of W. H. Auden and Christopher Isherwood, suggest how difficult this evasion can be. *The Family Reunion* (1939), *The Cocktail Party* (1949), *The Confidential Clerk* (1953), and *The Elder Statesman* (1958) all deploy a verbal order that, far from resisting realistic rhetoric, finally seems to be controlled by the scenic coherence of the realistic stage. In their interest in the evasions of "character" and their use of a heightened language that phrases this deeper consistency in terms of psychological motive, these plays finally seem not to impel a new form of theatricality, but to evoke a realism akin to that of Chekhov or Pinter. Depending on realistic procedures they invoke, parody, or subvert, Eliot's later plays dramatize the difficulty of trying to make a poetic theater without reconceiving the function of the text in the mise-en-scène. The plays seem precisely like realistic plays "done into verse."[1]

Eliot's effort to open a space for poetic drama illustrates the challenges that arise from conceiving of poetic theater solely in terms of the ordering of the text. Eliot finds himself on firmer ground when he follows the hard-won lead of Yeats's "plays for dancers," and concentrates his attention on the relation between signifying modes in the theater. Yeats, though more committed to verse drama than any of his successors, inaugurates the poetic theater's decisive area of innovation, the relation between the text, its enactment, and the audience. Speaking on the BBC in 1936, Eliot not only attributed the revival of poetic drama to Yeats but also cited Yeats's transformation of stage performance: "We have begun to see that the actor is more important than the scenery, that verse should be spoken as verse and not as prose, and that the actor should be in an intimacy of relation to the audience which had for a long time been the secret of the music-hall comedian"

---

1. Critics of Eliot's plays have increasingly come to conceive of Eliot's later drama as a problematic form of realism rather than as a distinct mode of "poetic drama"; as Katharine Worth suggests, "Eliot's central characters suffer from a troubling sense of division between their real selves and their acted selves. 'Real' self is a concept that still has force in his drama—here he separates from successors like Pinter—but the performing self is very much in the foreground, uneasily conscious of its liability to be taken over by the 'speechless self,' the mute, tough one" (*Revolutions* 55–56). See also Worth, *The Irish Drama of Europe*; Kenner 280; and Goldman, "Fear in the Way" 162–63.

("Need" 994). Eliot strikes several of Yeats's characteristic themes here, while replacing Yeats's preference for an aristocratic intimacy between spectacle and spectator with the more exuberant figure of the music hall. Rather than imitating a dimly "poetical" reality, poetic theater offers a specifically theatrical event, one that negotiates the staging of "poetry" through the physical, immediate, and personalizing forms of theater.

The real innovations of the poetic theater stem from its sustained investigation of how the text is rewritten by the stage. We don't often think of poetic theater as developing a theoretical inquiry into stage acting, but the most influential aspects of this theater depend immediately on the poets' meditation on the arts of performance. In "The Possibility of a Poetic Drama," Eliot opposed the "utter rout of the actor profession," and pointedly exposed the poetic theater's sometimes febrile efforts to "'get around' the actor, to envelop him in masks, to set up a few 'conventions' for him to stumble over, or even to develop little breeds of actors for some special Art drama" (*Sacred Wood* 69–70). Yet the automata of Yeats, Gordon Craig, Maurice Maeterlinck, and others witness the apparent necessity to depersonalize the actor's performance in order to subordinate it to the designs of the text. The vogue for actor-automata may seem remote to us, but it has analogies in the work of Meyerhold, in expressionist and dada performance, and in the actorless theater pieces of Robert Wilson, Heiner Müller, Richard Foreman, and others. Precisely because the realistic actor's "gestures and movements are not *regulated* by the text, but simply *inspired* by it" (Appia 52), poetic performance distinguishes acting from the mere reproduction of social life, performances that inscribe the text with the priorities of meaning latent in everyday behavior. If poetic theater, as Arthur Symons suggests, should evoke "the reaction of the imagination against the wholly prose theatre of Ibsen," then to perform such plays should call for a similar reaction, a marionette-like restraint, from actors who submit "passively to the passing through them of profound emotions, and the betrayal of these emotions in a few, reticent, and almost unwilling words" (*Plays* 77, 81). In marionettes and in marionette-like acting, the turn-of-the-century theater attempted to wrest the signification of the body from the codes of theatrical and social behavior and to engrave it instead with the regulating designs of the poet's text.

The sculptural images of the poetic theater might seem to hold little promise as models for acting, but the evident artificiality of marionettes helped to unseat the gestural authority of realistic performance, by foregrounding the gap between the drama and its stage production. Symons found the "symbolical buffoonery" of Alfred Jarry's *Ubu Roi* (1896)—whose marionette elements were largely preserved in Aurélien Lugné-Poe's production, which Symons attended with Yeats—"a sort of comic antithesis to Maeterlinck," less the premonition of the savage god than "the excuse, the occasion for an immense satire" (*Studies* 236, 238). And in "An Apology for Puppets," Symons clarified the relationship between actors and marionettes:

> The living actor, even when he condescends to subordinate himself to the requirements of pantomine, has always what he is proud to call his temperament; in other words, so much personal caprice, which for the most part means wilful misunderstanding; and in seeing his acting you have to consider this intrusive little personality of his as well as the author's. (*Plays* 3)

Symons is a brilliant critic of the stage and has left masterful accounts of Henry Irving, Eleonora Duse, Sarah Bernhardt, Constant Coquelin, and others. And yet even actors of such impressive variety and scope leave Symons unsatisfied, for unlike them, the "marionette may be relied upon." Symons admires marionettes because their actions seem not to interfere with the determinations of the authorial text; because they don't *act*, they can't be accused of representing the text, of translating the author's verbal design into the histrionic patterns of the actor's performance. The intrusion of the actor's personality, the extent to which his acting invariably identifies the author's words in the dynamics of his own self-presentation, offends Symons and leads him to an admiration of marionettes reminiscent of Gordon Craig: "Seen at a distance, the puppets cease to be an amusing piece of mechanism, imitating real people; there is no difference." On the other hand, to sit at a distance from the marionettes is to miss the point of theater entirely: "Choosing our place carefully, we shall have the satisfaction of always seeing the wires at their work, while I think we shall lose nothing of what is most savoury in the feast of the illusion" (*Plays* 4–5). Marionettes may be more predictable than actors, but their chief virtue lies in the perceptual "oscillation" produced by their enactment.[2] Although Yeats and Eliot would often deny it, the personality of the performer insistently troubles the theory of a poetic theater. Acting too easily conceals the "wires" of its art, assimilates the "personified gesture" of dramatic character to the personal style and conventional behavior of the actor. What attracts the poetic theater to marionettes is their "complication of view," the evident difference between the drama and its presentation crafted by their performance.[3]

The "external nullity" that Symons found in marionettes and in marionette-like acting is easily regulated by the poetic text, enabling the text to exert a more complete authority over the scene itself. Yet in some respects, marionettes represent a signal evasion of the human body's complex potentiality on the theater stage. Both Yeats and Eliot found in the dance a more subtle and suggestive paradigm of the performer's relation to the text. Eliot imagines a theater in which "only that is left to the actor which is properly the actor's part. The general movements are set for him. There are only limited movements that he can make, only a limited degree of emotion that he can express. He is not called upon for his personality." In this sense, "a true acting play is surely a play which does not depend upon the actor for anything but acting" (*Selected Essays* 95).

Eliot echoes Yeats here, but his program for performance also refigures the expressive dialectics of "Tradition and the Individual Talent," calling for a mode of enactment that is "not the expression of personality, but an escape from personality" (*Selected Essays* 10). Eliot finds a promising representative of this mode in the dancer Leonid Massine, for "Massine, the most completely unhuman, impersonal, abstract, belongs to the future stage" ("Dramatis Perso-

---

2. "Oscillation" is Anne Ubersfeld's term, "Notes sur la dénégation théâtrale" 19.

3. Reviewers often complained of this complication with regard to Yeats's plays. Writing in the *Dublin Evening Mail* of the 1905 production of *On Baile's Strand*, for example, Oliver St. John Gogarty criticized the actors for "their apparent theory that the audience should be constantly reminded that each actor is to maintain, as an actor, an individuality apart from that of the character represented" (Hogan and Kilroy 42). Eliot rejects the idea that actors can be replaced by automata or marionettes in "Four Elizabethan Dramatists," *Selected Essays* 96.

nae" 305). Like the marionettes, such a dancer is "a conventional being, a being which exists only in and for the work of art which is the ballet," an art whose conventions have been entirely abstracted from those of offstage behavior. In the theater, Massine's performance emulates the catalytic mind of the poet. Subordinating his person to convention, his performance creates a fictive "personality" that becomes the audience's point of interpretation, its focus for reading the spectacle and an instance of its own activity. Massine's performance clarifies the function of "personality" in the theater, in that "the man or the woman whom we admire is a being who exists only during the performances, that it is a personality, a vital flame which appears from nowhere, disappears into nothing and is complete and sufficient in its appearance" (*Selected Essays* 95). Neither Massine, the "character" he performs, nor the attentive audience escape from personality—this isn't marionette theater, after all—but neither do they perform "themselves." Instead, theatrical production constructs fictive personae which articulate the experience of theater, and the experience of the self as well, the "personality" represented in our performance.

As Eliot's discussion of Massine suggests, the dance provides a figure for the operation of poetic theater. In the dance, the poetic theater finds an emblem of nonrepresentational art, as well as a mode of theatricality capable of breaking the barrier between performer and audience, of undoing the machinery of realism and replacing it with a theater that acknowledges and requires the participation of its spectator. This kind of theater is more often associated with Antonin Artaud than with the poetic drama, yet in his description of the Balinese theater, Artaud provides a glimpse of the goal sought by the poetic stage:

> What is really curious about all these gestures, these angular and abruptly broken attitudes, these syncopated modulations formed at the back of the throat, these musical phrases that break off short, these flappings of insect wings, these rustlings of branches, these sounds of hollow drums, these creakings of robots, these dances of animated puppets, is this: that out of their labyrinth of gestures, attitudes, and sudden cries, out of gyrations and turns that leave no portion of the space on the stage unused, there emerges the sense of a new physical language based on signs rather than words. These actors with their geometric robes seem like animated hieroglyphs.
> (*Selected Writings* 215–16)

Artaud's hallucinatory theater subverts the determinations of language; to that extent—and, indeed, in its repudiation of the authorizing function of the text itself—it works against the claims of a poetic stage. Nonetheless, by disrupting the authority of realistic mimesis and recentering theatrical experience on the spectator, Artaud becomes the covert ally of the authors of *Sweeney Agonistes* (1935), *The Dance of Death* (1935), *Not I* (1972). When Rupert Doone wrote to Auden in 1932 with plans for the Group Theatre, he had in mind a company "committed to the possibilities of a 'total theatre' particularly suited to poetic drama" (Medley 131). And as Auden wrote in the program for the Group's 1935 production of *Sweeney Agonistes* and *The Dance of Death*, if "Drama began as the act of a whole community," then—as in Artaud's theater—"Ideally there would be no spectators." That such a theater brings into a focus a drama that is "essentially an art of the body" is not surprising, for by producing the text through an acting style more closely associated with "acrobatics, dancing, and all forms of physical skill," the poetic theater actively displaces the behavioral codes of realistic performance and the analysis of character which realistic theater takes as its main dramatic problem (Sidnell, "Auden" 497).

By altering the text's place in the discourse of the stage, poetic theater undertakes a political assault on realistic theatricality, self-evidently in the Brechtian spectacles of Auden and Isherwood, more implicitly in Eliot's *Sweeney Agonistes* and *Murder in the Cathedral* (1935) or in Yeats's aristocratic theater. By acknowledging the constitutive function of the stage in the production of the poetic text, poetic theater necessarily acknowledges the performance of the audience as well: "Because you are not moving or speaking, you are not therefore a passenger. If you are seeing and hearing you are co-operating," reads a Group Theatre prospectus from 1933 (Sidnell, "Auden" 491). Audiences were right to feel an antibourgeois edge to the performance of poetic theater, an aggression not confined to subject matter or dramatic style but extending to their own performance as well. As Michael Sayers remarked in a review of Auden's *The Dance of Death*, "The middle class element loathed it. Much preferable in its opinion, to be the Peeping Tom who pays for the privilege of prying through the fourth wall" (qtd. in Sidnell, *Dances* 127).

The production of the poetic theater, in contrast to the realistic effacement of the audience, works to figure and thematize the audience, to enable both actor and audience to become "part of the act," to discover a "vital flame" in their mutual "work of acting." Poetic theater, then, raises a variety of problems ranging far beyond the stylistic texture of dramatic language. Stephen Spender remarked in a review of the plays of Auden and Isherwood that it "is really a question of reviving the drama itself, which has fallen into a decadent 'naturalistic' tradition, confining itself, for the most part, to the presentation of faked-up photographic vignettes of the life of a small section of the unemployed rentier class." A "play for dancers," Yeats's *At the Hawk's Well* (1916) explores the constitution of the text as performance and suggests how the theological authority of text over performance is compromised when the text is distributed among several competing modes of realization—as speech, song, acting, dance, spectating. This experimental distribution of textual authority is the signal innovation that makes poetic theater possible and drives the most significant innovations of this kind. Eliot's *Murder in the Cathedral* also distributes the text among a variety of representational modes, fulfilling the promise opened by Auden's energetic example in the unstable and controversial *The Dance of Death*. More effectively than Auden, though, Eliot succeeds in thematizing the interpretive challenges offered by the performance in relation to the dramatic problems posed by Thomas's martyrdom. *Murder in the Cathedral* uses the text's production as poetry and as prose to engage the audience in the work of acting and the work of suffering that the play otherwise demonstrates on the stage. Although not written in verse, Samuel Beckett's drama might be said to address the central challenge of poetic theater most directly: the consequences of the body's marionette-like subjection to a depersonalizing text. By tracing the relations of textual authority that govern the dramatic action of Beckett's later drama, we can gain a sense of the place—and persistence—of the rhetoric of poetic theater on the contemporary stage.

THE DISCIPLINE OF SPEECH: YEATS'S DANCE DRAMA

"I have but one art," Yeats wrote at the opening of the Abbey, "that of speech" (*Explorations* 218). Yet throughout his career in the theater, Yeats sought to master the critical relationship between poetry, speech, acting, and the "discipline" of the "theatrical sense" (*Autobiographies* 469). This tension between the poetic text and its performance is dramatized by Yeats's most challenging plays, the "plays for dancers." The label is a provocative one: What is a "dance play"? How does it differ from narrative ballet? Or, more to the point, from an *acting* play? Although Yeats's search for "theatre's anti-self" often assimilates the incantatory gesture of ritual to the rhetorical patterns of the spoken word, the dance plays structure a dialogue between poetry and its incarnation in speech, song, acting, and dance (*Explorations* 257). Far from being theater-less drama, Yeats's plays break the realistic subordination of verbal to scenic representation and open a far-reaching investigation of how the language of the text can be inscribed in the practices of the stage.

As Pound noted in *The Classic Noh Theatre of Japan*, Yeats's theater is, like the Noh, "a stage where every subsidiary art is bent precisely upon holding the faintest shade of a difference" (Introduction 4). Yeats's early plays—*The Shadowy Waters* (1904), *Deirdre* (1906), even *On Baile's Strand* (1904)—exemplify a rhetorical strategy closely identified with the purpose of a "poetic drama": to subordinate theatrical practice to the formal and conceptual order of the verbal text. This renovation of stage practice is not confined to the mythological subjects and verbal flourishes usually associated with poetic drama. Yeats's "new kind of scenic art" systematically upsets the relation between text, actor, stage scene, and audience that sustains realistic representation, as Yeats recognized in the early essay, "The Play, the Player, and the Scene": "I have been the advocate of the poetry as against the actor, but I am the advocate of the actor as against the scenery." By situating the spoken word as the defining language of the spectacle, Yeats's early plays subordinate other theatrical enunciators—acting, gesture, movement, lighting, scene design—to "speech," indeed, to a variety of modes of enunciation prescribed by the text. The static stage tableaux, the ornamental or decorative backcloths, the marmoreal gestures and cantillated speech of these productions reflect Yeats's attempt to inscribe the pattern, rhythm, and euphony of the text in the material elements of the production: "That we may throw emphasis on the words in poetical drama . . . the actors must move, for the most part, slowly and quietly, and not very much, and there should be something in their movements decorative and rhythmical as if they were paintings on a frieze" (*Explorations* 176–77). The sensibility of Yeats's early plays is a pictorial one, and the plays tend to maintain the "realistic" division between the stage and audience, much as Maeterlinck's plays were sometimes performed behind a gauze sheer. The drama is perhaps magical and unreal, but the stage retains its objectifying otherness, projecting an exquisite series of pictures before its absent public.

With his discovery of the Noh, however, Yeats found a framework for rethinking the text's place in the poetics of performance. In the dance plays, Yeats felt that he had discovered "a new form by this combination of dance, speech, and music," a form whose intercalation of stage languages not only reversed the word/scene ratio of realism, but interrupted the "poetic" hierarchy of text-to-performance, word-to-speech as well (*Letters* 768). The rhetoric of the dance plays distributes the signifying modes of performance—speech, song, acting, dance—rather than assimilating them to the verbal code of the poetic text. Yeats's dance plays dramatize the process of the text's *staging*, how each mode of performance recomposes the verbal design of the text in its own idiom. In so doing, the performance implicates the audience in a fresh form of theatricality.

At the Hawk's Well outlines many of the ways in which the text can be made to constitute a poetic theater. The rhetoric of *At the Hawk's Well* is first characterized by the disposition of the playing area. The play opens against a *"patterned screen"* set against the wall of a drawing-room, and is lighted by *"the lighting we are most accustomed to in our rooms"*; the Musicians (*"their faces made up to resemble masks"*) enter, and sing the play's initial lyric as they unfold and refold the cloth (136–37). The first moves of the play evade the identifications of the realistic theater in several ways. *At the Hawk's Well* has been performed in theaters, but theatrical production suppresses an essential element of the play's confrontation with realism, its assertion that such a play should transpire in the midst of "life" and not be set apart within the confines of "theater." Unlike the darkened auditorium, which restricts the performance to the lighted stage and situates the spectator as an absent observer of both the drama and its theatrical presentation, Yeats's lighted room barely delineates the performance space from the spectators' living area. In this regard, the patterned screen is a notable development away from the ornamental backdrops of Yeats's earlier plays, or the mysterious settings of Maeterlinck's *symboliste* dramas. The scenery of the 1903 production of *The Hour-Glass*, as Maire Nic Shiubhlaigh recalled, "was calculated to centre the onlookers' attention principally on the dialogue and action," and so "merged" the design of costumes and properties "into the background" (33–34). While its pattern is reminiscent of such pre-Raphaelite decoration, the screen prevents rather than encourages the assimilation of the actors to an inaccessible dramatic fiction. The screen of the dance plays is a portable, openly theatrical backdrop, set up by the performers; it creates an unlocalized performance space in *"any bare space before a wall."*

The screen enables the material world surrounding the performance to spill into the play, signaling the performance without determining its distance from the audience. In a sense, the decorative patterning of the screen mirrors the artful posturing of Yeats's graceful public, "dressed in their evening best, the men immaculate in shiny sober black, the women gay and glittering in silk sonorous, and brilliant brocade." To Sean O'Casey, this self-regarding fragility typified the solipsism of Yeats's theater: the "grace" and "slender charm" of *At the Hawk's Well* "couldn't carry the stage to the drawing-room" (373–74); as Yeats suggests in "Certain Noble Plays of Japan," this kind of drama explicitly prevents the "disordered passion of nature"—and of the theater—from entering indecorously into our "sitting room." Yeats designs an elaborately conventional enactment, a "series of positions and movements" that imitates, intensifies, and reflects the rhythmic artifice of its elegant audience. The production relies on the actors and spectators, not on the theatrical scene and its scenery, to strike the shade of difference between drama, stage, and audience "by human means alone" (*Essays* 230, 221, 224).

The initial actions of the Musicians alert us to the registers of the play's performance, not to the details of the drama itself. Their masklike faces define a zone of identity midway between the various, changeable, and strongly individuated expressions of their audience and the fixed but generalized masks of the Old Man and Cuchulain. In "Literature and the Living Voice," Yeats remarks of musicians that the "minstrel never dramatised anybody but himself. . . . He will go no nearer to drama than we do in daily speech, and he will not allow you for any long time to forget himself"

(*Explorations* 214–15). In *At the Hawk's Well*, the Musicians don't *act*; they perform a boundary function, articulating the difference between the play's acting and its observation. They construct the theatrical site, arranging their instruments, attending to the lights, concealing the entrance of the Guardian. Since they don't participate in the drama, their singing of the lyrics need not characterize the Musicians, interpose a fictive "character" between performer and audience. Bert States has remarked that "song does not affect identity" in the way that impersonation does, but "simply alters the composure of identity" (159). For this reason, it seems unlikely that an audience need identify the lyrics either with the fictive "character" of the individual Musicians, or with the voices of the Old Man and Cuchulain, as critics have often done in reading the play. Instead, the lyrics themselves are poised between the theatrical and the dramatic scene, much like the Musicians, directing the action without entering into it. Like the unrolling and rewinding of the cloth, the frame of lyric poetry intercedes between stage and audience, marking a threshold between the acting and the acts of attention required to see it as drama.

The Musicians' liminal function in the performance is complicated by their articulation of the text as song *and* as speech. James Flannery rightly notes that the Noh generally enabled Yeats to "separate completely the actor from the singer of lyric passages" (204), but Yeats also discriminates between the Musicians' speech and their singing at the play's outset, a distinct advance over his earlier vocal experiments. Despite long work with gifted and sympathetic performers like Florence Farr and Frank Fay, Yeats's ideal of poetic speech seems not to have been achieved on the stage. The vocal style of the early plays most often disintegrated into a cacophonous quartet of speech, cantillation, recitation, and song. By interrupting song with speech, however, the dance plays deliberately lend a different theatrical purpose to each mode of the voice. In speech, the Musicians describe the dramatic setting, the time of day, the dry well, the Guardian, and the sound of the wind. Unlike the opening songs, which serve the theatrical purpose of covering the Guardian's stage entrance and orienting the audience to the play, the spoken descriptions seem part of the drama, filling in the fictive setting and acting as narrative stage directions within the scene. (The rhythms of speech and song differ as well; while the repeated triplets in Dulac's score embed a trimeter rhythm in the lyric passages, the spoken descriptions tend toward a more pronounced tetrameter.)[4]

Moreover, in speech, the Musicians react to the scene they describe. Producing the text as *speech* faintly "characterizes" the Musicians, marking a greater distance between the Musicians and the observing audience when they speak than when they sing—"I am afraid of this place," the Second Musician says before resuming his song (137). It is a faint difference, perhaps, but a signal one. The Musicians' speech is identified so closely with the dramatic "scene" that it is occasionally tempting to hear them as speaking for other characters, in the voice of the Old Man in particular. In its opening moments, *At the Hawk's Well* discriminates between two rhetorical functions of the voice: *speech* coordinates "character" and "scene," providing a dramatic context and perhaps even a symbolic cause for the action; *song* provides an interpretive perspective for the theater audience.[5] Although Yeats rigorously foregrounds the articulation of the word in his drama, each mode of enunciation strikes a different gestural relation between the drama and the attentive public, presents a different kind of access to the text, and raises different problems for our implication in the spectacle as a whole.

With the entrance of the Old Man, song and speech are counterpoised with acting as the play's means of presentation. Yeats's stage directions—the Old Man and Cuchulain are both masked, and both characters' "*movements . . . suggest a marionette*" (138)— again address the style of the actors' performance rather than specifying its "content" or "character." The actor inevitably skews performance toward a naturalistic imitation of behavior. Yeats combats this emphasis by identifying the acting with the formalized codes of expression already established by the Musicians. Yeats found a deeply symbolic meaning in the mask in his personal and poetic mythology, where the mask stands for that anti-self whose pursuit

---

4. See the Dulac score in Yeats, *Four Plays for Dancers*.
5. Denis Donoghue distinguishes between context and cause in *The Third Voice* 51. Donoghue's use of Burke to consider the scene/agent/act "ratio" of the play is exemplary; here, I am suggesting how the scene/agent/act "ratio" of theatrical performance articulates a "rhetoric" that shapes our view of the text's designs.

creates the self in action.[6] In the theater, Yeats intended the mask to prevent the irruption of the actor's personality into the performance, to hold dramatic character "at a distance" from the actor's presentation onstage, to bring the dramatic character into focus "nearer to us, and send the actors farther off," as Maeterlinck might have remarked (99).

Yeats's dance plays repudiate acting "that copies the accidental surface of life," to insist on a style of performance that emphasizes its status as acting, rather than as naturalistic behavior (*Essays* 18). The mask finally prevents the spectator from identifying the actor with the character he plays, because "no matter how close you go," the mask "is yet a work of art" (*Essays* 226). The mask fixes a minimal aesthetic distance between the actor and the role, a distance that is paradoxically annulled by the identity between realistic acting and social behavior outside the theater. The verisimilitude of realistic acting obscures our view of the actor's histrionic surface, by so closely identifying the style of theatrical representation with the gestural codes of social performance. Modern acting, like modern drama, "has been driven to make indirect its expression of the mind, which leaves it to be inferred from some commonplace sentence or gesture as we infer it in ordinary life" (*Essays* 334). In this view, "realistic" spectators avoid the labor of art by reading the spectacle much as they do in "ordinary life." The actor's mask, however, prevents us from identifying *our* performance—the way that we "infer" this scene—with the habitual forms of attention we practice outside the theater. Through the mask, Yeats presses the performances of both actor and spectator toward an art out of nature.

Like his use of masks, Yeats's orchestration of the actors' marionette-like movements to the taps of the drum can be seen to develop—and develop away from—earlier "poetic" techniques that attempted to regulate the actors like automata.[7] By masking

---

6. See Ellmann, and Flannery 11–17.

7. We may overemphasize the extent to which Yeats's directions really determine the actors' performances or conceal the actors from our view. During rehearsals of *At the Hawk's Well* in 1916, Yeats complained bitterly about his Cuchulain, Henry Ainley, to Lady Gregory: "The play goes on well except for Ainley, who waves his arms like a drowning kitten" (*Letters* 609).

his actors and dictating their movement, Yeats "complicates" our view of acting in *At the Hawk's Well*, and again marks a shift in the play's theatrical rhetoric.

> Why don't you speak to me? Why don't you say:
> 'Are you not weary gathering those sticks?'
> (138)

No doubt an inventive actor could "characterize" the Musician through his singing of the lyrics. The texts of the enacted roles, on the other hand, demand characterization. The Old Man's irritable, wheedling, and whining verse requires the performer to dramatize someone other than himself: the text itself provides a kind of mask. The text commands the actor to strike a relationship with another actor/character (the Guardian), and to express the Old Man's sensibility through a particular physical sensation (cold). The Old Man even speaks in a staccato that interrupts the verse meter. Much as lyric song sets the theatrical boundaries of the play, and narrative speech fills in the dramatic scene, acting—the impersonated word—defines the role of "character" in the drama: the actor decides the "appropriate distance from life" of the character he plays (*Four Plays* 87). The Old Man's querulous questions are instantly set against Cuchulain's vigorous self-assertion—"I am named Cuchulain, I am Sualtim's son" (139). Although masks and movement prevent a realistic identification between the actor's physical presentation onstage and the lineaments of his role, Yeats has keyed this part of the text to the ethical mode of acting. Through performance, the actor enables us to "infer" the dynamics of dramatic character.

Evocative song, descriptive narrative, personalizing acting: each identifies a different relation between text and performer, word and self. These relations are finally "complicated" in the play's climactic dance. The relation between word and gesture is critical to the dramatic climax of *At the Hawk's Well*, a point illustrated for Richard Allen Cave by a disappointing television production of the play:

> On the whole, however, the production was disappointing because the roles of Cuchulain and the Old Man were mimed throughout by dancers while the musicians spoke their parts for them; the resulting effect was fussy on the eye and declamatory on the ear. There was

no silence or repose to draw the spectator imaginatively into the experience; the intrusion of a supernatural force in the Hawk embodied in the dancer inevitably lacked climactic excitement here, despite a change in dance-idiom; and the passion of the verse semed cold, consciously elocuted, because it was not *seen* to spring from the same muscular and psychological tension as the movement. (139–40)

Yeats required a "minute intensity of movement in the dance of the hawk," the muscular and psychological tension that would sustain the spoken verse. In later plays such as *The Dreaming of the Bones* (1919), Yeats would insist that the dancer's part be "taken by a dancer who has the training of a dancer alone" (*Four Plays* 88, 129). Perhaps because of what Symons called "the particular elegance of the dance," the "intellectual as well as sensuous appeal of a living symbol, which can but reach the brain through the eyes, in the visual, concrete, imaginative way," it is difficult not to think of the dance alone as the culminating event of the play (*Studies* 246). The dancer embodies an image, rather than impersonating a "character," performing skilled movements rather than dramatic actions and the ethical dimension they imply. The wordless dance is less a mode of enacted character than of symbolic possession. In this sense, the dancer's enactment is more purely symbolic, a kind of meaning incommensurate with both speech and acting. Indeed, the dance, though hardly a gap in the performance, arises from a palpable lacuna in the text: "*The dance goes on for some time*" (142).[8]

In "The World as Ballet," Symons found dance to "concentrate in itself a good deal of the modern ideal in matters of artistic expression": "Nothing is stated, there is no intrusion of words used for the irrelevant purpose of describing" (*Studies* 246). At the moment of this dance play's climax, though, instead of suspending the other arts, Yeats brings speech, acting, and dance into a final coordination. Cuchulain continues to "act" the text, to project character through a "personated gesture." Actor and dancer are both framed by the response of the Musicians, who reassert their dual role in speech and song. Their striking lyric—"O God, protect me / From

8. Curtis Bradford notes that Yeats cut the First Musician's description of the dance from the play, because "no doubt the dance itself made the words seem inaccurate or redundant" (211, 203).

a horrible deathless body / Sliding through the veins of a sudden" (143)—again places the Musicians on the edge of the dramatic scene as a framing chorus (though described as *"singing or half-singing"* in the text, this speech is spoken in the Dulac score). Their function is a complex and divided one here, for while speech places the Musicians in the dramatic scene, song draws them toward the audience: their performance presents an analogy of the audience's own oscillating relation to the events in the drawing room. At the center, the symbolic gesture of the dancer confronts the impersonated, characterizing gesture of the actor. Speech and song stand outside the frame of action, mediating between the theatrical event and its reconstruction as drama in the eye of the mind.

To characterize the "complication" of our view Yeats prescribes here, we might recall his seminal early essay "At Stratford-on-Avon." Here, Yeats suggests that modern theatrical architecture should respond to the increased importance of pictorial effect in modern drama, particularly of visual perspective:

> Were our theatres of the shape of a half-closed fan, like Wagner's theatre, where the audience sit on seats that rise towards the broad end while the play is played at the narrow end, their pictures could be composed for eyes at a small number of points of view, instead of for eyes at many points of view, above and below and at the sides, and what is no better than a trade might become an art.
> (*Essays* 99–100)

Yeats calls for a more rigorous determination of perspective, but not to reinforce the conventional techniques of realistic scene painting. Instead, Yeats describes perspective as a means of placing the spectator precisely within the semiosis of theater, in order to reshape the relationship between the various agencies of the performance. In such a theater, "we could make our pictures with robes that contrasted with great masses of colour in the back-cloth and such severe or decorative forms of hills and trees and houses as would not overwhelm, as our naturalistic scenery does, the idealistic art of the poet" (*Essays* 99–100). Perspective, as Yeats later recognized, is too thoroughly identified with realism to accomplish this reordering of how the audience reads the play. In the lighted, foreshortened, nonillusionistic space before the patterned screen, Yeats is able to concentrate our attention on the relationship between the various arts of the stage and on how each interdependently rewrites the text in the playing.

The drama is not identified with any one code of performance or dimension of the text, with "language," "character," or "image." Yeats might be said to give poetry the last word, by closing the play with a lyric placed on the threshold between stage and audience. Yet even the final lyric does not subordinate performed to verbal meaning. The Musicians' final song for the unrolling and rewinding of the cloth voices a variety of perspectives on the dramatic action while the stage is cleared. The voice of the lyric is problematic, not fully identified with the sensibility of Cuchulain or of the Old Man, though reminiscent in places of each. Although the Musicians, in a sense, speak for the play's principal characters, Yeats is determined not to "characterize" the final lyric: the minstrels' *I* can be identified with any character in the play *except* the Musicians themselves. The words, that is, retain their status as words, stand apart from "character," as a lyric rewriting of the scene in the timeless "music of the beggar-man, Homer's music."[9] True, the play's final gesture is to translate the confrontation between acting and dance, character and image, into a summary verse. Yet though the word concludes *At the Hawk's Well*, its effect is prismatic, generative rather than reductive. To see the play through to its close, we reflect on the evocative but uncertain recapturing of the dramatic experience in poetry and on the shades of difference between the harmonies of the poetic text and the elusive incarnations of the theater.

In *At the Hawk's Well*, Yeats attempts to place the spectator within the process of drama; as at more formal rituals, "everyone who hears it is also a player" (*Explorations* 129). Yet as Eliot remarked in " 'Rhetoric' and Poetic Drama," theatrical play flows from the theater's "essential" division: "that we should preserve our position of spectators, and observe always from the outside though with complete understanding" (*Selected Essays* 28). We tend to think (and rightly, when we are thinking of Yeats's earlier plays) that the dance plays are typical of modern "poetic drama" insofar as they

9. See *The Death of Cuchulain* 439. On the difficulty of assigning characters' voices to the stanzas of the final lyric, see Vendler 212–16, and Friedman 106–10.

identify theatrical meaning entirely with the voicing of the word. The impersonality of the poetic "voice" governs an incantatory style of speaking; its rhythms inform a sculptural gestural style; metaphor and imagery are realized in an ornamental, symbolic, or abstract setting: the rhetoric of poetic drama casts the "languages of the stage" as echo, repeating or extending the design of the text. In the "plays for dancers," the text's theological authority is distributed among different means of enunciation, as lyric song, as narrative speech, as characterizing acting, as elegant ritual and symbolic dance; meaning arises at the interface between the text and its staging. By directing different registers of voice and movement in the dance plays, Yeats forces his audience to attend to the rhetoric of embodiment, the different ways in which the body can be shaped by the discipline of the poetic text. To see in this way, to suspend the habitual synthesis of word and gesture, is also to be identified by the rhetoric of the play, to be given a mask, a "second self" as spectator. Imagining "ourselves as different from what we are" (*Autobiographies* 469), we encounter the characteristic challenge of Yeats's poiesis, the quarrel between poetry and rhetoric that informs the rhetoric of the stage.[10]

THE DISCIPLINE OF PERFORMANCE: *THE DANCE OF DEATH* AND *MURDER IN THE CATHEDRAL*

Yeats's dance plays are a special mode of theater. Their scrupulous effort to reshape the relationship between the text and its production is achieved in a scope and with materials that may still seem precious, ethereal, untheatrical. A young W. H. Auden, at least, thought as much when reviewing Priscilla Thouless's *Modern Poetic Drama* for *The Listener* in 1934:

> This book is like an exhibition of perpetual motion models. Here they all are, labelled Phillips, Davidson, Yeats, some on the largest scale, some on the tiniest, some ingenious in design, some beautifully made, all suffering from only one defect—they won't go.

10. I also have in mind Yeats's famous epigram in *Per Amica Silentia Lunae*: "We make out of the quarrel with others, rhetoric, but of the quarrel with ourselves, poetry" (*Mythologies* 331).

Already involved in the development of the Group Theatre, Auden clearly speaks both to the limitations of the poetic stage currently in practice, and to his own sense of how a poetic theater might work. While Yeats avoids the popular in favor of the esoteric, Auden seeks to build a poetic theater that will "go," reclaiming the stage for poetry through the forms of theater "actually in use." Auden disclaims the available modes of poetic drama ("the romantic sham-Tudor," the "cosmic-philosophical," and the "high-brow chamber-music drama"), arguing that drama "is so essentially a social art that it is difficult to believe that the poets are really satisfied with this solution":

> The truth is that those who would write poetic drama, refuse to start from the only place where they can start, from the dramatic forms actually in use. These are the variety-show, the pantomime, the musical comedy and revue (Miss Thouless rightly discerns the relation between the success of "Hassan" and "Chu Chin Chow"), the thriller, the drama of ideas, the comedy of manners, and, standing somewhat eccentrically to these, the ballet.

Anticipating what would become an important strategy of innovation in the poetic theater, Auden argues that the "poetic" dimension of the text can only be realized onstage through the available means of theatrical performance. In this sense, Auden clarifies and extends Yeats's practice, recognizing that the practices of the poetic stage—speech, song, acting—do not operate in abstraction from their use in other kinds of theater. To Auden, the text's staging must be accomplished by directing the theater's legitimate, theatrical voices. As his collaborator Christopher Isherwood recalled, Auden thought that the "only remaining traces of theatrical art were to be found on the music-hall stage: the whole of modern realistic drama since Tchekhov had got to go; later, perhaps, something might be done with puppets" (214–15). This attraction to popular theater—mingled with a more recondite, even aristocratic impulse—sustains Auden's theater, from the Freudian panto-charade *Paid on Both Sides*, through the Cowardesque revue in *The Dance of Death*, to the variety of effects used in the plays written with Isherwood: the morality-drama format of *The Dog Beneath the Skin* (1936), the radio propaganda that interrupts the symbolic journey in *The Ascent of F6* (1937), the Brechtian fragmentation and satire of *On the Frontier* (1938). "The Music

Hall, the Christmas Pantomime, and the country house charade are the most living drama of to-day": the purpose of Auden's poetic theater is to find its voice in these popular idioms (qtd. in Sidnell, "Auden" 497).

Auden's career with the Group Theatre points to the poetic drama's central attention to the place of the spectator in the theater, an attention that emerges most clearly in the vigorous and controversial morality drama *The Dance of Death*. Although Auden's political vision is more pointed—to "present to you this evening a picture of the decline of a class"—the play's rhetoric owes a good deal to the perpetual-motion model of Yeats's drama.[11] The text is fragmented among a series of performance styles, providing a less meticulous, more popular version of Yeats's practice in the dance plays. The stage is bare; an Announcer sits above the action like a tennis umpire, speaking to the decaying middle-class Chorus of their upcoming demise. The Dancer leads the Chorus through a variety of transformations—beginning as seaside bathers, they become Fascist troops, Lawrentian nature-worshippers, spiritualists—before he dies, bequeathing his kingdom to the working class in a choral ballad sung to the tune of "Casey Jones." What is important about *The Dance of Death* is Auden's attempt to order the text's realization through popular stage forms, rather than through Yeats's more abstract ordering of speech, song, acting, and dance. The drama of *The Dance of Death* is staged not only through choral odes and the Announcer's directions, but as a revue, including snatches of doggerel, a farcical onstage commentary by the veteran team of Box and Cox, an updated *commedia dell' arte* routine, and a finale straight out of Christmas pantomime, in which Father Christmas is replaced by a panto Karl Marx (who intones over the dead Dancer, "The instruments of production have been too much for him. He is liquidated" 107).

As an effort to make the poetic drama "go," Auden uses the text to direct forms of popular theater, and so to direct the audience attitudes and responses they conventionally shape. "While BOX and

11. As Michael J. Sidnell suggests in his excellent study of the play in *Dances of Death*, Auden "was feeling his way, in fact, to the kind of juxtapositional structures that Yeats had adopted in his *Plays for Dancers* and Brecht in his use of lyrics to counterpoint rudimentary parabolic action" (64). See also Hynes, *The Auden Generation* 128.

COX *are speaking, the* AUDIENCE *should render the appropriate noises they describe"*—stamping their feet and swinging their arms, for instance. And while the spectators may balk at such calisthenics, Auden places members of the cast in the audience, who deliver a Cockney commentary on the action. The device is a clumsy one, but the planted audience's vigorous and outspoken activity suggests that Auden seeks a more lively version of Yeats's practice, enabling the audience to engage the text through its own performance of a familiar kind of theatrical behavior. Although the politics of the spectacle proved controversial, if not indeterminable, commentators on *The Dance of Death* agreed that the play's strongest effects emerged in performance, in the relation between stage and audience developed by the production.

It is somewhat easier to see Yeats's practice as poetic theater, in part because Yeats's text is more conventionally versified than the doggerel of *The Dance of Death.* Auden and Isherwood would later assimilate "bath-chairs, beer, boils, boots, calf-love, class-war, dope, egoism, farce, Fascism and fornication in a rambling theatrical entertainment," succeeding in some measure precisely "because they were concerned first, with theatrical entertainment" (Heppenstall). In the later plays, the problem is compounded, as Auden again follows Yeats in discriminating the uses of prose and verse but reserves verse mainly for thematic or atmospheric commentary. Noting that Eliot's summons to the poetic theater to learn its trade from popular arts like music hall had been carried out more completely by Auden and Isherwood, Stephen Spender nonetheless found that the "victory has not been gained without a certain number of concessions which amount perhaps to a loss to modern poetry"—namely bad verse (Auden's fault) and sketchy characterization (Isherwood's contribution). "What a relief it must have been to the undergraduate admirers of Auden's difficult *Poems* to discover that Mr. Auden had started writing in the manner of Cole Porter": Spender rightly charges Auden's drama with dissipating the intensity of poetic language and with wasting the poetic theater's one claim to innovation, using poetry to govern the many signifying activities of performance. *The Dance of Death,* like the later plays, is more cosmopolitan than Yeats's drama, more involved in European theatrical trends than Eliot's, and more popular than either. And while Auden's drama seems, finally, not to grasp the ratio between poetry and the stage as clearly as Yeats's, or to imagine the spectator's performance as clearly as Eliot's, it may be difficult for us now to recover precisely the kind of energy that *The Dance of Death* seemed to generate, its special "lucidity" in performance:

> In performance this piece has a lucidity which it lacks in print, and the general amusingness of the stage movement, the emphasis of the jazz band, and the singing and the dancing are aids, not hindrances, to the assimilation of the author's ideas. It all suggests an expressive and agreeable theatrical form which Mr. Auden, or some other modern poet, might some day richly load with ore.
> (Rev. of *The Dance of Death* and *Sweeney Agonistes*)

Auden was, perhaps, more expressive and agreeable, but Eliot more effectively pursued this theatrical form, coordinating the discourse of the stage and his designs upon the audience in the design of the play. As poetic theater, *Murder in the Cathedral* participates in the dialectic between "the act" and "the work of acting," organizing the fictive "personalities" of the theater—actor, character, spectator—as the expression of the "poetic" formalities of the text. For *Murder in the Cathedral* is a play *about* its audience, who, like the play's protagonist and like the choral audience onstage, come to know that "action is suffering / And suffering action" (*Murder* 17). Eliot's conception of a "native popular drama" nearer "to Shakespeare than to Ibsen or Chekhov," his attraction to a "mordant, ferocious, and personal" native theater like music hall, and his "Rome, Cambridge, and Harley Street" reading of ritual are often seen to motivate his drama, but Eliot's writing about such events tends to identify the effects of performance, without clarifying how such effects are produced.[12] Framing Eliot's plays as dramatized Frazer runs the risk of consigning them to the realm of lost ritual and forgotten theater, where poetic drama becomes simply a "conscious, 'pretty' piece of archaeology" ("The Ballet" 443). Much as in Yeats's plays for dancers, and even in Auden's exuberant moralities, the audience's engagement in suffering or acting is both

---

12. On native theater and drama, see "London Letter," *Dial* 70 (June 1921): 687; on ritual, see "The Ballet" 442. For an excellent reading of how Eliot's emphasis on ritual and music hall has preempted the recognition of other contexts of his drama, see Everett.

shaped and signaled by changes in the mode of the text—choral ode, verse dialogue, the Knights' prose—and in the performance it directs as choral speaking, individualized acting, soapbox oratory.

"From one point of view, the poet aspires to the condition of the music-hall comedian" (*Use* 22). Given the vaudevillian cast of characters in his earlier poetry and his own talent for self-dramatization, it is surprising to find Eliot—in "Poetry and Drama," the major essay on poetic theater—searching for a *"neutral"* verse style for his play, claiming that when poets turn to playwriting they are likely to find choral verse relatively familiar. Choral delivery seems to retain the role conventionally assigned to the text by poetic drama, producing the text as a generalized "speech," a verbal order distinct from the more personalizing effects of "acting." The celebrated choruses of Auden and Isherwood's *The Dog Beneath the Skin* work largely in this way, as descriptions of action, character, and theme. But Eliot's Chorus is not a marionette, an automaton, or a commentator, and it occupies a much more unsettling role in the drama and in the play's performance. Something like Yeats's Musicians, though without their evident artifice, Eliot's Chorus performs both as a "character" in the drama and as a "character" in the theater.[13] To play the Chorus requires a specifically histrionic—personalizing, characterizing, physicalizing—engagement with the text: "Here let us stand, close by the cathedral" (11). As actors have recognized, the Chorus must be conceived as a body of roles requiring individuation.[14] In this sense the Chorus becomes a character in the drama, a real community composed of "'individual threads of character'" as Elsie

---

13. Eliot was attracted to the Yeatsian mode, and wrote to Hallie Flanagan that her Vassar production of *Sweeney Agonistes* "should be stylised as in the Noh drama—see Ezra Pound's book and Yeats' preface and notes to *The Hawk's Well*." He thought that characters *"ought* to wear masks; the ones wearing old masks ought to give the impression of being young persons (as actors) and vice versa. Diction should not have too much expression. I had intended the whole play to be accompanied by light drum taps to accentuate the beats (esp. the chorus, which ought to have a noise like a street drill)" (Flanagan 83).

14. Hallie Flanagan describes the almost-Stanislavskian preparation of her students for the Chorus: "Individual actors built up their own characters, not only from the play, but from a study of the lives of women who had known 'oppression and torture, destitution, disease.' They pored over *These Are Our Lives, Have You Seen Their Faces,* and the drawings of Käthe Kollwitz" (129).

Fogerty put it, describing her training of the Chorus (Browne 86). Although the Chorus is composed exclusively of women, its members refer to the broader range of laborers, merchants, and others who inhabit their society, and so represent the "character" of Eliot's theater audience in general, a similar community composed of different individuals. Eliot had experimented with a more direct representation of the contemporary working classes in *The Rock;* the unsatisfactory results, perhaps compounded by Auden's example in *The Dance of Death,* turned him in a different direction. Placed as a spectator of the action, "forced to bear witness" in a role in which "there is no action," the Chorus's characterization shapes our initial understanding of the drama, in part by representing our activity within the play. Like the Chorus we may be content to be left alone, but the action both of the drama and of the theater works to prevent such solitude.

The characterization of the Chorus begins to blur the relation between inside and outside, suffering and acting, witnessing and performing. For the Chorus's performance not only represents a fictive character in the drama, it articulates the immediate theatrical continuity between stage and audience. The Chorus's text is the most insistently "poetic" text in the play. Its formal structure, density of imagery, range of reference, contextualizing function in the drama, remoteness from realistic stage language—as well as the fact that it is produced *as* a chorus—tend to prevent a complete subordination of the language to characterization. The Chorus's liminal oscillation between the dramatic fiction and the present audience is signaled by one of the persistent challenges of *Murder in the Cathedral* in production: striking a just balance between the Chorus as "character" and as "speaker" of poetic verse.[15] Characterizing the Chorus tends to insert it into the drama, and so to call into play familiar strategies of character interpretation: the search for motivation, for psychological integration, for social continuity, and so on. This dialectic—"women of Canterbury" or Chorus—emblematizes the theater audience's situation and creates one of the ongoing dificul-

---

15. Victor Turner's discussions of liminal and liminoid genres are now familiar; see *From Ritual to Theatre* 41. His study of Becket's confrontation with the king at the Council of Northampton provides an interesting alternative to Eliot's "ritual" construction in *Murder in the Cathedral.* See *Dramas, Fields, and Metaphors* 60–97.

ties of the play's reception. Onstage, most efforts to characterize the Chorus as medieval peasants fail, because the quality of their language and the formality of their speech provide a constant counterweight to "realistic" characterization.[16] This is not merely a technical flaw in individual productions but an aspect of Eliot's stage rhetoric, for the Chorus's part seems to require this instability, this dissonance. The inability to bring the Chorus fully into the drama is neither a failure of imagination on our part nor necessarily a failure of the production. Instead, much as the Chorus's represented emotions—fear, attraction—articulate the reactions of the audience, so the performance of the Chorus provides an index to the terms of the audience's enactment. Like the Chorus, to become fully complicit in the drama we also must assume a characterizing role, a fictive "personality" constructed as part of the spectacle, part of the act. Martyrdom, we are told, is "never an accident" in the design of God, never "the effect of a man's will" (33). Eliot's logos, the text revealed on the stage, similarly represents its audience at the intersection where accident and will are undecidable. The dialectics that produce the Chorus in the theater—expressed as character, constructed by the text—will, in a manner of speaking, come to shape our own performance if we are to enter into the play at all.

The acting of the verse text of Becket, the Priests, and the Tempters presents somewhat different problems, for we expect these texts to be more completely assimilated to the rhetoric of character-

---

16. Robert Speaight, while complimenting Elsie Fogerty's training of the original Canterbury Chorus, thought the women "remained middle-class young women from South Kensington. Nothing more remote from the medieval poor could have been imagined" (184). Helen Gardner assigns a similar dissatisfaction to the Chorus's costumes: "The power of the poetry triumphs over the curious costumes in which the 'poor women of Canterbury' are usually draped. They are made to look like young ladies who, for a charade, have done the best they could with a set of slightly old-fashioned artistic bedspreads" (138n). And Martin Esslin, reviewing the 1972 Royal Shakespeare Company production, remarks, "In this case the seven ladies of Canterbury sound as though they were reciting poems of T. S. Eliot which they had just learnt by heart. Their voices are far too middle class, their intonations far too Third Programme to make them believable medieval paupers of Canterbury." This use of anachronism may, in a sense, be Eliot's closest approximation of the theatrical community implied by medieval morality drama in the mode of *Everyman;* on the audience's role in medieval moralities, see Garner.

ization. Yet the First Priest's opening line repeats a line spoken earlier by the Chorus, a technique Eliot uses effectively throughout the play, most notably when the Fourth Tempter repeats Thomas's opening lines as his final temptation. Although each Priest is played by an individual actor, their roles are provided with relatively little definition; the Priests seem more like voices echoing a text than like characters in the conventional sense. In that they become even mildly individuated only when they engage the Chorus, it might be said that "character" emerges in the play only agonistically, only through conflict with others, or, as in the case of Thomas, with internalized others. Eliot's rhetoric of character seems to privilege this conflict by assigning to the Tempters and the Knights more clearly characterized roles than those assigned to the Priests.[17] Unlike the Priests, each of the Tempters has a distinct verse style, and a distinct speaking style as well. Each also accords with, and so dramatizes, one of Thomas's past roles: "Old Tom, gay Tom," the "master of policy," the "rough straightforward Englishman." By filling out the lineaments of character more fully in the text of the Tempters' speeches, Eliot's play emphasizes the reality of Thomas's internal struggle. And by articulating this conflict through rhetoric of realistic character, Eliot seems to claim that such expressionistic, inner struggle has a greater reality, is more dramatic, than the external relations between characters—between Thomas and the Priests, for instance.

"From this it follows that a mixture of prose and verse in the same play is generally to be avoided: each transition makes the auditor aware, with a jolt, of the medium" ("Poetry and Drama" 133). The first such jolt provided by the play is Thomas's sermon; the sermon also jolts the performance "medium" at this point as well, recalibrating the relationship between actor, text, and audience by altering the distance between the text and the "personality" of the performer. As Robert Speaight recognized, the sermon is "theatrically speaking, the *pièce de résistance* of the play," as any text that allows the actor to play to the audience usually is (186). The play's central theatrical conspiracy—to stage the audience's complicity in Thomas's murder—develops a new sharpness here, for the sermon provides the actor with the opportunity to bring a

---

17. See Whitaker, *Fields of Play* 147.

different kind of characterization to bear both on Thomas and on his audience. The sermon enacts the expected scene of Thomas's preaching to his flock on Christmas morning and provides a thematic center for the play in Thomas's oblique defense of his behavior and of the status of martyrdom. In the design of the performance, this is also the moment where the intrusive personality of the actor exerts its most palpable influence, in that the sermon provides an opportunity to *act* for the audience (rather than, say, to be acted upon by the Tempters), to produce "Thomas" for us through the charismatic expression of a stage personality. The colloquial prose invites both the actor and the audience to conceive Thomas through the conventions of realistic characterization, with the emphasis on motivation, cause, and origin that realistic interpretation requires.

This realism skews the performance in other ways as well. While the Chorus represents us within the drama, Thomas's "realistic" performance stages us in the scene of the drama itself, most evidently in the play's first production at the Canterbury chapter house. Through this realistic device, we engage Thomas's sermon in something closer to the unprotected immediacy of our offstage lives. The effect of this engagement is, however, to foreground Thomas's oratory *as* oratory, possibly as mere rhetoric. As a piece of realistic acting, Thomas's attempt to convince us that the martyr is "the instrument of God" requires the actor to persuade himself of the theatrical reality of the moment, in order to persuade us of the provisional reality of his characterization of Thomas (33). Oddly enough, by presenting the text of Thomas's sermon through the rhetoric of realistic performance, Eliot invites us to interpret Thomas in the way we interpret characters in realistic drama, and perhaps in the way we interpret others in the prosaic drama of our lives: by indirection, through the suspicion that motives are always falsified by their enactment. Is Thomas really persuaded of the role of martyrdom in God's design, or is he trying to persuade himself (and us) that he is not pursuing martyrdom in some way? As in realistic theater, we can never know, because neither Thomas nor the actor who plays him can say.

The drama becomes an instrument of community only in performance, and Eliot's uses of prose and verse tend to work differently in this regard and are more finely discriminated in their staging of the audience than the prose and verse of Auden and Isherwood's plays. The verse establishes a theatrical continuity between the performers and the audience; the prose tends to establish a continuity between the dramatic characters and a represented audience. The Chorus's characterized verse mediates between these positions, and emblematizes the audience's situation in the theater, torn by the sometimes conflicting demands of the drama and the performance. This dichotomy in the ways in which the "vital flame" of the audience's personality is implied in performance is confirmed and extended by the Knights' apology. The Knights' direct address was perhaps Eliot's "main reason for writing the play," and despite the tang of Shaw's *Saint Joan* (1923), the Knights produce a very un-Shavian spectacle.[18] The Knights work less to educate us than to offend us, arguing with us in a series of sinister yet pacifying platitudes. The Knights ask for sympathy from the audience, inviting us to treat the murder as we treat other blasphemies of modern life, as "merely a department of bad form" ("Personality" 94). This identification again arises through Eliot's use of a realistic rhetoric. For unlike the formal language of Thomas's sermon, the Knights' text is composed in a recognizable, even contemporary idiom, one that requires a more relaxed, physically nonchalant gestural style of the performer. Engaging us in our own vacant clichés ("we had taken on a pretty stiff job"), the Knights again establish a continuity between dramatic character and a represented spectator. By speaking in our tongue, the Knights claim a kinship with the conventional morality that guides our everyday lives. To play our part, to "witness" the drama of martyrdom, we must reject this identification, this construction of our performance in the theater. The play invites an ironic performance from us, one in which we learn to see differently than we do in our lives.

Without trivializing the significance of martyrdom, I would like to suggest that the process of Eliot's theater is designed to provide a kind of simulation, not of martyrdom, but of the spiritual educa-

---

18. The sense in which the Knights' address forges a real community—i.e., one of diverse opinion—is perhaps suggested by another incident reported by Hoellering that occurred during the filming of *Murder in the Cathedral*: "When, towards the end of the play, we came to the speeches in which the three Knights justify themselves before the crowd, the sound recordist suddenly turned round to Mr Eliot and, completely forgetting his control switches, said excitedly, 'Aren't they right, sir? What do you think?' Mr Eliot, needless to say, was highly amused" (Hoellering 82–83).

tion necessary for a modern faith. Like the Chorus, perhaps, we want to have a "theatrical" relationship to events like martyrdom, to see them without having to witness them, without having to be transformed by them. Watching *Murder in the Cathedral*, we are urged briefly to forsake our other parts for the role of the audience, a demanding part which requires our direct engagement in the "work of acting" if we are to comprehend the play's designs on us. In this tiny figure is inscribed not only the sign of the greater revolution that the play dramatizes—Thomas's performance of the "design of God"—but also the suggestion, again in little, of what witnessing such an act might really mean for us. This is, it seems to me, partly the burden of the final chorus, the prayer that asks forgiveness both for the Chorus and for the contemporary audience, the "sightseers come with guide-books" to Canterbury (53–54). The prayer depends precisely upon the "personalities" the play has evoked throughout the performance, for as the audience is invited to assume a specific role in the drama—to raise the possibility of martyrdom by rejecting the Knights' defense—the Chorus also undergoes a change. The Chorus is converted into a community of our contemporaries, part of the community we have, through the rhetoric of the play's production, become.

"I see myself emerging / From my spectral existence into something like reality": like Lord Claverton in *The Elder Statesman*, the audience of *Murder in the Cathedral* emerges from a ghostly absence, into a "real" relation to the events of the stage (341). I have come some way from the rhetoric of poetic theater, and I would like to return to it for a moment as a way of suggesting the place of *Murder in the Cathedral* in the rhetoric of modern theatricality. In a review of the play published in Eliot's *Criterion* in 1936, Michael Sayers posed the question of the play's permanence in these terms: "It may occasion a revolution in popular thought and theatre through subsequent imitations, and by its direct influence similar to that brought about by the comedies of Shaw. Or it may go down to the popular limbo as one of the curiosities of a moribund theatre" (655). Although the experimental rhetoric of *Murder in the Cathedral* is "too incisive, too original, too mordant" to be ignored, Eliot's drama—like the plays of Maeterlinck, of Auden, of Auden and Isherwood, of Christopher Fry, and, to a certain extent, of Yeats as well—has indeed slipped into the limbo of "poetic drama," or possibly someplace worse. Yeats may be a more original dramatist, and certainly Yeats had a more sure sense of the stage, but in some respects *Murder in the Cathedral* undertakes a more radical displacement of the authority of the text than Yeats's, Auden's, or Beckett's plays do, precisely because Eliot contaminates the "poetic" spectacle with a prose that is traced by the dynamics of realistic stage production, realistic acting. *Murder in the Cathedral* surrenders some of the text's "poetic" authority and acknowledges that meaning in the theater arises in the necessary rewriting of "poetry" in the various, competing "languages" of stage performance.

In this regard, Eliot's poetic theater not only challenges realism, it also partly challenges the privileged status of the word in the semiosis of poetic theater. Eliot's drama strategically designs the spectator's performance as an essential part of the meaning of the theatrical event. Yeats preconceives his aristocratic audiences, and Auden seats stage-Cockneys in the auditorium, but Eliot builds a form for the audience's "collaboration." Eliot's attention to the spectator, his attempt to evoke the spectator's performance in the play's design, to provide a theatrical "escape" from the habitual "personality" with which we confront the world at large, may point surprisingly enough in a different direction, toward a theatrical rhetoric more overtly engaged in the production of the audience as "subject": the rhetoric of political theater. For like poetry, the rhetoric of poetic theater "may effect revolutions in sensibility such as are periodically needed; may help to break up the conventional modes of perception and valuation which are perpetually forming, and make people see the world afresh, or some new part of it" (*Use* 149).

THE DISCIPLINE OF THE TEXT: BECKETT'S THEATER

> "The text is the text."
> —Rick Cluchey, reporting Beckett's refusal to incorporate production changes into the published text of *Waiting for Godot* (qtd. in Duckworth 185)

To begin a discussion of Beckett's relation to the rhetoric of "poetic theater," we might reflect for a moment on a relatively unpoetic play,

Catastrophe (1982). *Catastrophe* is hardly "poetic" in any conventional sense; the verbal texture of the play is, if anything, rather less rich than that of plays like *Waiting for Godot* (1953) or *Rockaby* (1981). *Catastrophe*, it seems, has more to do with the ideology of the image than with that of the word, to concern the systems of authority—textual, theatrical, and political authority—that operate in and on the body of performance. In his efforts to bare, whiten, and sculpt the body of the Protagonist, the Director produces a spectacle for us, inscribing the body of the performer with an unspoken code, the code within which we recognize "our catastrophe" (300). As Pierre Chabert suggests, the body of the Protagonist—both actor and character—becomes emblematic of the role that the body performs in much of Beckett's theater: "It is *worked*, violated even, much like the raw materials of the painter or sculptor, in the service of a systematic exploration of all possible relationships between the body and movement, the body and space, the body and objects, the body and light and the body and words" ("The body" 23). It is this final "working" of the body of the Protagonist that most interests me here, how the body's subjection to textual authority reveals the rhetoric of Beckett's theater.

Beckett's most punishing plays tend toward an abstract visual composition at the expense of realistic mimesis: to reduce the lively movement of the body to a grim geometry, to efface character and abandon action. In this and in other respects, Beckett's theater puts the conception of the "poetic" stage that I have been developing to the test. Of course, Beckett's plays do not appear in verse form on the page. Yet insofar as the understanding of poetic theater I have developed here emphasizes the text's function in the stage production, this aspect of the text's appearance may not be critical. Many of Beckett's plays have the densely imagistic texture we associate with "poetic" drama. More important, stylistic features of the texts govern the plays' physical articulation on the stage, as the actors and the entire mise-en-scène are used—as in the poetic theater—to present the drama as a poetic "object." The antiphonal quality of dialogue in *Waiting for Godot*, the interspersed voices in *That Time* (1976), the interaction of speech and music in *Cascando* (1963), the poised periods of *Rockaby*: many of Beckett's plays articulate the text in performance in ways that are indistinguishable from the practice of poetic theater. And when Beckett claims that the "best possible play is one in which there are no actors, only the text" (Bair 513), he seems most the inheritor of Maeterlinck, Craig, Yeats, and of the *symboliste* theater of which they are a part.[19] It is, finally, in the authority assigned to the text's verbal organization that Beckett's drama enters, and complicates, the realm of poetic theater.

Although the vitality of the poetic stage may in fact be clear to us now as the result of Beckett's theater, the process of Beckett's dramatic action emerges for us in a different cultural horizon from the poetic drama of Yeats or Eliot, and perhaps exposes more effectively the place of its rhetoric in our own culture. The aesthetics of Beckett's stage seem to contain their own Foucauldian "microphysics of power," traced both within the dramatic action and in the process of theatrical representation (26). Beckett's drama often explores the poetics of torture, and is preoccupied with the speaking of a justifying "text," words that can define an order, an explanation, and so an end to a painfully interminable spectacle. To render this text in the play often requires the rending of the protagonist. Both actor and dramatic character submit to the signifying formalities of torture, suffering "the works" until they "say it," "confess" a text that may or may not release them (*What Where* 312–13). The spectacle also tests our endurance, our prolonged postponement of an essentially narrative closure, the "text" of our experience rewritten as interpretation. For even though "we do not know ... what exactly it is we are after" (*Rough for Radio II* 122), this "sign or set of words" promises to free us as well as our victims, to empower us to write the events of the stage as drama from our special vantage as spectators: "Audience privileged / actors tortured" as the director George Devine put it, describing *Play* (1963).[20]

Where we are placed in Beckett's rhetoric is the issue I would like to consider here, how our performance is traced within the differential power ascribed to the texts of Beckett's theater. The text's interest in locating our performance both marks another fea-

---

19. I am thinking here not only of the approximation of *The Cat and the Moon* in *Rough for Theatre I* and the allusions to Yeats in *Godot*, *Happy Days*, and *...but the clouds...*, but also of Katharine Worth's suggestive remarks on the resemblance between Beckett's plays and Maeterlinck's "drama of the interior." See *The Irish Drama of Europe*, passim.

20. Qtd. in Knowlson, *Samuel Beckett: An Exhibition* 91.

ture of Beckett's implication in the rhetoric of poetic theater and locates that rhetoric in the world beyond the stage. Elaine Scarry urgently reminds us that our situation as spectators of the torturous production of fictions may have an appalling likeness to other realms of torment: "In torture, it is in part the obsessive display of agency that permits one person's body to be translated into another person's voice, that allows real human pain to be converted into a regime's fiction of power" (18).[21] Are we subject to the text like the Protagonist, or identified with its authority, like the Director, like Godot? How does our performance expose the relations of power inscribed in the project of the poetic stage? Are we the victims of the spectacle, or, chillingly enough, the authors of the catastrophe?

Rough for Radio II, an early and relatively minor radio play first broadcast in 1976, provides a model of the differential power ascribed to texts in Beckett's theater. The play is something of a study for *Catastrophe*, concerning a male "Animator," who interrogates the victim Fox and supervises the transcription of the confession by a female Stenographer; we also hear the labor of Dick, who whips Fox into speech. At the opening, the Stenographer delivers a report on the previous day's unacceptable results, a report that outlines today's inquiry: to "refrain from recording mere animal cries," to "provide a strictly literal transcript, the meanest syllable has, or may have, its importance," and to "ensure full neutralization of subject when not in session, especially with regard to the gag," since the "least word let fall in solitude . . . *may be it*" (116). Yet as the play proceeds, it becomes difficult in some ways to decide who is the victim of the interrogation. Although the Animator confesses that "we do not know, any more than you, what exactly it is we are after, what sign or set of words," he increasingly prompts Fox to deliver a specific confession: "Someone, perhaps that is what is wanting, someone who once saw you...(*Abating*)...go by. . . .

---

21. The relations between theater and torture seem complex and multiple. Scarry also notes that it "is not accidental that in the torturers' idiom the room in which the brutality occurs was called the 'production room' in the Philippines, the 'cinema room' in South Vietnam, and the 'blue lit stage' in Chile: built on these repeated acts of display and having as its purpose the production of a fantastic illusion of power, torture is a grotesque piece of compensatory drama" (28).

Even though it is not true! . . . A father, a mother, a friend, a...Beatrice—no, that is asking too much" (122). Unfortunately, when Fox confesses, his narrative seems more figural than actual, resistant to the Animator's desire to plot a recognition scene. The Animator forces the Stenographer to amend her account to include the phrase *"between two kisses"* that would characterize the "Maud" that Fox mentions: "'Maud would say, *between two kisses,* etc.'" (124). Fox's oblique speech prolongs his suffering and the Animator's inquisition and encourages a frequent activity in Beckett's drama—fabulation. Providing the text with narrative coherence, the Animator hopes to placate his offstage authorities and bring an end to his own inquisitorial captivity: "Tomorrow, who knows, we may be free."

Rough for Radio II provides an instance of how the production of text as performance encodes the power relations of Beckett's drama. The body is subjected to the theater of pain in order to produce a text, a text which becomes significant only when it is inserted into the absent designs of a captor narrative. Neither Fox nor the hounding Animator knows which syllable *"may be it,"* might constitute their "catastrophe"; both are held within the absent text's fictions of power. To say that the protagonist is depersonalized is hardly adequate. The body becomes the instrument and container of a text which has its origin and meaning only elsewhere, as part of another's writing. The *staged* texts—I am thinking here of the many self-displacing narratives of Beckett's drama—betray a familiar anxiety about the ability of the stage to represent and preserve the authority of verbal art. Like the Animator torturing his foxy poet, the stage always misrepresents the poet's verbal design.

In the stage plays, the function of this master text is assumed to a large degree by another unspoken text—Beckett's directions—and it is in the relation between these two texts that Beckett most strikingly engages the formalities of the poetic stage. As a text for theater, *Play* anticipates the design of many of Beckett's later plays in containing two modes of textuality, words designing the structure of the performance, and words to be spoken on the stage, "in character," or at least "as character." In general, stage directions describe a possible disposition of the set, actors' movements, intonation, and expression. Yet *as* description they tend to convey a texture of effects, to locate meaning in a retrospective, narrative mode rather than in the incipient mode of the theater. They tell a reader how a character behaves or reacts, informing us of the content of his behavior, rather than addressing the actor, telling him or her how to produce the text. In *Play* and elsewhere, however, Beckett's directions determine the conditions within which the text, the performance, and our playing will be articulated: "The source of light is single and must not be situated outside the ideal space (stage) occupied by its victims," "In order for the urns to be only one yard high, it is necessary either that traps be used, enabling the actors to stand below stage level, or that they kneel throughout play, the urns being open at the back," and so on (158–59). Much like the disembodied voice in *What Where* (1983), emanating from beyond the pale arena of the drama, this text constructs its protagonists from outside the frame of the stage, transferring the authority of presence from the stage to the immanent region of an (unspoken) script.

The direction-text displaces the means of the actors' charismatic self-presentation: it prohibits gesture, movement, facial expression, vocal inflection, tonality and rhythm, even their uninterrupted visibility before the audience. The protagonists are sculpted, hollowed out by the text of the mise-en-scène. This functioning of the actors as images becomes invasive at the point where the text is transformed into speech: the voice. "The voice," as Helga Finter remarks, "is *par excellence* the 'object' of theatricalization because of its status as *between*: inscribed in a text, the voice indicates a carrying *externality* . . . which links it to the singular body or to a disposition of the subject" (505). Proscribing expression, intonation, intentionality, Beckett's drama displaces the voice as a sign of the actor-character's subjectivity: the actors abandon expression for a *"toneless,"* even *"unintelligible"* speech driven at a *"rapid tempo throughout"* (147). The directions even erase "speech" as a sign of volition or spontaneity. Not only is the actors' delivery *"provoked"* by the spotlight, but the spotlight also controls the volume of their speaking. The only vocal quality left to their command—loudness—is produced as an effect of the mise-en-scène as well: *"Faint spots"* produce *"Voices faint, largely unintelligible,"* while *"Strong spots"* produce *"Voices normal strength"* (147–48). Finally, the power of the unspoken text of the mise-en-scène over the presentation is registered by the language of the play itself, that stagey dialogue ("swore by all I held most sacred" 148) so relentlessly stripped of its actorly emphasis.

Emptied as a sign of the protagonist's expressive presence, speech provides an index of Beckett's exhaustion of other means of representing the text. Beckett's deconstruction of speech does not imply an implacable critique of the authority of language in the spectacle. Beckett's *word* retains its authority by refusing to be represented in the personalizing voice, as "language" as it is generally understood. Like the poetic theater, with its characteristic resort to marionettes and marionette-like acting, Beckett's theater attempts to preserve the authority of a kind of poetry by withholding it from representation as a "stage" language, as song, as acting, as theater. Beckett's recent video plays urgently convey the sense that the image forecloses the function of language. Martin Esslin suggests that in these dramas the television image "can embody and preserve the poet's imagery without having to rely on language as its primary medium, and, in the end, even enable him to dispense with it altogether" ("Towards" 47). The result, in plays like ...*but the clouds*... (1977), *Ghost Trio* (1977), and—notoriously—*Quad* (1982), is a text that violates our notions of "literature" precisely by distributing the authority of verbal language in unexpected ways, assigning it not to the dramatized speech, but to the constitutive, unspoken, offstage text of the stage directions. This sense that the theater interferes with the poetic text by representing it as acting drives the deepest dream that Beckett shares with the poetic stage, the desire for a pure "poetry" of images, scripted but unmediated by the languages of theatrical production. Rather than refiguring the text in the theater's scenic arts, Beckett's text withholds the authority of poiesis from the stage itself.[22]

It is perhaps too easy for the "summary static images" of Beckett's theater to be taken solely as the signs of "the permanent, causeless and unchanging universal condition of mere existence,"

---

22. It might be remarked that this question, the authority of stage directions over spoken text, seemed to inform some of the controversies regarding the staging of his plays in which Beckett became involved. In one case, it was not tampering with the spoken text that drew Beckett's ire, but rather tampering with the circumstances of its production: altering the setting of *Endgame* in the controversial Joann Akalaitis/American Repertory Theater production in 1985.

as critics have tended to do, too easy because such a reading avoids the most significant feature of this rhetoric, its likeness to the torture it represents (McMillan 99). To its protagonists, the symptoms of Beckett's theater are despair, deprivation, and breakdown. As Ben Barnes suggests, one of the principal tasks of a director is to convince "the actor to forfeit the notion of character in the service of poetic stage-images"; indeed, the actors must "accept this depersonalisation before any progress can be made" (86,87). Depersonalizing the actor's voice is, of course, only part of Beckett's more general machining of his performers. Winnie in *Happy Days* (1962) is progressively earthed; in *Play* the actors are metaphorically disembodied, yet "trembling" with stress in their narrow urns; in *Footfalls* (1976), May's "walking should be like a metronome." In *Not I* (1972), the actress both represents and is imprisoned within an infernal speaking machine. As Billie Whitelaw reports, in "the first couple of rehearsal performances, when the blindfold went on and I was stuck half-way up the stage, I think I had sensory deprivation. The very first time I did it, I went to pieces. I felt I had no body; I could not relate to where I was; and, going at that speed, I was becoming very dizzy and felt like an astronaut tumbling into space."[23]

This machinery of depersonalization is, in a sense, offstage, invisible in *Not I*, concealed as part of the productive actuality of the theater we overlook to see the fictive drama. Yet its effect both on the body and on the "self" signified by the voice is palpable: "The goal of the torturer is to make the one, the body, emphatically and crushingly *present* by destroying it, and to make the other, the voice, *absent* by destroying it" (Scarry 49). What "position she was in!" may be of immediate concern to the actress, but it remains concealed from us in the theater audience; we receive only the fictive "confession" of the character Mouth, whose vocalizations have been erased as voicings, as signs of presence. And yet to ignore the fact that the theater operates like an instrument of torture on the protagonists, in order to concentrate our attention on

23. Billie Whitelaw reports "trembling" in *Play* in "From Billie Whitelaw." Enoch Brater quotes Beckett's production notebook describing May's walk in *Beyond Minimalism* 71. And Billie Whitelaw describes acting in *Not I* in an interview with James Knowlson, "Extracts" 87.

the incomplete, fictive text of the drama, should, perhaps, give us pause. Such a deconversion of an instrument of civility and sociality into a weapon is precisely the mode of torture itself, in which all of the victim's extensions—the room, her own body, the voice—are used to destroy her, and to take the "fact of civilization" along with them.[24]

Corps physique dépossédé par la parole: voir Artaud" (Chabert, "Samuel Beckett" 82). The desire to textualize experience and so to provide it with narrative closure is a desire that Beckett's drama cruelly withholds from its characters and seems to invite of its spectators. In *Play*, the characters hope for a "conceivable dark and silence in the end" (*Disjecta* 111), one that could be supplied by the completion of their purgatorial text, a hope endlessly deferred by the unspoken text's final direction, "*Repeat play.*" Although the play's visual structure suggests an inquisition, in fact it is the characters who interrogate the spotlight. As W1 remarks, there may be "Nothing being asked at all. No one asking me for anything at all" (154). And much as the spotlight represents our attention within "the ideal space (stage) occupied by its victims" (158), the characters—motionless, cramped, allowed a largely visual experience—also recapitulate our situation. The characters not only narrate a conventional romantic intrigue, they also interrogate their current circumstances in order to impose a familiar shape on them, to interpret them. W2, for example, sees a rather malign capriciousness in the light, even while admitting that she may be making "the same mistake as when it was

---

24. Scarry's account of this process is compelling: "The room, both in its structure and its content, is converted into a weapon, deconverted, undone. Made to participate in the annihilation of the prisoners, made to demonstrate that everything is a weapon, the objects themselves, and with them the fact of civilization, are annihilated: there is no wall, no window, no door, no bathtub, no refrigerator, no chair, no bed"—only weapons (41). That the theater can become, to some small degree, such a weapon inflicted upon the performers may be implied by the experience of rehearsing plays like *Not I* and *Footfalls*. Billie Whitelaw reports rehearsing *Not I*: "I don't know what happened. I just stood there with tears pouring down my face. And then I saw Beckett himself walking towards the back of the theatre with his head in his hands. After a while he came back and reached up and held me. 'Oh, Billie,' he said, 'what have I done to you?' He's a wonderful man, compassionate and kind" (qtd. in Cohn 200). On the machinery used for restricting the movement of the actress's mouth in various productions, see Bair 623–30.

the sun that shone, of looking for sense where possibly there is none": "Someday you will tire of me." W1, on the other hand, more often addresses the light as part of "this," as an agent in a wider context of meaning, a purgatorial environment or system: "Penitence, yes, at a pinch, atonement, one was resigned, but no, that does not seem to be the point either." W2 and W1 model familiar habits of attention for us, for they are those of the realistic audience, attempting to discover the drama of events in the disposition of character or in the determining features of an environmental process.

What does it mean to observe such a process as drama and as theater; what where do *we* occupy in the spectacle? At the moment that the characters most closely resemble the audience, textualizing their experience, that activity is represented as a strategy of displacement, of evasion, of placation. The authority of the spoken drama in *Play* is compromised by the play's final brilliant direction: "Repeat play." Regardless of whether the repeat is played in exact imitation of the first scene—as Beckett finally seemed to favor—or intentionally varied in tonality, pace, order, or illumination, "*Repeat play*" insists on the controlling authority of the text to govern the play.[25] Beckett's text, not the characters' narration or our sense of impatience, determines when, how, and if the play will end. Like the poetic theater, Beckett's *Play* deploys the actors' bodies for their imagistic value. But the spoken words lack the authority ascribed to the text in poetic theater, those lyrics or choruses that serve to explain, rearticulate, or restate the action as "poetry." The spoken text is transformed into a kind of aural object, emptied of the rhythms, intonations, and emphases that carry much of the burden of spoken communication. Much as the actors are rendered as objects, so the words they speak are also staged as objects, "just 'things' that come out of their mouths" as George Devine commented. And yet this direction—"*Repeat play*"—also operates on us, the audience, placing us in our seats not as patrons, but as "things" in the spectacle. The rhetoric of *Play* identifies us in two incompatible and fragmentary ways: it empowers us in relation to the dramatic fiction; it objectifies us as victims of the theater.

We would expect the authority of the word in poetic theater to be paramount, that words would not be transformed into objects

---

25. On Beckett's sense of the "repeat" in *Play*, see Blackman 103.

like the other "properties" on the stage but would retain a kind of transcendent value and meaning. And yet as Yeats and Eliot make clear, it is not the text's verbal design alone that renders it as a "poem" in the theater. Instead, it seems to be in the relationship between the text's design and the means of its enunciation that the power of "poetry" emerges onstage. I would like, finally, to return to *Catastrophe* as a way of suggesting some of the implications this kind of thinking about Beckett's theater has for us, both in relation to the project of poetic theater and more generally. In his obsession with a precise stage image, his minute attention to the architecture of the body, his autocratic control of the production, the Director's practice in *Catastrophe* is reminiscent of Beckett's own work as director, and they share a common interest in the audience as well. Like the Protagonist, the audience of *Catastrophe* is staged by Beckett's drama: the *"Distant storm of applause"* that greets the Director's final image both represents our attention to the drama—we *will*, in fact, soon be applauding—and displaces us, renders our performance as a figure in the design of Beckett's play. The taped applause represents our subjection to the Director's authority; our silence, like the Protagonist's fixed gaze, signals our refusal to be scripted in this manner. And yet this refusal is more apparent than actual, for our eventual applause functions in Beckett's theater in much the manner that the taped applause works in the Director's fictive one: in the end, our applause affirms the Director's staged "catastrophe," whether we approve of his inhuman designs or not. Silent, slightly conspiratorial, attentive and restive by turns, Beckett's drama captures us in an uncanny quarter by constituting each of us as a *spectator*, author and object, interrogator and victim, a vanishing point in the play's perspective.

To conceive of Beckett's drama in this way is to work directly against Beckett's reception in the canon of modernism. Although Beckett insists on the aesthetic autonomy of his plays—"I produce an object. What people make of it is not my concern" (McMillan and Fehsenfeld 15)—the theatrical procedure of plays like *Play* and *Catastrophe* challenges the autonomy of the stage and of the drama it contains.[26] Beckett's theater no longer displays aesthetic objects

---

26. The classic statement of Beckett's "autonomous" relation to politics and culture is Theodor Adorno, "Commitment."

disinterestedly before a willing audience, if it ever did. It seems instead to assume a more rhetorical function, manifestly subjecting the public to its own mastery. In *Play*, and in *Not I, What Where, Catastrophe*, and other plays, Beckett recomposes the audience's performance in the theater, dramatizing the power of the text to evacuate, fragment, and deform its protagonists, characters, actors, and spectators. In so doing, Beckett's theatricality appears to engage a cultural field from which Beckett's drama is usually held to be distinct: a field in which representation pursues an instrumental function; in which its subjects are qualified by and painfully inspected for a "text" that invades, objectifies, replaces, and destroys them; a field that includes both the legitimate theater and the illegitimate theatricality of advertising, propaganda, pornography, and torture. To continue to read Beckett as our contemporary may finally require a complex archaeology, one that penetrates the "existential" inertia of Beckett's drama to recover the repressed complicity between the dynamics of postmodern culture and the strategies of Beckett's stage. It may, finally, require an exhumation of the field of poetic theater itself, an effort to see the relations of authority inherent in this theater as signs of a certain will to power, a power as always based on its distance from the body, from the bodies it would control as much as from those it would entertain.

4

Political Theater: Staging the Spectator

TRANSFORMING THE FIELD OF THEATER

> Do not despair—many are happy much of the time; more eat than starve, more are healthy than sick, more curable than dying; not so many dying as dead; and one of the thieves was saved. Hell's bells and all's well—half the world is at peace with itself, and so is the other half; vast areas are unpolluted; millions of children grow up without suffering deprivation, and millions, while deprived, grow up without suffering cruelties, and millions, while deprived and cruelly treated, none the less grow up. No laughter is sad and many tears are joyful. At the graveside the undertaker doffs his top hat and impregnates the prettiest mourner. Wham, bam, thank you Sam. (87)

Recall for a moment the brilliant coda of Tom Stoppard's *Jumpers* (1972). The hallucinatory symposium concludes with Archie Jumper's dizzying pastiche of *Waiting for Godot*, a theft, really, both of Didi's bleak image of the brevity of life and of Beckett's famous Augustinian parable on the play.[1] The allusion to Beckett here presents Archie's audience with a kind of interpretive paradox, a paradigm, perhaps, of Stoppard's vertiginous assault on the audience throughout the play. Wham, bam—just what is Sam being thanked for?

As with much else in *Jumpers*, this question poses a problem of theatrical hermeneutics, a theatrical analogy of the interpretive

---

1. Stoppard pairs Didi's "Astride of a grave and a difficult birth . . ." with Beckett's now-familiar anecdote: "I am interested in the shape of ideas even if I do not believe them. There is a wonderful sentence in Augustine. I wish I could remember the Latin. It is even finer in Latin than in English. 'Do not despair; one of the thieves was saved. Do not presume[;] one of the thieves was damned.' That sentence has a wonderful shape. It is the shape that matters." See *Waiting for Godot* 58; and "Samuel Beckett—Dramatist of the Year," McMillan and Fehsenfeld 58–59.

problems confronted by the characters in the play. The action of *Jumpers* turns obsessively on a series of epistemological paradoxes, confusing our ability to decide whether truth (or certainty, morality, reality) is simply a function of how we look at it or somehow transcends the means of its representation. How should we read a man who answers the door half-shaven and holding a bow and arrow and a tortoise? Is he mad, or only illustrating a problem in moral philosophy? Is it really a case of murder when the victim appears to have committed suicide neatly in a plastic bag? When is a cry for help "just exhibitionism: what we psychiatrists call 'a cry for help'" (66)? That is, the action of *Jumpers* extravagantly elaborates the anecdote that George Moore (but not *the* George Moore) tells us toward the end of the play:

> Meeting a friend in a corridor, Wittgenstein said: "Tell me, why do people always say it was *natural* for men to assume that the sun went round the earth rather than that the earth was rotating?" His friend said, "Well, obviously, because it just *looks* as if the sun is going round the earth." To which the philosopher replied, "Well, what would it have looked like if it had looked as if the earth was rotating"? (75)

Interpretive validity—let alone "truth"—is inseparable from the system that generates it. The play forces its audience into a dazzling series of such recognitions, as our own experience is constantly revised. And as Archie reminds us, this theatrical principle is much like life: "Unlike mystery novels, life does not guarantee a denouement; and if it came, how would one know whether to believe it?" (81).

Life is not a mystery novel, nor is it philosophical acrobatics. *Jumpers* lends this interpretive issue dramatic urgency by phrasing it in more pressing terms, translating the notion that moral imperatives are not absolute but only "categories of our own making" into the more passionate actions of lived experience: murder, marriage, careerist ambition, failure, love and betrayal, heroism and cowardice. Thomas R. Whitaker nicely summarizes the play's "interplay of three modes of interpreting life" as the form of our interpretive experience of the play: "an agnostic empiricism that serves the will to power; an anxious religious demand or faith that can be practically and ethically blind; and a spontaneous and compassionate ethical response that helps to guide us through the play's action.

Each mode has its own kind of jumping—amoral, anxious, or theatrical—which contributes to the kaleidoscopic whirl of performance" (*Tom Stoppard* 102). These paradoxes have broader consequences in the play, though, for hermeneutics necessarily come to influence the more public, political world we produce as the result of our own conduct. The consequences of Duncan McFee's position, "that moral judgements belong to the same class as aesthetic judgements," are dramatized by the fortunes of his corpse, transformed by gymnastic sleight of hand from homicide victim to tidy, aesthetic suicide (52–53). Such philosophical acrobatics seem to lie behind the menacing political upheaval taking place just offstage: the installation of a new government, jailing of newspaper editors, replacing the police with the army, frequent air force demonstrations and military parades, even the promotion of the agriculture spokesman to Archbishop of Canterbury.

How is Archie's invocation of Beckett framed by this larger context? In one sense, the rewriting of Beckett's parable of "divine apathia divine athambia divine aphasia" (to use Lucky's terms) as a justification of moral and social callousness seems directed both against Archie and against the revolution he seems to support. Stoppard appears to invite us to measure the philosophical world of the play and the political world it shapes against the more urgent moral example of Beckett and *Godot*, in part by having that world's chief advocate convert Beckett's existential neutrality into a program of opportunistic indifference. Yet although the allusion to Beckett ironically qualifies its speaker, the fact that Beckett can be absorbed by Archie's rhetoric suggests that the irony may run in another direction as well. We might also ask whether the audience is also being criticized, much as Archie is, for seeking a kind of solace in Beckett's existential status quo. Rather than standing ironically apart from Archie, is the design of Beckett's drama too easily assimilable to the ethics of an amoral police state, of a world in which there is "nothing to be done" precisely because we have become resigned to it? Does Stoppard's invocation of *Godot* present Beckett as a kind of moral guide, available to the audience but not to the characters? Or is the absurd texture of moral and political life in the play partly attributable to Beckett, whose existential drama and theater provide a surprisingly pacifying rationale that justifies Archie's world?

I am not certain that *Jumpers* gives us the means to choose between these possibilities, though the position we choose will unavoidably implicate each of us as members and agents of a particular kind of world. The politics of this interpretive choice—and it is political: the consequences are visible in the play—arise only in part from the determinations of the text, or from the internal balance and emphasis of the drama. The politics of Stoppard's theater exceed the politics of the drama and require us to reflect on our own production in and by the theater, as its patrons, witnesses, audience. How we read Beckett's figure in the design of *Jumpers* may depend on where we sit.

Political theater is often described as an effect, a side effect, perhaps, of the thematic content of the drama, as though an explicitly "ideological," tendentious, thesis drama were needed for an openly political theater. Yet, like the drama, theatrical performance already occupies an ideological field, a field often independent from the claims of the texts it brings to the stage. Modern political theater is distinctive only in the degree to which it is an openly rhetorical, interested production of the drama, working against the naturalized "objectivity" of theatrical realism. The politics of political theater emerge not only in the themes of the drama but more searchingly in the disclosure of the working of ideology in the making of meaning in the theater, in the formation of the audience's experience and so, in a manner of speaking, in the formation of the audience itself. Any theatrical rhetoric provides the terms and procedures that enable us to interpret the performance; stage rhetoric implicitly "qualifies" us, attributes qualities to us as spectators that we provisionally assume in order to undertake appropriate ("qualified") participation in its entertainment.[2] As we have

---

2. I am much indebted to Göran Therborn's discussion of subjection and qualification here. "The reproduction of any social organization, be it an exploitative society or a revolutionary party, entails a basic correspondence between subjection and qualification. Those who have been subjected to a particular patterning of their capacities, to a particular discipline, qualify for the given roles and are capable of carrying them out" (17). To Therborn, ideology operates less as a fixed text than as a body of rules, habits, attitudes, and practices for determining meanings and so for determining ourselves. In and out of the theater, ideologies "function neither as bodies of thought that we possess and invest in our actions, nor as elaborate texts" but "as *ongoing social processes*" that continually address us and

seen, the theater frames our interpretive activity and so frames "who we are" as an audience. To redirect a well-known phrase of Louis Althusser's, the material conditions of our attendance in the theater are refigured, represented in the "imaginary relationship" between actors, characters, and spectators (162). For this reason, modern political theater is only in part about innovations in dramatic style or about initiating action outside the theater. Political theater works to transform the field of theatrical relations, to dramatize the implication of actors and spectators in the social process of the theater and in the representation of the world it at once stages and reproduces.

Much as poetic theater develops by reversing the realistic theater's subordination of the word to the scene, so the rhetoric of political theater opens by subverting the "realistic" qualification of the audience and its interpretive prerogatives. Of course, stage realism itself originated in an assault on the assumptions of romantic and classical drama, and on the society that sustained it, and later drama in this mode retains more than a trace of this insurgency, still visible in plays like *Death of a Salesman* (1949), *Look Back in Anger* (1956), or Marsha Norman's *Getting Out* (1977). Yet while the action of such plays is often critical of the social order, in the theater such criticism is blunted by the rhetoric of realistic production, which represses the actual character of the audience's performance in order to insist on its "objective" absence from the scene it observes. Masking the "real conditions" of the audience's attention in order to claim its freedom to act, judge, and interpret objectively, the realistic theater duplicates the social structure often criticized in this drama, in which the characters' desire for freedom from their material conditions marks their deepest enslavement to them, their immersion in pipe dreams, in castles in the air, even in utopian munitions works. The modern theater regains political agency when it regains the ability to stage the activities of theatrical production (acting, action, participation) as parts of an explicitly political event, an event that produces individuals (actor, character, spec-

---

so "unceasingly constitute and reconstitute who we are" (77–78). See also Raymond Williams's discussion of ideology as "the production of meanings and ideas" in *Marxism and Literature* 55.

tator) as subjects negotiating the terms of an immediate social and cultural order—the order of the theater itself.

The Anglo-Irish-American theater has undergone several "political" phases—the Abbey at the turn of the century, workers' theater in the 1920s and 1930s, the New York Group Theater, London's angry young men and women in the late 1950s, labor theaters like El Teatro Campesino in the 1960s, the "fringe" of the 1970s, the theater of Northern Ireland today. In the contemporary theater, the production of the "spectator" in the "politics" of the theater has become a central dramatic problem. Bertolt Brecht's influence in this area is massive and undeniable, extending far beyond the superficial stylistic quirks or heavily didactic themes usually taken to signal "Brechtian" or political drama. Before turning to contemporary political drama we will need to consider the contours of this influence, particularly Brecht's placement of the audience in the theory and practice of a political stage. Brecht calls for the theater to dramatize its own rhetoricity as a social practice, to show how staging theatrical experience *for* the spectator necessitates the staging *of* a spectator or spectators, the reproduction of material individuals as an interpreting, interpretable, ideologically packed "audience." Although Brecht's use of dramatic parables and the spare theatricality of his stage style are everywhere visible in contemporary performance, it might be argued that Brecht's most decisive contribution to modern political theater is his canny assault on the complacent "invisibility" of the absent public.

Brecht's originality lies in his varied and systematic interrogation of the rhetoric of realism, of the theoretical possibility of the materials of stage production and how they might be retrained in the work they perform. Recognizing that the "bourgeois theatre emphasized the timelessness of its objects," and that its "representation of people is bound by the alleged 'eternally human,'" Brecht sought everywhere to suspend the identification between theatrical behavior and the universal, the natural, and the human qualities it claimed to represent (*Brecht on Theatre* 96). As a result, Brecht's stage theory earnestly unravels the body of identifications characteristic of realistic performance. Brecht's "radical *separation of the elements*" (*Brecht on Theatre* 37) unbinds the "realistic" relationship between actor and character, stage and setting, individual and spectator, and so calls into question the transparency of realistic production, the objective interpretation it enables, and the unconstructed freedom of the audience. In Brecht's theater, "What the audience sees in fact is a battle between theatre and play" (*Brecht on Theatre* 22). Dialecticizing theatrical activity and dramatic action, Brecht fashions the absent, voyeuristic spectator of the realistic theater as an agent of the production. In terms of acting, this battle pits the demonstrative aspect of performance against realistic empathy, or Stanislavskian "emotion memory," as justifying the relation between the character, the actor's performance, and the spectator's attention. This model of acting also alters the relationship between stage and audience, similarly transforming the audience's activity into a kind of *gest:* an apparently private or individual behavior shown in its public determinants and consequences.

Brecht's theater, that is, subjects the two zones of privacy produced by the realistic theater—actor/character, individual/spectator—to a dialectical reconsideration: how is this privacy the effect of public activity, the product of theater and society? As far as acting is concerned, Brecht's most controversial prescriptions occur at just this point, at the relation between identity and expression, fictive "character" and its enactment onstage. Brecht's theater decenters reified "character" as the object of the actor's representation or of the spectator's attention. Brecht urges actors to emphasize the contradictoriness of the dramatic role, to avoid assimilating the role's patterns of action to a predigested motivational source, a "super-objective" that serves as both origin and goal of action and meaning. Although "the dramatic actor . . . has his character established from the first and simply exposes it to the inclemencies of the world and the tragedy, the epic actor lets his character grow before the spectator's eyes out of the way in which he behaves" (*Brecht on Theatre* 56). The political actor is not the vehicle of feigned sensibility whose labor disappears into his product (the "character"), but the demonstrator of a public, social project of making "character." This demonstration coordinates the actor's work, the character's actions, and the spectator's attention in an explicitly political event—the *gest. Gestic* acting constructs "character" in the context of all its conditions, not only the conditions of the drama, but in the theatrical interaction between stage and audience as well.

Gestic acting opens a fissure between actor and character. While

Stanislavski urges actors to work toward a feeling of "I am" in performance (273), Brecht's actor asserts a vigorous "I am not": the meaning of Brechtian acting arises through difference from the character/subject rather than identity with it.[3] To accomplish this, Brecht develops a theory of performance that compromises the authority of the private "self": "Emotions, instincts, impulses are generally presented as being deeper, more eternal, less easily influenced by society than ideas, but this is in no way true" (*Brecht on Theatre* 101). Political theater, in Brecht's view, should interrogate the explanatory power assigned to "emotions, instincts, impulses," as part of the actor's performance of "character" or as definitive of the spectator's response. In *A Short Organum*, Brecht vividly places empathy within the dialectic of "alienation": "that truly rending contradiction between experience and portrayal, empathy and demonstration, justification and criticism, which is what is aimed at." Demonstration and empathy are in practice "two mutually hostile processes which fuse in the actor's work; his performance is not just composed of a bit of the one and a bit of the other. His particular effectiveness comes from the tussle and tension of the two opposites, and also from their depth" (*Brecht on Theatre* 277–78). While the realistic theater defines empathy as the sign of effective (enjoyable, entertaining, realistic) acting and spectating (think of the American Method's attitude toward "indicating" emotion or behavior), Brecht's theater regards both acting and spectating as dialectical procedures, in which empathy and detachment define and qualify one another. For this reason, "Neither the public nor the actor must be stopped from taking part emotionally; the representation of emotions must not be hampered, nor must the actor's use of emotions be frustrated" (*Messingkauf Dialogues* 57).

The demonstrated *gest* dramatizes the social relations between performer and spectator in the theater, mediated by the dramatic fiction they share. As Brecht suggests in his most familiar epitome

---

3. Brecht does, however, tend to simplify and homogenize the kind of identification invited by realistic theatrical production: "Everyone (including every spectator) is then carried away by the momentum of the events portrayed, so that in a performance of *Oedipus* one has for all practical purposes an auditorium full of little Oedipuses, an auditorium full of Emperor Joneses for a performance of *The Emperor Jones*" (*Brecht on Theatre* 87).

of epic theater, "The Street Scene," the spectator's performance is also part of the *gest*. The demonstrative actor "behaves naturally as a demonstrator, and he lets the subject of the demonstration behave naturally too. . . . That is to say, what the audience sees is not a fusion between demonstrator and subject, not some third, independent, uncontradictory entity with isolated features of (a) demonstrator and (b) subject, such as the orthodox theatre puts before us in its productions" (*Brecht on Theatre* 125). Since the dramatic subject ("character") can only be seen through a performance marked as "demonstration," we can never see demonstrator and subject, actor and character, as entirely independent of one another. Realistic performance elides the difference between actor and character by privileging psychological interiority, affective identity as the sign of good, "realistic" acting. Brecht's actor builds her character in the public, social circumstances of the theater. As a result, the performer's authority is independent of the text and of the action, an independence that alters her responsibility and relation to the audience: "The actress must not make the sentence her own affair, she must hand it over for criticism, she must help us to understand its causes and protest" (*Brecht on Theatre* 98). Reversing the performer's relation to the role becomes the first step in Brecht's refashioning of the entire theatrical exchange: "His actors weren't waiters who must serve up the meat and have their private, personal feelings treated as gross importunities. They were servants neither of the writer nor of the audience" (*Messingkauf Dialogues* 71).

Much as he does for the actor, Brecht requires a public performance from his audience, one that responds both to the fictive life of the dramatic character and to the material reality of the actor's performance. The "two faces overlapping" of the actor's performance reflect those of the spectator, who attends both to the dramatic fiction and to the actor's visible labor (*Messingkauf Dialogues* 76). The actor uses his or her "countenance as a blank sheet, to be inscribed by the gest of the body"; so too the spectator's performance responds to the immediate and acknowledged circumstances of the theater: "The audience identifies itself with the actor as being an observer, and accordingly develops his attitude of observing or looking on" (*Brecht on Theatre* 92–93). The individual's functional refiguration *as* a spectator throws into question the interpretive attitudes natural to the realistic theater: empathy, for instance, is shown to emerge as a rhetorical effect of a certain kind of theatricality, rather than as something necessarily "deeper, more eternal." Brecht dialecticizes both zones of privacy produced by the realistic theater, the mysterious inner life of the actor/character and the solitary and secret freedom of the abstract spectator. Like the character's actions and the actor's work, the spectator's activity assumes the quality of a *gest*, an action whose meaning lies in its public significance.[4]

Brecht's effort to stage the spectator can be seen throughout his work, in his experimental approach to playwriting, his career as a director, and his extensive, often occasional theoretical writing about the stage. To talk about the rhetoric of political theater in postwar Britain and America is necessarily to ask how Brecht's theory and practice have been challenged, extended, and refined.[5] In part because of the immediacy and duration of the Berliner Ensemble's impact, the British theater has developed a more critical response to Brecht, a confrontation that informs the theatrical rhetoric of its own powerfully political drama. This response, though, frequently recasts Brecht's dialectical assault on the rhetoric of realism as a polemical dichotomy, and so preempts much of Brecht's real force. In one version, Brecht's theatrical and dramatic technique is read as recapitulating traditional values, and is divorced from Brecht's theater theory, which is dismissed as doctrinaire, inartistic, dull, and incapable of being realized in practice. Harold Hobson, for example, reviewing the National Theatre's 1963 "Brechtian" production of George Farquhar's classic comedy, *The Recruiting Officer*, takes a representative position: "Brecht was a considerable dramatist whose value lay in the tension between his genius and his theories. I will be sad if at the National Theatre we get the theories without genius" (142). Alert to Brecht's vivid theatricality, Hobson moves to contain that potentially "instructive" vigor as "entertainment," while consigning its politics to the stuffy, nondramatic realm of an unstageworthy theory. This polarity—the "public exhibition of im-

---

4. As Elizabeth Wright remarks, the spectator resembles the actor insofar as "he is forced to acknowledge his split subject-hood and shown that he too is part-object, part-subject" (57).
5. On Brecht's reception in America, see Bathrick.

mense talent pitted against a self-defeating theory"—suffuses stage criticism of Brecht in the 1960s, echoed whenever critics praise the "lyricism," the "sense of poetry and wonder" so evident in Brecht's theater at the expense of the overtly political and theoretical claims that lyricism makes on our attention (Bornemann 147, 152).

A second strategy distinguishes between Brecht's stagecraft and Brecht's playwriting—between theater and drama, rather than theater and theory. Reviewing the Berliner Ensemble production of *The Caucasian Chalk Circle* in 1956, for instance, *The Times* found the performance to be "a triumph of theatrical collaboration; and the impression it gives is not of earnest experiment, nor of political engagement—but of a joke as big as a thunderclap." The review distinguishes stage technique from the politics that inform it, finding that the play's theatricality has more to do with "the Marx Brothers" than with Marx. Similarly, the production of *Mother Courage* "affords a rare aesthetic pleasure," an instance of the "triumph of team acting. . . . However unwilling we may be to enter into the spirit of thesis drama conditioned by Marxism the compulsion of the exquisite playing is not to be resisted, and we adjust our minds to the theory on which it is based as best we can." In *Trumpets and Drums*, what impresses the reviewer "is not the special interpretation of life which the play tries to establish. It is the practiced team work of the Berliner Ensemble and the clearness of the speaking." The triumphs of the theater, those stagey pleasures and that exquisite playing, are what prevail with the critics. The actors' political engagement with the audience and with the politics of the dramatic text are dispensable side effects of an otherwise impressive "aesthetic" experience. Brecht's influence as the bogey of boring theory and/or pietistic Marxist drama is habitually invoked whenever a play appears to gesture toward Brecht's political agenda. T. C. Worsley, for instance, complains that John Osborne's *The Entertainer* (1957) is "singularly careless" in construction, "perhaps deliberately so in pursuit of some Brechtian purpose." Harold Hobson similarly lauds John Arden's *The Workhouse Donkey* (1963) by contrasting Brecht's tendentious theater with the "freedom" of the realistic spectator: "the freedom of thought given by Brecht is, of course, illusory. By his employment of alienation he instructs his audience to think: but he clearly indicates to them what conclusion their thought should reach. This is why he is such a reassuring dramatist. He asks the question, and supplies the answer" (Evans and Evans 119).[6]

As Roland Barthes suggests, "in order to 'humanize' Brecht, the theoretical part of his work is discredited or at least minimized: the plays are great *despite* Brecht's systematic views on epic theater, the actor, alienation, etc.: here we encounter one of the basic theorems of *petit-bourgeois* culture, the romantic contrast between heart and head, between intuition and reflection, between the ineffable and the rational—an opposition which ultimately masks a magical conception of art" (*Critical Essays* 72–73). Indeed, while the Brechtian mode provides the style of choice for many recent playwrights—bare stage, episodic structure, rapid shifts in tonality, deemphasis on naturalistic psychology—its rhetorical implications have met with the kind of resistance that Barthes outlines. The political theater's open designs on the spectator move directly against the realistic theater's fiction of a disinterested, free subject, the empowered privacy of the consuming audience. As Edward Bond argues, "Political subjects in themselves do not make political theatre . . . you can have a play dealing with racism, or sexism, or fascism, and if that subject is dealt with in, let's say, an Ibsen-like way, then the audience is left with nothing to do in working on the problem; you might just as well read about the subject in a newspaper. That is not political theatre" ("British Secret" 8). True enough; yet Bond's scrupulous regard for the complex working of ideology in the theater nonetheless recapitulates a familiar critical convention where Brecht is concerned: "I rather admire Brecht, actually. I think his

---

6. This effort to depoliticize theater by reifying the politics of performance—either in a suspect "theory" or in an "ideological drama"—even informs the assimilation of a "Brecht style" to the scenic vocabulary of stage design and directing. This influence can be traced in the British theater largely to the work of influential directors like William Gaskill and designers like Jocelyn Herbert, and more pervasively to Peter Hall's institution of a cool, quasi-Brechtian house style at the Royal Shakespeare Company during the late 1960s and 1970s. Brecht's theatrical style, that is, has been transformed from a rhetorical activity into an aesthetic object, a commodified "look" rather than a process of engagement with the drama and with the audience. In so doing, the rhetorical process of performance is displaced as the site of attention or of political engagement and reflection. Like the politics of the text, the politics of performance are fixed within the inert textuality of a "Brecht style," rather than within the relation between actors, the play, and the audience.

naivety covers painful knowledge. The nearest thing to a Brecht play in English *is* the Victorian melodrama, with its wicked landlord and pure labourer's daughter and all the rest of it" ("Drama" 13). Bond, in a sense, recalls the stigma attached to "thesis drama" by William Archer, Brander Matthews, and others at the turn of the century, for he locates Brecht's politics in the moral structure of the drama rather than in the activity of its production. Like many of his contemporaries, Bond here seems nearly to echo the realistic theater's marginalization of political theater as "theater for instruction," as eccentric to the stage's natural purpose, to provide "theater for pleasure." Bond's ambivalence reflects, perhaps, the pervasive and ongoing influence of realistic rhetoric in the theater, an influence most powerfully felt not in terms of dramatic or production style, but at just the point contested by Brecht: its production of the audience.[7]

To carve a place for political theater has required the most delicate negotiation of Brecht, because the private freedom of the spectator is the political theater's principal point of attack. In practice, the rhetoric of political theater has worked to stage the spectator's performance as part of the point of the spectacle. In Britain, political theater has often adopted the strategy of John Osborne's *The Entertainer,* juxtaposing popular performance traditions with the conventions of the legitimate stage as a way of foregrounding the audience's performance.[8] The music hall frame of the play—each scene is given a "number" on the bill, and scenes of Archie Rice's family life are interrupted by his turns at the "local Empire"—images an allegory of imperial decline, while it enacts the process

---

7. Bond's ambivalent response to Brecht is typical of a generation of political dramatists, whose dramatic and theatrical aims seem close to Brecht's. David Hare, for instance, rephrases Hobson when distinguishing his own goals from the impression he has of Brecht's: the "impression, the godlike feeling that the questions have been answered before the play has begun" ("A Lecture" 63). And Howard Brenton, who adapted Brecht's *Galileo* for the National Theatre in 1980, nonetheless claims that Brecht's dramatic "influence is wholly to the bad" ("Petrol Bombs" 14). On Brenton's work with "the great post-war play," a "socialist classic," and on the National Theatre production, see Hiley, *Theatre at Work.*

8. On the theater's use of popular and "populist" culture, see Edgar. For a reading of the dramatic use of music hall, and of the attitude toward the working-class audience it embodies, see Harrop.

of ideological formation in postwar Britain. Within the play, class interests are objectified and polarized. Archie's tatty hymns to a stripper-Britannia both denude British imperial authority and assert the pieties of a bygone nationalism for the consumption of a socially captive audience. As Kenneth Tynan remarked, "With his blue patter and jingo songs he [Archie] is a licensed pedlar of emotional dope to every audience in Britain" (Evans and Evans 59). Yet Tynan's comment betrays a desire to see the play as about music hall, rather than as using music hall as a strategy to place the Royal Court audience within the political process of performance. To see "the popular culture and theatre that Britain lost with the music halls" (Bryden) as the play's subject works to preserve the audience's distance from the spectacle of lower-class life, a freedom that the play marks as the sign of class power. Archie clearly doesn't sell "to every audience in Britain." His audiences are principally the working classes, who—like Mick, the son lost in the Suez—are both instructed and seduced by this impoverished vision of empire. Brother Bill and Graham Dodd, on the other hand—as "well dressed, assured, well educated" as the audience ("If you can't recognize [them], it's for one reason only")—would not be caught dead either in Archie's "Empire" or in the Suez fiasco. They have "an all-defying inability to associate themselves with anyone in circumstances even slightly dissimlar to their own" (*Entertainer* 83).

By casting the audience, even briefly, in the unfamiliar "circumstances" of the music hall public, Osborne traces the covert ideological process that is otherwise displaced by the divisions of class. The "popular culture" of the music hall is usually taken as an emblem of the unifying interests of the nation, a view represented in the play by the generation of Billy Rice and George Robey: "We had our own style, our own songs—and we were all English. What's more, we spoke English. It was different. We all knew what the rules were" (81). Perhaps it really was different. In *The Entertainer*, though, music hall has lost its innocent populism. By using music hall to insert the Royal Court spectator within the rhetorical design of the "local Empire," *The Entertainer* dramatizes the reappropriation of resistant "popular" entertainments like music hall by the ruling class: Brother Bill becomes Archie's audience, authorizing the "emotional dope" he peddles elsewhere. Brother Bill, his class, his Empire, and his audience are all nakedly "out for good old Number One" (86).[9]

The drama of the 1970s and 1980s follows the lead offered by *The Entertainer*, and the theater has worked in a variety of ways to bring the spectator into a more urgent and actual relation to the stage. Osborne's exposure of the function of class in British imperial expansion has its echo in the pervasively historical cast of political drama in the postwar era, particularly in the important series of plays that examine the war and its immediate aftermath in England. In Howard Brenton's *Hitler Dances* and *The Churchill Play*, the spectators themselves undertake a critical replaying of the drama of recent history. The most striking formal feature of *The Entertainer*—its use of popular music hall in a "straight" play—provides another common strategy, as playwrights investigate the power of genre to refashion the spectator's relation to the stage. The fragmentation of the apparatus of stage production also sustains a principal strategy in much feminist theater, which represents the relations of theatrical realism as themselves complicit in the politics of gender oppression; here I consider the gendering of the spectator in Caryl Churchill's *Cloud Nine* and Maria Irene Fornes's *Fefu and Her Friends*. These plays only touch on the range of subjects and strategies that the political theater currently brings to the stage, but I hope they will suggest how the theater has mapped the theoretical terrain opened by Brecht, the politicization of our performance in the theater. For it is, finally, in transforming the field of theatrical relations that the theater subjects its own rhetoric to scrutiny:

> We need a type of theatre which not only releases the feelings, insights and impulses possible within the particular historical field of

---

9. The relationship between a performance of Osborne's play and music hall is dialogic rather than nostalgic. As Fredric Jameson argues, "the stress on the dialogical then allows us to reread or rewrite the hegemonic forms themselves; they also can be grasped as a process of the reappropriation and neutralization, the cooptation and class transformation, the cultural universalization, of forms which originally expressed the situation of 'popular,' subordinate, or dominated groups" (*The Political Unconscious* 86). This process is revealed in part by the fact that Frank's song in Number Nine, which was "both booed and cheered on the opening night," was "dropped for the west-end transfer" (Sinfield 261).

human relations in which the action takes place, but employs and encourages those thoughts and feelings which help transform the field itself. (*Brecht on Theatre* 190)

BREAKING THE FRAME OF HISTORY: *HITLER DANCES* AND *THE CHURCHILL PLAY*

A powerful gambit for dramatizing the spectator's share is the renegotiation of "history" on the stage. Despite the predominance of lush costume drama as the standard for historical dramatization on film and television, the standard practice of theatricalized history has become much more fragmentary, audience-directed, and disruptive. Plays as diverse as Arthur Kopit's *Indians* (1969), Howard Brenton's *Scott of the Antarctic* (1971), Caryl Churchill's *Vinegar Tom* (1976), David Hare's *Plenty* (1978), David Henry Hwang's *M. Butterfly* (1988), Pam Gems's *Queen Christina* (1977), Trevor Griffiths's *Occupations* (1970), Frank McGuinness's *Observe the Sons of Ulster Marching to the Somme* (1985), and Carlos Morton's *Rancho Hollywood* (published 1979) might be taken as instances of the range of contemporary historical dramaturgy. History is no longer disclosed to the audience as a fait accompli. In restaging history, the drama invites and often compels the audience to play its part in the reconstruction of this narrative, and of the social order it represents and sustains.

Since his early plays for the Portable Theatre, Howard Brenton has consistently turned to the problems of dramatized history, how the staging of history traces the sign of performance in the material events of the past. Christie's horrific exhumation from a pen of crumpled newspaper in *Christie in Love* (1969) is only one in a series of images in Brenton's scrutiny of historical process: of the function of individualism in *Scott of the Antarctic* and *Bloody Poetry* (1984); of history and class behavior in *Weapons of Happiness* (1976); of the relation between myth and history in *The Romans in Britain* (1980); of the "news" in *Pravda* (1985, written with David Hare); even of the possibility of utopia in *Greenland* (1988). Brenton's continued experimentation with sites of performance—the ice rink of *Scott*, for instance—and with various experimental or fringe companies suggests that staging "history" is only part of his larger effort to recharge the political interaction between stage and audience. Two of Brenton's most direct engagements with the problem of historical dramatization, *Hitler Dances* (1972) and *The Churchill Play* (1974), resemble his more overtly "public plays" in their attempt to articulate "the space between people" that "defines the actual physical theatre, the space between the audience itself and the actors" as "an almost moral force in the writing and in the presentation" ("Petrol Bombs" 10). Replaying the war and its immediate aftermath, *Hitler Dances* and *The Churchill Play* interrogate the reenactment, consumption, and transmission of "history" as theater.

Hitler Dances is striking not so much for the formal experimentation of its dramatic design as for its use of innovative theatrical procedures. Conceived as a workshop by the Traverse Theatre of Edinburgh, *Hitler Dances* originated as a series of exercises in which the actors confronted their experience and recollection of wartime England. Several of the actors, however, shared Carole Hayman's limited familiarity with the war ("I know almost nothing about it," she said), and most of the actors' memories were diffuse, mere affectual traces: "'The line I say about my father having been shot down in France was certainly true. I was born three months after his death. . . . We are left with this terrible residue of our families having been twisted and decimated by events which took place before we were born.'" As the performers themselves recognized, their war exists neither as history nor as memory, but only in the imagery of popular media bent on producing a "total myth about the Second World War." Wartime events have been so fully absorbed into the images of the screen that the ordinary behavior of their parents has become "inconceivable" (Ansorge).[10]

To confront the "seemingly dead and buried subject" of history and to present this confrontation as part of the *actors'* play, Brenton sought a theatrical image that would enable the actors to use their individual responses to the war as part of their performance. Brenton found this performative frame while on tour with the Portable Theatre:

> I saw children in Eindhoven, which was flattened twice during the war, first by the Germans and then by the Allies, and is now the home of the world headquarters of the Philips Electrical Company. And at night in Eindhoven, the huge Philips sign, like a weird em-

10. On Brenton's treatment of post-war Britain, see Bull.

blem, flashes everywhere in the sky. I saw a bomb-site there with children playing on it, while we were touring *Fruit*, and there the idea was lodged in my mind, because it was like children playing on this heap of rubble—history. And the idea of a German soldier coming out of the ground became meaningful. ("Petrol Bombs" 14)

The scene provides the play's core improvisation: a group of children unearth a dead German soldier, who comes to life and, before beginning his march back to Germany, tells the story of a brave woman's resistance activity in France, a story taken from the 1958 film *Carve Her Name with Pride*. Each of the roles provides a field of playful inquiry, for the actors each take the opportunity to enact several major parts—German soldier, resistance fighter, Nazi officer, modern child. The actors continually adjust the relationship between personal and public history through roleplaying, revising themselves in their relation to history through the complex engagement and disengagement offered by the mask of "character."

Hitler Dances invokes the performative rhetoric of the participatory theater of the late 1960s and 1970s as a structuring and heuristic device. The "poor theater" enabled Brenton to sidestep the standards of British Brecht—the "Bond-Gaskill-Jocelyn Herbert" tradition—and to strike a "more emotional, uncool" stance toward the audience ("Petrol Bombs" 14). This strategy may at first seem unpromising. Although the Artaud-Grotowski style of American participatory theater has an aggressively "emotional, uncool" edge, its characteristic emphasis on the "paradise now" of unmediated self-presence for actors and audiences seems at odds with the decentered character-subjects of an openly Marxist theater like Brenton's. Even though "history" of a kind appears in Spalding Gray's performance narratives, in the Performance Group's *Dionysus in 69* (1969), in the Living Theater's *Paradise Now* (1968), and in the Kennedy-King assassination sections of the Open Theater/Van Itallie *The Serpent* (1968), this history is either strongly colored as personal recollection or immediately rekeyed in the register of myth. Moreover, the exploratory-confessional mode of acting in this theater would seem to frustrate the goal of reinterpreting history as a public narrative formed by a powerful cultural machinery. In order to represent "history" as a collective construction but *not* as personal mythology, *Hitler Dances* modifies the rhetoric of participatory theater, dramatizing the actors' confrontation with the materials of history while repressing the zone of personal subjectivity—actors' and characters'—as critical to the dramatic action or the audience's interpretation. The play suspends the defining moment of such participatory acting, the self-consciously charismatic identification of actor and character. Instead, the play requires acting in a variety of modes, and indeed represents a variety of performance forms, drawn from television and film as well as theater, to suggest that, even in live performance, "history" is a function of its means of representation. History is always already written, as memory, as literature, as television, and as film; in *Hitler Dances*, we await its investiture in the bodies of the performers.

Hitler Dances refigures the "total act" required of actors in the participatory mode by striking a dialectical relationship between actor and "character." The play opens with the actors masking and costuming the first actor to play "Hans"—Kevin Costello, in the Traverse production. The investment of Kevin in the role of "Hans" is accompanied by two frames of acting. In one, the actors recite the narrative underlying the scene: "At the end of the Second World War, the German soldiers walked home." In the second, the actors respond to the character of Kevin/"Hans." To play the death of a German soldier, on the last day of the war, the actors mask and dress Kevin as "Hans," cower back from him, and then proceed to indulge in a ritualized frenzy of "Bosch" beating. The play insists that all actors participate in characterizing Hans as the stereotypical Nazi villain that Kevin/"Hans" in fact becomes: "Hot black blood sausage! Sauerkraut, steaming! Black coffee boiling! Beer all frothy!" (3). To be addressed as a Nazi soldier fundamentally interrupts the actor's self-presence, requiring a reorientation to the body ("*KEVIN, both hands to his mouth, fingers exploring inside his cheeks*" 3), to the voice, and to the society on- and offstage. No one actor is responsible for the "character" of the Nazi soldier; all subsequently "*in turn impose tiredness, cold*" on him, and the actor modifies his performance accordingly (5). Since each of the male actors will play "Hans" and each of the women will play "Violette," characterization in *Hitler Dances* avoids both the calculated psychological interiority of realistic performance and the more spontaneous and charismatic possession of participatory theater. Although *Hitler Dances* retains the idiom of "poor theater," it shows both actor and character in their social relations.

The actors enter the field of history as a field of play. History speaks only a dead language, as Kevin stands with the "Hans" costume at his feet, speaking to it as though it could explain the significance of a once-familiar lexicon, "Blitzkrieg—Warsaw—shell shock—pattern bombing, Rotterdam Dresden Hamburg" (7). Yet the war's erasure from our language is offset by its reconstitution in other media. Much as he juxtaposes "Hans's" resurrection with a television horror show, Brenton juxtaposes the film heroine of *Carve Her Name with Pride* with her stage reenactment, a conflation of narrative, enacted, and film versions of the war that signals the transformation of history into the pastiche of popular images. The film, as *Variety* noted in 1958, "pays tribute to the real life exploits of Violette Szabo, a beautiful young woman who became a British cloak-and-dagger agent in France and won a posthumous George Cross after being tortured and executed in Ravensbruck camp." Notable for an understated "ordinariness," the film nonetheless emphasizes "the brand of courage which lifted an ordinary girl, with all her fears and her emotions, to the stars, and flecked her with glory." The film devotes a leisurely development to Violette's relation with her lover Etienne. Brenton eviscerates this motivation from the play's narrative, representing the film's action in a foreshortened, cartoon-like idiom: meeting, love at first sight (with cymbal clash), whirlwind romance, and wedding in a few brief minutes of stage time. The play further distances the film narrative by having the actresses both narrate and enact Violette's actions, and by seating a working-class couple onstage who watch and comment on Violette's progress as though it were a television program. Something like the opening sequence of Jean-Claude Van Itallie's *The Serpent*, in which actors mime scenes from the familiar film of the Kennedy assassination, here film "history" becomes the text of the the actors' performance.

Hitler Dances invokes the romantic heroine of the film but displaces her personal motivation as the focus of our response. Brenton underplays character and emphasizes the action by having all the women of the cast play "Violette," and by foregrounding their performance as openly theatrical play, rather than as possession. Throughout the play, the actress uses third-person narration to disperse the "subject" of characterization ("And these were the thoughts of Violette, and she became a heroine" 41), an interruption conveyed in her performance as well. In scene 13, for example, Carole and Amaryllis discuss the random violence of contemporary life, the prospect of sudden rape, the suicide of friends, the prominence of grotesque mutilation in recent films. Suddenly, "*A bright spot slams on,*" and while Amaryllis narrates, Carole performs "Violette": "I wanna kill a German!" (43). Here, the attempt to translate the inconceivable behavior of a previous generation into a conceivable modern equivalent is undertaken in social rather than personal terms. "Violette" is not given an internalized motive; the performance of the actress is keyed to the external context of contemporary social life.

The relationship between history, film, and the stage is dramatized in the play's final scenes, in which the torture scenes of *Carve Her Name with Pride* are replayed as black Nazi farce ("Ja wohl donnerundblitzen zieg heil.... Ludwig Van Beethoven Eine Kleine Nachtmusik" 67). The play suggests that our knowledge of historical events is inevitably interceded by the images with which we identify the past, images continually appropriated to new purposes. As Sabin/"Keiffer," Violette's guard, remarks, "Nazi Gestapo Torturer Victim. After the War, torturer and victim will be seen as something sexy" (73). Keiffer's interrogation of Violette points up the inadequacy of a history that fails to acknowledge its basis in ideology, and reveals how the film transforms the history it claims to represent:

> Please hear why the Gestapo never tortured you, in the Avenue Foch. Why that scene in the film, never took place. Because...Of administrative confusion. They lost your papers, Violette. That is why you were never sent for again, by Hans Josef Keiffer. *A small bow.* (74)

Hitler Dances dramatizes the relationship between history and its representation: "Oh Vi, there's no 'magnificent gesture' that can't be defiled. Mucked. Messed. Believe me" (74). Irving Wardle, reviewing the play for *The Times*, remarks that Brenton's refiguration of history is at once brilliant and inchoate: Brenton seems to "fall into the trap of being engulfed in the myths he is trying to manipulate," to the degree that the interinvolving of parody, play, history, myth, horror show, and kitsch becomes "too intricate and unrestrained." The point of *Hitler Dances*, though, is not so much to parody or defile the magnificent gestures of the war but to open those gestures—and the gestures that recreate them onstage—to our inspection. This is the question posed by the play's theatrical rhetoric and by its unresolved, open, inconclusive dramatic structure: does the juxtaposition of performative modes enable a revision of history by dramatizing the variety of ways—live acting, film, television—in which it has been encoded, or does it more simply provide what Fredric Jameson terms a *pastiche*, a history subordinated to the signifiers of style?

To Jameson, pastiche locates the postmodern aesthetic firmly in the moment of consumer capitalism: the "transformation of reality into images, the fragmentation of time into a series of perpetual presents" illustrates "the disappearance of a sense of history, the way in which our entire contemporary social system has little by little begun to lose its capacity to retain its own past, has begun to live in a perpetual present and in a perpetual change that obliterates traditions of the kind which all earlier social formations have had in one way or another to preserve" ("Postmodernism" 125). *Hitler Dances* exhumes the past as theater, as parody, play, myth, horror show, TV show, and as kitsch, but as pastiche the performance provides no frame of value or reference, no means of ordering those images, of assimilating them to a mode of access to the past. This may be in part the result of the play's performance rhetoric, its brittle conjunction of the mode of Jerzy Grotowski's "poor theater"—which casts the audience as a present witness—and a more traditionally realistic notion of the spectator as voyeur. *Hitler Dances* invites the audience to consider the process of history and the complicity of entertainment in the representation of historical "fact." Oddly enough, though, the audience's play—unlike the actors'—remains largely vicarious; our own relation to the actors' exposure remains outside the process of history onstage, a notable departure from the environmental aesthetic of the Performance Group, Grotowski, and so on. *Hitler Dances* casts the spectator outside the frame of performance, and so outside the frame of history. We stand before or above the materials of culture rather than making cultural history even in our performance as audience, as perhaps the actors themselves have done. In this sense the proscenium operates as a "moral force," but largely by intervening between the drama of history, the stage of its production, and the audience in the theater.

The Churchill Play undertakes a more direct examination of the work of political theater in a society where theater is marginalized as "recreation" and made within an explicit hierarchy of power relations—that is, in a society something like our own. By creating a dramatic frame for the rewriting of history in the prisoners' "Churchill play," Brenton addresses not so much the acting of political theater but its function in a specific social context, one that embraces the performers, the onstage audience, and the theatrical audience they come to represent. *The Churchill Play* provides an exemplary critique of historical drama as political theater.

The Churchill Play opens "Back 'ere! Inna nineteen-bloody-sixties," at the funeral of Winston Churchill, the catafalque flanked by an army private, a marine, an airman, and a seaman. After some bitter discussion of Churchill, a knocking is heard, the bier shudders, and Churchill bursts out, cigar at the ready "Onto...Mah History's stage," raving about "England! Y' stupid old woman. Clapped out. Undeserving. Unthankful. After all I did for you" (9–13).[11] This crude, fiercely funny scene is suddenly interrupted when Churchill begins to flirt with the sailor ("Give us a kiss, Jolly Jack Tar"), at which point the lights come up on the flanks of the stage, to reveal that we are not the play's immediate audience. The players are surrounded by armed guards and are performing before the officers of a concentration camp, Camp Churchill, somewhere in England.

This is a stunning moment, a condensed vignette of how history—and its theater—encodes a structure of political power in the relationship between stage and audience. The play opens in much the way that we expect of political theater, with a rewriting of the myths of the past in an apparently Brechtian style. Within moments, the apparent freedom of that activity is sharply circumscribed by its audience, its patrons and captors. *The Churchill Play* represents the "moral force" of the relationship between stage and audience, dramatizing the function of political theater in a society where theatrical performance is at once an act of submission and of transgression. Those who live to please must please to

---

11. Page references are to the 1974 edition, but readers should consult the version of *The Churchill Play* collected in Brenton's *Plays: One* for several revisions made in the text for its 1978 RSC revival. On the 1988 revival, see Lustig.

live: in the economy of the contemporary theater, the gesture of instruction must be contained as pleasure. "The men put the play together themselves. It is recreation," claims the liberal physician Captain Thompson, defending the play to the camp's commander, Colonel Ball (18). As "recreation" the play falls under Thompson's purview, as part of his mission to care for the physical and mental health of the inmates. Like all their activities, the prisoners' recreation works to legitimate their captors, for the play is being rehearsed before the camp's officers to preview it for its real audience, a Select Committee of the House of Commons, which is looking into the recreational facilities of the camp. As Ball suggests, the play serves to empower its invisible audience, not its players: "Water it down, cut it about. . . . Put a few . . . patriotic remarks...About England...In it. That is an order" (19). The performance necessarily defines a "moral force" between stage and audience, for the prisoners' performance is figured as the sign of their "moral" and righteous subjection: "I mean what are we? Performing bears? To stand up in our chains?" (36). Contained as pleasure, theater is identified as submission, regardless of its revisionary instructive content.

As an allegory of the function of political theater in the wider theatrical economy, *The Churchill Play* implies that the performance environment inevitably invests the drama with its own ideological pressure. Whether political theater can reshape the dynamics of the realistic stage is the principal challenge offered by the prisoners' production of their "Churchill play" in act 4. First, in a strategy reminiscent of Genet's *The Blacks*, the play's production becomes a diversion, a part of the prisoners' insurrection. Moreover, the prisoner-players foreground the fact that the materials of theater—words in particular—are already marked with the sign of their subjection. The captor-audience determines the significance and consequences of any verbal act; the audience has the power to render any word as the sign of dissent, a punishable offense. As a result, the political stage must avail itself of means of expression marginal to the codes of the "legitimate" stage, even if they seem—as perhaps they must—to be inarticulate or incomprehensible. As Furry announces to the audience, when "there's a dirty word, in play...Stead of yer gerrin' dirty word in yer face, I hit my gong. . . . So (*He hits the dustbin lid*) to you all" (67).

The audience deprives the political stage of its language; as the prisoners' "Churchill play" demonstrates, the audience erases the politics of history as well. The "Churchill play" repudiates postwar history in order to dramatize the use of history to enforce the privileges of class. When, for example, the "Churchill" character recalls being "dazzled" by his reception in Glasgow in 1945, his recollections are immediately offset by the prisoners' account of the city, which details the extent of the devastation and the scope of their suffering. "Of twelve thousand dwellings, seven only hit. Of forty-seven thousand souls, thirty-five thousand homeless. From that time on, for many months, but for a few, the whole population went to the moor at night" (72).[12] Ronald Hayman complains that Brenton's "war never eclipsed the class war," but this is really only half the truth (*British Theatre* 97). As the earlier scenes between Thompson and Sergeant Baxter suggest, the class war continues but has been concealed from public view by Churchill's rhetorical integration of class interests in a national mythology. Churchill's image of a unified "Island Race" urges a common national interest, but in practice this myth reduces the working classes to minstrel-show puppets, acted on by historical forces that they cannot presume to change. The "cloth caps and waving flags" that define the working classes from Churchill's perspective are as much a prison as Camp Churchill itself: their experience, too, is unseen, trivial, and forgotten.

"Historical truth. In all 'er vulnerability" (47) is less at issue here than the process by which history is made. Furry lowers a white sheet with the legend "We can take it, Guv. Give it 'em back." On the screen, the prisoners project scenes taking us "Back through England"—Churchill's funeral, the first Wilson government, Eden, Suez, Potsdam, Yalta, and so on—to December 29, 1940, the night of the second great fire. The central scene of their play concerns one of Churchill's many visits to the East End. Mike's "Uncle Ern and Annie," working-class Londoners left homeless by the bombing, are visited by Churchill, who narrates

---

12. Like that of many of his contemporaries, Brenton's view of the war has been shaped by Angus Calder's *The People's War*. Here, for instance, Brenton transcribes two passages from Calder's study; see 579–80, and 210. See also Johnstone, and Sinfield chapter 2.

the scene: "And I saw these good people, at the side of the crater. And they cried out to me":

ANNIE: Look. He's crying for us.
ERNIE: Good old Winnie.
ANNIE: We thought you'd come and see us.
ERNIE: We can take it.
ANNIE: Give it 'em back. (79)

Acts of sacrifice and solidarity among otherwise competing class interests were critical to British survival, but official history transforms the working classes into *"doll-like"* figures, subjected by the perspective that was privileged and qualified for historical narrative: Churchill's. When the prisoners restage the scene, Ern and Annie are shown attempting to salvage a life from the rubble, but this time it is Churchill who appears to them as unreal, like a "myth. Standing there. Like he'd come down from a cinema screen, out of a film show." Ernie also recalls making a different speech to Churchill: "And I said, I swear to this day I said . . . We can take it. . . . But we just might give it back to you one day" (80).

"And in his book on war he wrote it down as... Give it 'em back": much as Churchillian history embodies a gesture of legitimation, so the prisoners' play both revises history and stages an act of social aggression. The Union Jack curtain rises to reveal the play's finale: the sergeant bound and the Select Committee captive under the watchful eyes of machine-gun–bearing prisoners ready to break out. To present revised images of history is not enough. A political theater must wrest the stage from the physical and ideological control of the social audience. Yet despite seizing the stage, the prisoners finally have "Nowhere to break out to," since the world beyond the camp is itself a prison (89). In a play whose most brilliant device is the parodic restaging of recent history, this static ending seems anticlimactic. *The Churchill Play* appears to suggest that political theater itself has "nowhere to break out to": the best that it can offer is to open a narrow fissure in the machinery of social control. The play invites the audience to consider the process of history and the complicity of drama, entertainment, and theatrical production in its representation. Finally to alter the process of historical drama, as Brecht suggests, will require a transformation of "the field itself." Something like Brenton's prisoners, political drama will have to stage the

spectators, as a means of disarming them and of altering the field of social relations inside and outside the theater.

HISTORY AND THE FRAME OF GENRE: *LAUGHTER!* AND *POPPY*

The Churchill Play offers a parable of the theater in a politically repressive society, a parable that allegorizes the more indistinct means by which our own theater is governed. Much of the argument of *The Churchill Play* is, in this sense, also directed against the hegemony of realistic theater and the social order it represents: the prisoners' play not only invokes the disruptive discontinuities of Brechtian drama, it provides the weapon that discloses the captor-audience and, for a moment at least, delivers it from the darkness into the prisoners' hands. Representing the techniques of Brechtian theater onstage, *The Churchill Play* illustrates a staple gambit in the rhetoric of political theater. For in plays like *The Entertainer*, Theatre Workshop's *Oh, What a Lovely War* (1963), Trevor Griffiths's *Comedians* (1975), Caryl Churchill's *Cloud Nine* (1979)—and two plays I want to discuss here, Peter Barnes's *Laughter!* (1978) and Peter Nichols's *Poppy* (1982)—the drama begins by refashioning a familiar stage genre and the rhetoric it embodies, as a way to dramatize the audience's performance.

"Like Brecht's Galileo, Jonson was an intellectual sensualist": writing of a playwright he has admired, imitated, and adapted for the stage, Peter Barnes might easily be speaking of his own work in the theater ("Still standing" 206). Like Jonson's drama, Barnes's plays—*The Ruling Class* (1968), *The Bewitched* (1974), *Red Noses* (1985)—burst with a stagey vitality, a baroque delight in extravagant language and incident, a shrewd skepticism, and a ferocious moral and sensuous intelligence. I want to pause here, though, over only part of one play, Barnes's most problematic restaging of history, the "Auschwitz" section of *Laughter!* Barnes's depiction of the bureaucracy of genocide in *Laughter!* has been rightly criticized for "setting out to wring humour from a subject like Auschwitz" (Hiley, "Liberating" 16). We might ask, though, whether the subject of *Laughter!* is Auschwitz, or something else, the audience it provokes to laughter. To read *Laughter!* as about Auschwitz alone is crucially to misread the play's theatrical design, which depends in large measure on the way that popular performance genres inscribe a kind of activity for the audience in the performance itself. Unlike plays working within the realistic stage/audience division, *Laughter!* stages the spectator's performance as part of its critique of history. *Laughter!* places the audience before the spectacle of the holocaust, and identifies our performance as its theatrical—and historical—cause.

It may be useful to compare *Laughter!* with more widely disseminated treatments of "comical" Nazis, such as Chaplin's *The Great Dictator*, the "Springtime for Hitler" spoof in *The Producers*, or the television sitcom *Hogan's Heroes*. Recall the TV series for a moment: the easygoing and omnicompetent GIs continually outwit their captors, apparently remaining in prison from week to week only for the purpose of humiliating the Reich. The series rewrites the war as farce, a matter of much irritation in the mid-1960s to many veterans of the war, the POW camps, and the death camps. The sitcom genre articulates a powerful postwar ideology, one that replaces historical and political causality with an ethical motive, the effortless success of the American "character": those casual and clever, regular guys somehow overcome all obstacles, not least the series's troubling setting and subject matter, mostly by making us laugh— "I see NUTTINK," indeed.

This is some remove from Barnes's savage farce, which works to expose the conventions of comedy as a politically neutralizing device, complicit in the construction—literally, since the play takes place in a requisitions office—of an Auschwitz, a Dachau, a Buchenwald. In the prologue of the play, the Author delivers an impassioned tirade against laughter as the "ally of tyrants" but is defeated, in his efforts to "root it out," by the machinery of vaudeville—his whirling bowtie, squirting flower, and elusive pants provoke a laughter that his lecture can't stifle. In the "Auschwitz" section, Barnes extends this dissonance by characterizing the Nazis through a range of familiar comic devices and stereotypes. The Nazis' pratfalls, their Hitler jokes, their mania for "heiling," and so forth, become a kind of schtick. Barnes broadens his critique of laughter by repeatedly associating it with other kinds of conventionalized response. The bureaucrats, for example, speak in a kind of officialese—the play opens with Cranach's dictation: "WVHA Amt C1 (Building) to WVHA Amt D1/1. Your reference ADS/MNO our reference EZ 14/102/01. Copies WVHA Amt D IV/2, Amt D IV/4: RSHA OMIII: Reich Ministry PRV 24/6D" (48). Barnes's Nazis are compulsively orderly and neat, and in their concern for propriety they most seem to rival Wilde's Cecily and Gwendolen, and generally to recall comedy of manners:

> GOTTLEB: According to Hoflich of the "Schwarzes Korps" it is customary when Heiling Hitler to raise the right arm at an angle so the palm of the hand is visible.
>
> CRANACH: Hoflich also wrote "if one encounters a person socially inferior, when Heiling Hitler, then the right arm is raised only to eye-level, so the palm of the hand is hidden." (377)

A familiar situation, a familiar slur, a familiar laugh; as in *Hogan's Heroes*, such comic obsessions work to displace the more troublesome facts of anti-Semitism and genocide.

If laughter—our laughter—is the ally of tyrants, Barnes must dramatize the social consequences of laughter in the events of the stage. To accomplish this, Barnes juxtaposes the evasions of laughter against the confrontational seeing of theater. First, Gottleb identifies the evasive language of the bureaucracy: "CP3(m) described in regulation E(5) is the new concrete flue for the crematoriums" (401). He then opens the eyes of the bureaucrats, and of the audience, "to the sights, sounds, smells of Auschwitz." The filing cabinets lining the upstage area part, bodies spill forward onto the stage, and two horrific figures step out of the smoke, wearing gas masks and rubber suits: "*As they clump forward, they hit the dummies with thick wooden clubs. Each time they do so there is the splintering sound of a skull being smashed*" (405).

This is no laughing matter, but the play's bureaucrats desperately attempt to transform it into one, in order once again to "hide behind the words and symbols" of their self-protective administrative jargon. Indeed, Cranach leads Stroop and Else in a bureaucratic chant, the ritual effacement of the dead, "Future cases of death shall be given consecutive Roman numbers with subsidiary Arabic numbers. The first case Roman numeral I/1 the second the Roman numeral I/2 . . ." (407). As he does so, the files are closed, and all four characters return to the comic business of the play's opening: Gottleb (having been thrown from the office) "*pops his head in*" and "*deliberately sticks his Hitler moustache back on his upper lip* . . .—HAAA.

Top that!" (408–09). Barnes restores the brittle vaudeville of the opening of the scene, but the consequences of the audience's laughter have been brought into view. Laughter at the comic Nazis is reconstituted as a sign of complicity with their project, an acceptance of conventional "words and symbols"—the comic conventions of the stage—and so of the work they do. The bureaucrats' language, the manipulative devices of comedy, and the audience's theatrical response lead to a common, final solution: the gas chamber.

Cranach proceeds to consider how centuries to come will explain the ruins at Auschwitz: "They'll find it hard to believe they weren't heroic visionaries, mighty rulers, but ordinary people, people who liked people, people like them, you, me, us." People like you, me, us. With Cranach's final word, the circle of laughter is complete. "Ideology represents the imaginary relationship of individuals to their real conditions of existence" (Althusser 162); only when our "imaginary" absence from the dramatic spectacle has been reconstituted as an authorizing complicity are we prepared for Barnes's epilogue: the vaudeville routine of "the Boffo Boys of Birkenau, Abe Bimko and Hymie Bierberstein," played while they expire under the gas. Barnes wants to root out the laughter that allows "anything" to be "possible," and the obscene fantasy of a vaudeville routine in the gas chamber is Barnes's attempt to "dramatize" both cause and effect, action and consequence. It might plausibly be said that Barnes shows the Jews going happily to their fate, responsible for their own victimization; such a reading, I think, misconceives how the interpretive relations of performance structure the meaning of this event.[13] For in the epilogue, the comedians

---

13. Barnes has suggested that the play questions "the old cliché that runs if we can laugh at our miseries and at the injustices that afflict us, somehow laughing alleviates those injustices and those miseries and makes it bearable." He continues, "One of the reasons the second part of *Laughter* is about Auschwitz is because the Jews have a great reputation of being able to laugh and make the most marvelous one-line jokes about their situation. I wonder if one of the reasons they have been persecuted (not the only reason of course) and haven't done anything about it is because of their ability to laugh at it, laugh at the terrors that have afflicted them" (Bly and Wager 46). I want to be very clear about this: I have no desire to salvage the scene that Barnes describes here, in which the Jews' laughter, rather than the Nazis' brutality or the Allies' indifference, is said to cause the holocaust. The issue is whether the dramatic scene that Barnes describes is the scene that is produced in the theater.

don't laugh. Onstage, *Laughter!* shows the Boffo Boys performing for *our* entertainment, not to soothe their own fears. Surely it's not funny; yet the scene presents us with the essential situation of stand-up comedy—comic, joke, audience. The Boffo Boys don't "slay" us, "kill" us with their routine. We execute them by assenting to the role of comic audience; the final cause of the scene is less their joking than the audience's potential for laughter. Representing the idiom of the comic, *Laughter!* stages our laughter as a *gest*, an action figured in a social and historical framework. Subject to the performance, we become the subject of the drama, and of the history it brings to the stage. The passive audience becomes the author of the spectacle of genocide.

Laughter! stages the spectator as captor, dramatizes the ideological work performed by the conventions of comedy and the laughter they channel. Peter Nichols's *Poppy* stages the spectator by examining how the working of a theatrical genre duplicates and extends the genres of social action. *Poppy* concerns the economy of the Opium Wars, England's promotion of Indian opium in China as a means of securing the tea trade and reversing a damaging trade imbalance. In the play, an impoverished young aristocrat, Dick, contracts to marry into a wealthy mercantile family. To prove his business sense he takes a trading assignment in the Far East, accompanied by his faithful servant Jack and his lovelorn ward Sally. When he arrives in India, he finds out that he has engaged to trade opium, and that he must open the China market as well. Dick swallows his scruples, and we see him pursuing dangerous expeditions, negotiating trade agreements in the splendid Manchu court, and getting caught up in the fighting as the British brutally quell Chinese resistance and sack the Summer Palace. His moral compromise eventually exacts its price, for Sally—without a fortune, an unthinkable match for Dick—becomes an addict and must be married off to rustic Jack before both are sent off to America. For his pains, Dick is rewarded by the queen and finally marries the merchant's daughter.

The foreign setting, the class tension suffusing personal relations, the ritual snobbery of the Chinese aristocrats and the British traders, the background of actual events: as an episode in Victorian colonial expansion, the Opium Wars invite the plush, cultivated soap-opera treatment of *Masterpiece Theatre*. Nichols, though, designs the play's political substance more directly in the relations of performance, for *Poppy* examines the imperial economy in the rhetoric of the quintessential Victorian theatrical genre, the English pantomime. Queen Victoria—who, as the panto "good fairy," assumes a variety of guises in the play—appropriately defines the conventions of English pantomime, explaining them to her principal adversary in *Poppy*, the Chinese Emperor:

> I fear I must detain
> You yet a minute longer to explain
> That regular immortal intervention
> 's a vital part of pantomime convention.
> Another is a superfluity
> Of blatant sexual ambiguity.
> A man, for instance, always plays a Dame—
> Yet he may have a son who by the same
> Perverse tradition struts on high-heeled shoes
> And flaunts an ample bosom . . .
>
> (31)

Dick is of course Dick Whittington, "principal boy" of the classic Christmas panto, now the decayed descendant of the famous Lord Mayor. Played by a woman, he is paired with the panto "dame," the dowager Lady Whittington (Dodo), played by a man, and accompanied by his faithful servant Jack Idle, his ward Sally, and their blue panto ponies.[14] Along with *Aladdin, Cinderella, The Babes*

---

14. For details see Coveney. The traditional legend, which dates from the sixteenth century, is a parable of capitalist investment. Dick Whittington leaves rural poverty for service in London. He comes into the employ of the merchant Fitzwarren, and his happiness is clouded only by regular beatings from the cook, and by the mice and rats that infest his bedroom. For a penny, he buys a cat, which rids him of the vermin. The merchant, preparing an argosy, invites each of his servants to invest some property. Since Whittington has only the cat to invest, he does so; the vermin return, the cook's beatings worsen, and Dick sadly leaves London. Meanwhile, the ship lands in Barbary to trade. The captain and crew are feasted by the Barbary king, but before they can eat, hordes of mice and rats swarm over the feast and consume it. The captain strikes a deal with the king, and when Dick's cat drives away the vermin, the king buys the cat and all the goods on the ship as well, paying "ten times as much money as the ship's whole cargo." When Dick changes his mind and returns to London, he discovers that his investment has produced a huge return, and that he is wealthy. With such good fortune, Dick grows up to become the renowned Lord Mayor, knighted by Henry V, and known for his public munificence. For illustration, I quote from *The History of Dick Whittington* [c. 1814].

in the Woods, Puss-in-Boots, and *Robin Hood, Dick Whittington and His Cat* provides one of the perennial pantomime plots, and in its bawdy couplets and horrific puns, music and dance numbers, special effects and "transformation scenes," dramatic structure and tone, *Poppy* everywhere deploys the traditional devices of Boxing Day fare.[15] "Deciphering the British pantomime" is the critical activity of the play, for *Poppy* invites us to see panto as representative of the ideological process sustaining both the Victorian and the contemporary social order: "Good honest folk subliminally know / That romance helps maintain the status quo" (31).

Nichols's scrupulous attention to the rhetoric of pantomime implies that the politics of *Poppy* arise from the way that English panto traditionally addresses its audience. Despite its fantastic spectacle and audience of children, pantomime has always verged on "good Aristophanic satire," as Leigh Hunt put it (qtd. in Booth 5: 46). What distinguishes pantomime from other theatrical genres is not its topicality but its rhetorical elasticity in performance. Pantomime's mishmash of spectacle, song and dance, ballet, slapstick, and cross-dressing tends to interrupt the fictive surface of the drama, and of the fourth wall separating the actors from their audience. Rather than assigning a fixed performance style to the production, and so fixing a relationship between stage and spectator, pantomime constantly alters its strategy of address, as when the Cook was played as a "New Woman" in an 1894 *Dick Whittington*, or when Jack Idle joked about the Barbican's air-conditioning and parking facilities during *Poppy*'s run with the Royal Shakespeare Company.[16] Not only is the audience acknowledged, it is often invited to play a part in the drama. At one moment in Fred Locke's *Dick Whittington* (Edinburgh, 1893), Dick asks, "Is it a crime to have an empty purse?" to which Jack, encouraging the audience

---

15. On pantomime, see Booth 5: 46. Booth's introduction provides an informative account both of the development of pantomime in the nineteenth century and of its relation to other spectacular genres such as burlesque and extravaganza.

16. Since such topical remarks must arise from current events, they are, naturally, not to be found in the published text of *Poppy*; Jack Idle's comments on the Barbican are reported by Michael Coveney in his review. On the "New Woman," see the photograph of Herbert Campbell and Dan Leno in the 1894 Drury Lane *Dick Whittington* in Mander and Mitchenson plate 135.

to join him, replies, "A crime! Society knows nothing worse." Brecht recognized that such "radical *separation of the elements* . . . always brings up the question 'which is the pretext for what' " (*Brecht on Theatre* 37). By decentering the dramatic representation as the motive "pretext" for the performance, pantomime builds an active and actual relationship between the spectator, the drama, and its performance.

The pantomime audience authorizes the spectacle, and often quite literally enables it to proceed. Panto frankly addresses us as spectators, and it implicitly addresses us as *paying* spectators, since the holiday pantomime has traditionally offset the expenses of the "legitimate" drama. W. S. Gilbert noted that the theater manager "looks upon the pantomime he is about to produce as the only source of important profit that the year will bring him. Its duty is to recoup him for the losses attendant upon two or three trashy sensation plays, a feeble comedy, and a heavy Shakespearian revival" (qtd. in Booth 5: 55). Although for some theaters the pantomime subsidy has been replaced by one from the government, panto remains popular in London—*Dick Whittington* was staged there during the Christmas season prior to the opening of *Poppy,* as were *Aladdin* and *Cinderella*—and in the provinces, and becomes profitable in the traditional manner: by widening the class composition of the audience.[17] Panto is usually recalled with nostalgia, as "ideal family entertainment because it combines a children's story with a great deal of sexual innuendo which the parents can enjoy while it remains unnoticed by the children" ("Pantomime").[18] Yet the fairy world of panto is firmly rooted in the economics of theatrical survival. Pantomime author John Morley remarks that the "only time working-class people go to the theatre is in the Christmas season," which lends panto its populist flavor. Even though the "real national theatre is not on the South Bank at all. It's in the provinces, at pantomime time," panto is widely regarded as a genre "mounted with cynicism, and executed without art," offered each Christmas to the "more conservative proclivities" of a dramatically naive audi-

---

17. On the continued popularity of panto in the provinces and in London, see "Dame for a laugh."

18. Yet as Stanley Baxter—a pantomime pro—describes them, the children watching his *Cinderella* hardly seem so innocent: "They scream obscenities their parents never imagined they knew!"; see Hiley, "Revolution" 15.

ence.[19] While panto identifies its children as "innocent," it identifies its adult audience as childish, easily seduced into financing the "legitimate" theater that largely eludes or excludes them—"What signify Dick's riches, fame, and glory, / If they—our patrons—relish not our story?" (Locke). Although pantomime claims to serve its public, it witholds "patron" status from the audience that underwrites the theater's more artistic endeavors. Drama and entertainment, patron and consumer: pantomime conceals its patronizing innuendo within the "popular" and profitable gusto of good dirty fun.

Poppy relates the performance conventions of pantomime to Victorian imperialism, in order to identify our performance in the audience with our conduct outside the theater. The conventions of panto include the audience in the dramatic action, much as when Obadiah Upward gleefully explains the opium economy to us, the "boys and girls" in the house:

> Your cuppa's what it's all about. Your English cuppa China tea. We needed that but they never wanted anything of ours. Not Derbyshire porcelain nor the latest mousetraps nor cotton drawers from Manchester. So all the time we paid for tea with hard cash it was a drain on our currency reserves. We had to discover something they wanted as urgently as we wanted their tea. Are you with me so far?
>
> (45)

Rolling a huge crate of opium balls onstage, pulling down a chart from the flies, surrounded by calculating clerks, Upward transforms the traditional *Dick Whittington* scene in Fitzwarren's countinghouse into an illustration of how the English instigated and monopolized the opium trade: "John Chinaman is already paying more for his pipe than John Bull's paying for his cuppa. We've achieved a balance of payments!" (47).

Poppy shrewdly identifies us as—economically speaking—chil-

---

19. Hiley, "Revolution" 15, 12. In their 1969 survey of the audience of the subsidized Citizens' Theatre of Glasgow, Roy Wilkie and David Bradley imply the extent to which the pantomime audience differs from the usual audience of subsidy theaters. The Glasgow audience identified itself as largely composed of students and professionals: 68% identified themselves as either students, professionals, or teachers. Of this audience, 32% had attended the opera during the previous year, while only 16% had seen a pantomime (39, 56).

dren, needing a graphic illustration of the coercive principles of free trade. Although *Poppy* assigns us a childish grasp of the ways of the world economy, it refuses to allow us to hide behind childlike sentiment. The play reverses the usual disjunction between panto's "innocence" and the economic calculation it conceals. Much as in Barrie's *Peter Pan* (1904), the audience's "belief" is put to the test, but in a way that casts theatrical participation as social complicity. Late in the play, for instance, Upward and Lady Dodo sing a rousing song about the sacking of the Summer Palace. Since the "finale's not ready yet," the song must be repeated, and, as Upward complains, "Well, if we're going to sing it again, we're going to need some help from the boys and girls." Upward and Dodo divide the house in two, pull lyrics down from the flies, and lead the audience in a song, miming a machine-gun accompaniment: "The sound you hear's the fusiliers / Shooting the crystal chandeliers" (108). As John Russell Taylor reported, "It is a sight to behold": " 'Rat-tat-tat-tat! Ker-pow, ker-splat!' cry the bejewelled women and dinner-jacketed men enthusiastically, aiming with a will their imaginary gatling guns and hand-grenades at one another."[20]

Audience participation of this kind is a traditional part of pantomime "fun," one that explicitly characterizes the audience's performance as part of the dramatic action. William Archer reports that "Miss Ada Blanche made a very popular Robinson Crusoe" in Sir Augustus Harris's 1894 panto, ministering "to that patriotism which is one of the holiest feelings of our nature, by exterminating a huddled crowd of savages with a machine-gun" (1894 7). Raising the house lights always alters the spectators' sense of the spectacle, momentarily revealing an intimacy both enabled and structured by the performance we have shared. Here, Nichols decisively qualifies that intimacy. We applaud the theatrical spectacle, confirming its success. Our performance also authorizes, and literally advances, both the plot of the drama *and* its theatrical presentation. Our activity strips away the layers of "innuendo" that are the real subject of *Poppy*, dramatizing our ongoing addiction to the rhetoric of empire. *Poppy* invites us to play out both a political act and its inscription as ideology, to sing for ourselves the song of domination.

20. John Russell Taylor, rev. of *Poppy, Plays and Players* (December 1982).

In the theater, *Poppy* dramatizes both the process of imperial expansion, and its "transformation" to entertainment. In this regard, the stage illusions of pantomime are also shown to have an ideological function. The Chinese play the part of the panto primitives in the *Whittington* genre. In *Poppy*, though, the Chinese also provide most of the play's best special effects.[21] In the opening scene, the Chinese Emperor appears to the sound of a gong, flying in a throne suspended high above a mist-swirled stage, chastising Victoria before he disappears in a burst of flame, smoke, and music. Throughout the play, the Emperor relies on his magnificent stage magic; at the moment of Canton's final collapse, the Emperor performs *"a series of impressive illusions, conjuring* WARRIORS *in antique garb from traps and flies. . . . invoking* DEMONS, SPIDERS *and* FIGURES *from Chinese classical theatre. Smoke and drums"* (98–99). As the Emperor discovers, "Such gestures aren't to be relied upon" (67). The imperial pantomime constitutes Chinese power as illusion, mere mystification. In defeat, the Emperor's magic is defeated, too: after his fall, the Emperor slowly rises from the trap, *"No flash, no smoke. He juggles with three cigar boxes, drops one and throws them in disgust down the hole"* (105). To the English, and to the audience, the Chinese are not barbaric; their culture and society are simply unreal, an "illusion" within the codes of theater and power shared by the English characters and their audience. Of all of the theater's participants, only the Chinese are unable to decipher the British pantomime. Only for them is Dick's gender subject to an unreadable code—is he a man, woman, or "Foreign Devil Eunuch" (62–63)?

In its thorough refiguration of the rhetoric of pantomime, *Poppy* dramatizes the continuity between the fictions of the stage and our own. To suggest the historical progress of colonization, Nichols occasionally interrupts the panto mode, intercalating moments of Savoyard light opera, Broadway musical, and the officious narra-

21. The cultural misunderstandings typical of the English encounter with the inhabitants of Barbary are transformed in *Poppy* into a misunderstanding of the basis of opium economy—the Emperor argues, "Without our tea and rhubarb your whole nation / Will die in agonies of constipation" (3). Nichols, in fine panto manner, works the rhubarb/opium "shit" joke for all it is worth and more. In Locke's *Whittington*, a similar situation develops when the native king Rustifustican develops an ambiguous passion for the Cook: "She's not half bad-looking. I'll mash her, and if she's a failure as a wife, she'll always come in handy for the larder" (42).

tive voice of 1940s newsreels ("To the likes of you and me it may look like nothing more than a common wild flower but to old Abdul and his hardpressed family it means full stomachs and a safe future" 33). This sequence comes to a climax in the panto's finale, the transformation scene:

> DICK and LUCY are twentieth century City-of-London people: he in dark suit, bowler, rolled umbrella, Financial Times. She a City man's wife in dowdy dress.
>
> They all turn upstage and above, VICTORIA appears as ELIZABETH the SECOND, waving in the royal way. (115)

Instead of the traditional harlequinade, the play trains its panto magic on the audience once again. Dick and his rapacious contemporaries are transformed into staid moderns, the play argues, precisely because nothing is really changed: the Victorian adventurer and the modern banker are convertible within the imperial "romance" that maintains the status quo. When Dick is transformed into one of us, and the cast turns upstage to wave to Victoria/Elizabeth, *Poppy* enacts another, more subtle change. The "characters" are transformed into modern "spectators," while we—as our playing has implied throughout—are explicitly converted to "characters," an extension of the onstage audience waving at the queen. Like the transformation of the Victorians into moderns, this conversion also urges a substantial likeness between characters and spectators, by claiming the "spectator" as a kind of character, a site of performance grounded within the procedures of the theater and its society. Our activity, our wave of acknowledgment, provides the play's concluding harlequinade.

Or at least *Poppy* might stage us in this way. Nichols has inscribed the politics of *Poppy* in the rhetoric of its staging; changing that rhetoric unavoidably alters our performance, and the political process of the play. This problem was illustrated by the RSC's 1982 production. Perhaps because of the size of the Barbican, which seemed to thwart the intimacy needed for pantomime, director Terry Hands inflated, polished, and smoothed out the play's style, rephrasing the homely dialect of English panto in the brassy idiom of Broadway musical. This compromise between Broadway and the London Palladium reversed the play's theatrical politics: "The Royal Shakespeare Company's spirited and well-drilled performance allows almost no time for any intrusion by sombre realities. . . . if you can forget what [*Poppy*] is actually supposed to be about you will find this jolly romp quite suitable—give or take a few blasphemies and four-letter words—to bring all the family to for a Boxing Day treat" (Hayter). Rather than capturing the spectator within the politics of pantomime, Nichols's Aristophanic panto became a complacent "celebration of Britishness," just some "jolly good fun"; if that fun could make enough money to subsidize all that dreary Shakespeare, so much the better.[22] Small wonder that Nichols vowed to leave the stage: *Poppy* was transformed into a "jolly romp," brilliant technique emptied of social implication, a golden haze through which we might see, faintly, the trace of politics. Theater for pleasure *or* theater for instruction: both the direction and the critical reception of *Poppy* reveal a desire to resume the privileged, invisible power assigned to the audience of the realistic theater. In this production, at least, the spectators' "jolly good fun" remained distinct from the field of human relations constructed by the performance. The patrons were encouraged to believe in their child-like privilege, their freedom above and beyond the spectacle of exploitation.

FRAMING GENDER: *CLOUD NINE* AND *FEFU AND HER FRIENDS*

I want to conclude this outline of the rhetoric of contemporary political theater by turning to the production of women onstage. We have examined political theater in terms of its rhetoric of production, its ways of resituating the spectator vis-à-vis the stage. What renders this reorientation political is the sense that the spectator is so placed in order to question received wisdom, how things are, the "dominant ideology." It would be as absurd to deny a complicity between the rhetoric and experienced "content" of political theater as it would be to deny such a complicity on the "apolitical" stage. This complicity is particularly and necessarily evident in feminist theater, for the production of gender on the stage has been so fully naturalized to partriarchal norms that a critical staging of gender politics has needed to disrupt the theater's ways of produc-

22. Quotations are from reviews by Christy and by Mervyn Jones.

ing gendered performers, on the stage and in the audience. This disruption has, not surprisingly, confronted the practice of theatrical realism. Elin Diamond rightly argues that exposing the covert gender bias of stage realism must operate on two fronts: both suspending the structure of identifications that relate the dramatic fiction to its offstage reality and inspecting how realism "*produces* 'reality' by positioning its spectator to recognize and verify its truths" ("Mimesis" 60). In playwriting, production, and theoretical practice, feminist theater has recognized the mutually sustaining relation between the rhetoric of the realistic stage and more general strategies of gender subjection in the surrounding culture. Feminist theater is rightly taken to oppose "the patriarchal encodings in the dominant system of representation," a system in which realism still, in all areas of dramatic production, exerts a kind of hegemony (Case, *Feminism* 121).

The critical controversy surrounding Marsha Norman's plays, for example, arises in part from this sense that the rhetoric of realistic production, its assumption of "universality" and of a genderless (i.e., male, heterosexual) spectator, too easily compromises the critical or subversive dimensions of the plays it stages.[23] The unspoken rhetoric of realism works like the male loudspeaker voice in Wendy Wasserstein's *Uncommon Women and Others* (1977)—the voice that recites the rules of the college catalogue—to enforce the rules of our conduct in the theater, the forms of our representation and so of our interpretation. As Sue-Ellen Case argues, "symbolic systems" like realistic theater implicitly "masculinize" the audience-subject and reciprocally "masculinize the content" of the women they objectify onstage.[24] Apart from *'night, Mother,* Norman's plays can be numbered with those of Tina Howe, Pam Gems, Caryl Churchill, Corinne Jacker, Sarah Daniels, and of several other playwrights, as

---

23. For a fine overview of the politics of reception in the case of Norman's *'night, Mother,* see Dolan chapter 2. As Dolan argues, "Norman's play can be considered for canonical membership because Norman is still writing for male spectators under the guise of universality" (39).

24. Case remarks, "As symbolic systems masculinize the subject (perhaps most simply demonstrated by the use of the 'universal' pronoun 'he' for the subject of action), structuralizing male dominance in systems of thought, so do male images of the subject and female images of the object masculinize the content" ("From Split Subject to Split Britches" 129).

realistic plays which attempt to avoid this duplication of patriarchial subjection in the theater by searching out ways of infiltrating the narrative order of realism, the mystified external order (the environment), and the internal zone (the spirit or psyche) that it emphasizes as the drama's cause. This critical realism works to expose the rhetoric of realistic production and the spectatorial detachment on which it depends for its realization.

Not surprisingly, a number of feminist theater companies—Monstrous Regiment, Split Britches, and many others—have redesigned the performance conventions of the popular theater, using cabaret, stand-up comedy, and variety-show routines to evoke a collusion between stage and audience (see Wandor). One of the most influential examples of such work is Caryl Churchill's *Cloud Nine* (1979), which deploys a spectacular pastiche of melodrama, Gilbert and Sullivan operetta, and contemporary realistic dramaturgy in the mode of Pinter or Daniels to examine the construction of gender in the theater and its society. *Cloud Nine* presents a "parallel between colonial and sexual oppression" by examining the political formation of individual subjects in both spheres: the first act of the play takes place in Victorian colonial Africa; the second takes place twenty-five years later (anachronistically in the 1970s), and concerns the children of act 1, who are now young adults. The play implies that gender is both a biological and an ideological effect, by framing a continuity between the farcical hypocrisy of its light-opera Victorians and the more subtle deceptions of contemporary sexual politics. The most striking feature of the play is its performance design, for Churchill specifies that several roles are to be systematically cross-dressed, and that all of the roles of act 2 are to be doubled with actors from act 1.[25]

The play's cross-dressing and doubling of parts suspends the realistic assimilation of actor to character, stage presence to dra-

---

25. On devising *Cloud Nine*, see Keyssar chapter 4. Although the "doubling can be done in any way that seems right" (Introduction 247), Churchill prefers the paradigm of the original Joint Stock production; although the Joint Stock/Royal Court revival (1980) and the New York production (1981) altered this doubling plan, all productions retain Churchill's direction that Betty be played by a man in act 1, Joshua by a white man, Edward by a woman, and Cathy by an adult man. See Caryl Churchill, *Cloud 9* (New York: Methuen, 1984) v–viii. On the "ideological nature of the seeable" in Churchill, see Diamond, "(In)Visible Bodies."

matic representation, by staging both the race or gender of the fictive character and the race or gender of the performer as signifiers within the drama and within the discourse of Victorian, and contemporary, imperialism. As Elin Diamond rightly points out, Churchill historicizes the actor's body, showing how it enters history and representation: "In its conventional iconicity, theatre laminates body to character, but the body in historicization stands visibly and palpably separate from the 'role' of the actor as well as the role of the character; it is always insufficient and open" ("Brechtian Theory" 89). Rather than naturalizing the signs of "character" to the performer's bodily presence, Churchill's strategy converts the performer's body into a signifier that stands apart from "character" and enters into a dialectical relation with the dramatic fiction and its theatrical representation.

To be more exact, Churchill forces us to recognize that the body is always already a signifier, ideologically traced and textualized. In the case of Joshua, for example, the *character's* subservient behavior is what realizes him as a black man in the white society of the play, while the *actor's* white skin signifies the degree to which Joshua has been subjected to the colonial perspective, the sign of Joshua's desire "to be what whites want him to be" (245). The characters see a black man who is literally invisible, nonexistent; his race is assigned to the ideological register where it can be colonized and erased. But the actor's race isn't only a sign of Joshua's internalization of white attitudes, a sign, that is, of the *character's* subjection. The theater audience also reads Joshua as a white man, in exactly the way that Clive and the characters onstage do. In this theater—both the Savoyard pastiche and the modern theater in which *Cloud Nine* is performed—the other remains unseen, imaginable but invisible to the colonial eye/"I."

The ideological contouring of the visible body is surely one of Churchill's most important theatrical subjects, and provides the central problem of *Cloud Nine* in performance. In *Cloud Nine*, both the actor's self-presentation and the representation of a fictive character are suspended as points of self-present identity. Both are seen to be ideological texts within the frame of social performance. A related kind of unpacking takes place with regard to the staging of gender in the play. Playing Betty, the male performer's realization of a female character again takes place in an ideological register, as the re-presentation of the "real conditions" of his gender in an "imaginary" key: "We see a man representing a woman, mouthing her inanities, making typically female fluttering gestures with distinctly male arms. . . . The point is not that the male is feminized but that the female is absent," much as blackness is absent from the staging of Joshua (Diamond, "Refusing" 277–78).

While the white actor's playing of Joshua and the male actor's playing of Betty work to assert the subjection of racial and gender difference to imperial and patriarchal ideology, the enactment of Edward claims a different relationship between actor and character as signifiers, and so articulates the performer's body in another fashion. Played by a woman, Edward's difference from gender and sexual norms is signaled rather than concealed by the actress's presentation onstage. The actress's gender doesn't signify an unmediated feminine "identity" beneath "Edward's" masculine exterior: the play is hardly claiming that gay men are somehow women in disguise. Churchill suggests in her introduction to the play that "Edward, Clive's son, is played by a woman for a different reason—partly to do with the stage convention of having boys played by women (Peter Pan, radio plays, etc.) and partly with highlighting the way Clive tries to impose traditional male behavior on him. Clive struggles throughout the act to maintain the world he wants to see—a faithful wife, a manly son" (245). The bodies of the performers of "Joshua" and "Betty" are like "Clive's" body, signaling the extent to which Clive's culture maps all others onto the paradigm of white, male, European experience, a mapping that claims the other as a kind of fiction at the same time that it enforces its submission. Unlike "Joshua" and "Betty," though, "Edward's" *difference* is registered by the gender of the performer: Edward's sexuality is not convertible, it seems, to Clive's paradigm.

This ordering of the representation of gender and sexuality is confirmed by the performance of "Harry Bagley," where the white, male actor's performance is also denaturalized. When Bagley is misled into seducing Clive, both he and Clive agree that Bagley's sexuality is disgusting, shameful, that Bagley is "like a man born crippled" (283). Whereas Edward's actions—here and in act 2—stand apart from patriarchal ideology, Bagley's efforts are continually to become like Clive, an effort which he carries too far for

Clive's taste. After the acting of "Joshua," "Edward," and "Betty," we can hardly read "Bagley's" performance innocently. Played by a white man, Bagley is finally complicit in the colonial and sexual order that Clive represents. In this sense, it's not surprising that he reinforces Clive's notions of order by offering to marry Mrs. Saunders, nor that the casting plan calls for this actor to play Martin in act 2, the superficially "liberated man."

The play's political assault lies to an unusual degree not in the content of the text, but in the contours of performance and, as in *Poppy*, performance style can radically change the play's politics. How does the dialectic between identity and ideology that informs the staging of "Joshua," "Betty," "Edward," and "Bagley" shape the audience's engagements with the politics of race, gender, and sexuality? The spirited comedy of act 1 often draws productions into a kind of parody, in which Joshua is played in minstrel-show style and Betty is played in travesty, somewhere between Milton Berle and a campy drag queen. This kind of performance works counter to the process of the play's inception, in which Churchill and a selected group of actors "talked, read texts on sexual politics and worked through exercises exploring gender and sexuality" in order to "educate each other about the diversity of sexual possibilities and to unfix these categories and their own identifications with them" (Keyssar 93). A parodic production, of course, tends to confirm these categories, as the audience's laughter dramatizes the continued power of Clive's perspective in our culture: the threat to patriarchal hegemony posed by black, female, gay male, and lesbian experience is both denied and neutralized by rendering that experience laughable, inferior, trivial, and finally invisible. Travestying Edward and Betty—in the Bagley-Edward and Ellen-Betty seduction scenes of act 1, for instance—denigrates the reality of gay and lesbian sexuality, in part by using gestural reference to the actors' bodies to recuperate the transaction between the characters for the imperial/patriarchal/heterosexual audience. Parody, that is, "legitimates" homoeroticism by showing it to be "substantially" heterosexual: it's really a man and a woman, after all. In so doing, "essential" difference is wrongly made to underwrite homosexual activity in the audience's experience of the play, to render it invisible in much the way that race and gender are erased in the enactment of "Joshua" and "Betty."

Is it possible to avoid this kind of recuperation, the containment of Churchill's disruptive politics by the conventions of stage performance? Perhaps not, or not entirely. Loren Kruger has argued that even the most scrupulous production can hardly avoid invoking the machinery of gender and sexual oppression inscribed in conventional uses of cross-playing. As result, stage production solicits "the audience's *assent* to this spectacle rather than its criticism of gender stereotyping outside the theater," titillating the audience "with the *display* of a 'concern for gender' rather than offering a dramatic *interaction* of these concerns that might challenge the audience to think about them differently" (34). Yet this reading seems to foreclose the possibility that stage conventions can change in the work they can perform, and in the meanings they are capable of generating, as their place, function, and use in culture itself changes. The cross-playing in *Cloud Nine* ought to challenge the constructions of race, gender, and sexuality by challenging the means of their production as theatrical behavior (as is often currently done in gay and lesbian performance): this would mean challenging both a superficially "Brechtian" form of enactment as well as more traditional versions of cross-playing. Churchill has committed the politics of *Cloud Nine* to the arena of its stage production to an extraordinary degree. The politics of the play may well become clear only when the possibilities of the stage and its audiences have been more searchingly explored.

In *Cloud Nine, Top Girls* (1982), and other plays, Churchill carefully crafts strategies for disturbing the privilege and power assigned to the realistic theater audience. Despite the possibility of misappropriation, the use of performance to disrupt the assimilation of actor to character has become something of a staple in feminist theater. This exploration of the ideological working of the mise-en-scène is especially characteristic of Maria Irene Fornes's plays. *Tango Palace* (1963) parodies the traditional authority of the dramatic text, as a clown tosses off witty repartee, while tossing away the cards on which his lines are written; in *The Danube* (1983), the charismatic presence of the performers is suspended, when a love scene is played first by actors, and then by puppets they manipulate; and in a stunning scene from *Fefu and Her Friends* (1977), the audience sits in a semicircle around a woman desperately negotiating with invisible tormentors, becoming themselves the woman's unseen, sadistic judges. Despite their variety, Fornes's experiments share a common impulse: to explore the operation of the mise-en-scène on the audience's representation in the theater.

Fornes's most assured play, *Fefu and Her Friends*, brings the gendering of the realistic spectator fully into view, revealing "his" covert control of the women of the stage. The play opens at a country house in 1935. Fefu has invited a group of women to her home to rehearse a brief series of skits for a charity benefit to raise money for a newly founded organization. In the first scene, the women arrive and are introduced. Many seem to have been college friends, two seem to be lovers, or ex-lovers. Much of the action of the scene centers on Julia, who is confined to a wheelchair as the result of a mysterious hunting accident: although the bullet missed her, she is paralyzed from the waist down. In part 2, Fornes breaks the audience into four groups, who tour Fefu's home—garden, study, bedroom, and kitchen: "These scenes are performed simultaneously. When the scenes are completed the audience moves to the next space and the scenes are performed again. This is repeated four times until each group has seen all four scenes" (*Fefu* 6). In part 3, the audience is returned to the auditorium. The women rehearse and decide the order of their program, Fefu goes outside to clean her gun, and suddenly a shot rings out; Julia falls dead, bleeding, though again the bullet seems to have gone elsewhere.

The play examines the theatrical poetics of the feminine not only as theme, but in the visible protocols of the spectacle as well, by unseating the invisible spectator of realism and by dramatizing "his" authority over the construction of stage gender. Early in the play, for instance, Fefu looks offstage and sees her husband approaching: "*FEFU reaches for the gun, aims and shoots. CHRISTINA hides behind the couch. She and CINDY scream. . . . FEFU smiles proudly. She blows on the mouth of the barrel. She puts down the gun and looks out again*" (9). As Fefu explains once Phillip has regained his feet, "It's a game we play. I shoot and he falls. Whenever he hears the blast he falls. No matter where he is, he falls." Although Phillip is never seen in the play, his attitudes constantly intrude on the action— "My husband married me to have a constant reminder of how loathsome women are" (7)—and mark the presence of a powerful, masculine, destructive authority lurking just offstage. The shells may be live or only blanks ("I'm never sure," says Fefu), but it hardly matters. The exchange of power takes place through the "sighting" of the other.[26]

The power of the absent male is everywhere evident in *Fefu*, and particularly imaged in Julia's paralysis. As Cindy suggests when she describes the accident, Julia's malady is a version of Fefu's "game": "I thought the bullet hit her, but it didn't . . . the hunter aimed...at the deer. He shot":

> Julia and the deer fell. . . . I screamed for help and the hunter came and examined Julia. He said, "She is not hurt." Julia's forehead was bleeding. He said, "It is a surface wound. I didn't hurt her." I know it wasn't he who hurt her. It was someone else. . . . Apparently there was a spinal nerve injury but the doctors are puzzled because it doesn't seem her spine was hurt when she fell. She hit her head and she suffered a concussion but that would not affect the spinal nerve. So there seems to be no reason for the paralysis. She blanks out and that is caused by the blow on the head. It's a scar in the brain.
>
> (14–15)

The women of *Fefu and Her Friends* share Julia's invisible "scar," the mark of their paralyzing subjection to a patriarchy that operates on the "imaginary," ideological plane. The hunter is kin to Julia's hallucinatory "voices" in part 2, the "judges" who enforce her psychic dismemberment: "They clubbed me. They broke my head. They broke my will. They broke my hands. They tore my eyes out. They took away my voice." Julia's bodily identification is broken down and reordered according to the "aesthetic" canons prescribed by the male voice, the silent voice that characterizes women as "loathsome." This internalized "guardian" rewrites Julia's identity at the interface of the body itself, where the masculine voice materializes itself in the woman's flesh. The subliminal voice infiltrates the

---

26. The gun business derives from a joke, as Fornes reports in "Notes": "There are two Mexicans in sombreros sitting at a bullfight and one says to the other, 'Isn't she beautiful, the one in yellow?' and he points to a woman on the other side of the arena crowded with people. The other one says, 'Which one?' and the first takes his gun and shoots her and says, 'The one that falls.' In the first draft of the play Fefu explains that she started playing this game with her husband as a joke. But in rewriting the play I took out this explanation." It's notable that the gun business dates from Fornes's original work on the play in 1964, as Fornes suggests in "Interview." For a fuller reading of Fornes's theater, see Worthen, "*Still playing games.*"

deepest levels of psychological and physiological identification, enforcing a crippling gesture of submission:

> (*Her head moves as if slapped.*)
> JULIA: Don't hit me. Didn't I just say my prayer?
> (*A smaller slap.*)
> JULIA: I believe it. (25)

As Fornes remarked to Gayle Austin, "Julia is really not mad at all. She's telling the truth. The only madness is, instead of saying her experience was 'as if' there was a court that condemned her, she says that they did" (Austin 80).

Fornes suggests that "Julia is the mind of the play," and Julia's scene articulates the shaping vision of *Fefu* as a whole, as well as organizing the dramatic structure of part 2 ("Notes"). The action of *Fefu and Her Friends* takes place under watchful eyes of Phillip, of the hunter, of Julia's "guardians," a gaze that constructs, enables, and thwarts the women of the stage: "Our sight is a form they take. That is why we take pleasure in seeing things" (35). In the theater, of course, there is another invisible voyeur, whose performance is both powerful and "imaginary." *Fefu and Her Friends* extends the function of the spectator beyond the metaphorical register, by decentering "his" implicit ordering of the theatricality of the feminine. First performed by the New York Theater Strategy in a SoHo loft, the play originally invited the spectators to explore the space of Fefu's home. In the American Place Theater production, the spectators were invited, row by row, to different areas of the theater—a backstage kitchen, an upstairs bedroom, the garden and the study sets—before being returned to the auditorium, but not to their original seats. At first glance, Fornes's staging may seem simply a gimmick, a formalist exercise in multiple perspective something like Alan Ayckbourn's *The Norman Conquests* (1973). Yet Ayckbourn's trilogy—each play takes a different set of soundings from the events of a single weekend—implies that there could be, in some mammoth play, a single ordering of events, one "drama" expressed by a single plot and visible from a single perspective. *Fefu and Her Friends*, though, bears little confidence in the adequacy or authority of the single viewing subject characteristic of both film and of fourth-wall realism, and more closely approximates the decentering disorientation of environmental theater.[27] Different spectators see the drama in a different sequence and in fact see different plays, as variations invariably enter into the actors' performances. Fornes not only draws the audience into the performance space, violating the privacy of the stage, she actively challenges and suspends the epistemological priorities of realistic vision and its privileged, private subject: the invisible, singular, motionless, masculine "I." By reordering the audience's function in the theatrical process, *Fefu* reorders its relation to, and interpretation of, the dramatic process it shapes.

As Cecilia says at the opening of part 3, after we have returned to the living room, "we each have our own system of receiving information, placing it, responding to it. That system can function with such a bias that it could take any situation and translate it into one formula" (29). In performance, *Fefu and Her Friends* dramatizes and displaces the theatrical system that renders woman visible: the predication of feminine identity on the sight of the spectator, a "judge" multiplied from the singular "he" into an audience of "them." In this sense, Fornes's theatrical strategy works to replace the "objective" and objectifying relations of realistic vision with the more "fluid boundaries" sometimes said to describe women's experience of themselves and others. Writing the play, Fornes sought to avoid "writing in a linear manner, moving forward," and instead undertook a series of centrifugal experiments, exploring characterization by writing a series of improvisational, extraneous scenes (Cummings 53).[28] Perhaps as a result, the staging of *Fefu* challenges

27. Stanley Kauffman's reading of the play's filmic texture is at once shrewd and, in this sense, misapplied: "I doubt very much that Fornes thought of this four-part walk-around as a gimmick. Probably it signified for her an explanation of simultaneity (since all four scenes are done simultaneously four times for the four groups), a union of play and audience through kinetics, some adoption by the theater of cinematic flexibility and montage. But since the small content in these scenes would in no way be damaged by traditional serial construction, since this insistence on reminding us that people actually have related/unrelated conversations simultaneously in different rooms of the same house is banal, we are left with the *feeling* of gimmick."
28. It should be noted that Fornes also remarks, "I don't mean linear in terms of what the feminists claim about the way the male mind works." For the phrase, "fluid boundaries," and for much of my understanding of feminist psychoanalytic theory, I am indebted to my late colleague Joan

the institutional "objectivity," the controlling partitions of realistic vision. The play not only realizes Julia's absent voices, it reshapes the audience's relation to the drama, requiring an interpretive activity that subordinates "plot" to "atmosphere" or "environment," one that refuses recourse to a single, external point of view.

In *Fefu and Her Friends*, vision is achieved only through displacement, by standing outside the theatrical formula of realism. The play undertakes to dramatize both the results of realistic bias—in the various deformations suffered by Julia, Fefu, and their friends—and to enact the "other" formula that has been suppressed, the formula that becomes the audience's mode of vision in the theater. To see *Fefu* is not to imagine an ideal order, a single, causal "plot" constituted specifically by our absence from the performance; not only are there several "plots," but we have shared the space in which they have been enacted. *Fefu* sharply illustrates how a "subversive text" can open up theatrical rhetoric, exposing "the negotiation of meanings to contradictions, circularity, multiple viewpoints" (Forte 117). *Fefu and Her Friends* decenters the absent "spectator" as the site of authentic interpretation, replacing "him" with a self-evidently theatricalized body, an "audience," a community sharing irreconcilable yet interdependent experiences. In *Fefu*, Fornes provides what Glaspell could not discover in *Trifles*: a means of politicizing our interpretive activity as spectators. The environmental design of the play invokes the realistic ideal of verisimilitude even as it renders any sense of spectatorial "objectivity" impossible. The perspective offered by the realistic box appears to construct a community of witnesses but is in fact grounded in the sight of a single observer: the realistic audience sees with a single eye. *Fefu* challenges the "theory" of realistic theater at its source, by dramatizing—and displacing—the covert authority of the constitutive *theoros* of realism and the social order it reproduces: the offstage man.[29] In this regard,

---

Lidoff. Patrocinio Schweickart argues, referring to the work of Nancy Chodorow and Carol Gilligan, that "men define themselves through individuation and separation from others, while women have more flexible ego boundaries and define and experience themselves in terms of their affiliations and relationships with others" (54–55).

29. See Jane Gallop's description of the oculocentrism of theory "from the Greek *theoria*, from *theoros*, 'spectator,' from *thea*, 'a viewing' " (36–37). It should be noted that theater of this kind is, in the careful sense developed by Benjamin Bennett, anti-Fascist, in that it not only opposes the

Fornes's theater shares its rhetoric with the theater of Brenton, Barnes, Churchill, Osborne, Kennedy, and many others who work to stage our performance as a political act. The genius of *Fefu and Her Friends* lies in the way that Fornes renders the relations of visibility palpable, dramatizing their coercive force and the gender bias they inscribe within our own performance of the play.

---

imagined uniformity of response latent in the single perspective of realism and the single "personality" produced by poetic theater, but it also forces the audience to negotiate its own variety of responses as part of the play's condition of meaning. See *Theater as Problem* chapter 4, esp. 159–63.

POSTSCRIPT

Sidi's Image:
Theater and the Frame of Culture

I opened this reading of the rhetoric of modern theatricality by recalling the camera that Chekhov placed onstage in *Three Sisters*. As the prevailing metaphor for the turn-of-the-century theater's claim to reproduce an uninflected slice of life, the camera works in Chekhov's play to expose the rhetorical, suasive character of realistic theatricality. Chekhov's irony is enabled by the habitual collocation of the two arts, an intricate ideological interrelation that sought to define theatrical production by identifying it with the "objective" apparatus of photography. Staging the camera, Chekhov invokes this relation between photography and theatrical realism as part of the substance of his drama. Of course, relations between the arts, as between other social institutions, constantly shift in their lines of affiliation; photography and theater may no longer intersect in quite this way, if they intersect at all. Think, for instance, of the very different relations between film images and theatrical production that emerge in Robert Wilson's work, in plays like Adrienne Kennedy's *A Movie Star Has to Star in Black and White* (1976) or Sarah Daniels's *Masterpieces* (1989), or in Athol Fugard, John Kani, and Winston Ntshona's *Sizwe Bansi is Dead* (1972). Much as roleplaying and plays-within-plays in Elizabethan drama pointed to the complicity of the stage in forms of culture outside the theater, so staged photography relates the rhetoric of theatrical production to the most pervasive visual means of reproducing our social order, the technologies (photography, film, video, print) of the image.

    The complicity of theater and photography stands at the heart of the final play I wish to discuss here, Wole Soyinka's *The Lion and the Jewel* (1959). This is a complex and challenging play, and one that occupies an increasingly problematic place on the horizons of contemporary theater and culture; here, I want to ask how it refracts the rhetoric of theatrical production as part of the larger working of European culture. Praised as "an amusing African variation of the classic love triangle" (Lindfors 200), *The Lion and the Jewel* plays a significant and sometimes negative role in criticism of Soyinka's writing, his politics, and his status as an African writer. The play itself may come to seem an instance of the Eurocentric "progress" it appears to criticize: the figuration of Africa through European conventions of dramatic representation (the "classic love triangle" of romantic comedy) invariably subjects African culture to the perspective of European values and authority ("an amusing African variation"). Soyinka's long dialogue with the West and his apparent approval of a "traditional," perhaps even "romanticized," African culture spurs the sharpest criticism of this kind, which finds a suspiciously European orientation displayed in his drama. This attitude appears mainly in Soyinka's efforts to reprise Western drama in African dress—Dylan Thomas's *Under Milkwood* lurks behind *Camwood on the Leaves* (1960); Brecht's *Threepenny Opera* provides the model for *Opera Wonyosi* (1977); classical drama inspires Soyinka's *The Bacchae of Euripides* (1973), and perhaps even the *Oresteia* motif of *Death and the King's Horseman* (1976)—but it can also be found, perhaps, to underlie Soyinka's treatment of postcolonial dictators in *Kongi's Harvest* (1965) and *A Play of Giants* (1985).[1]

Such readings of Soyinka's career—which I do not endorse—could well be capped by remarking on the inclusion of *The Lion and the Jewel* in the fifth Continental edition of *The Norton Anthology of World Masterpieces*, as though the editors' grouping of the play among a handful of non-European works were the sign of Soyinka's imitative belatedness to European culture. Yet the presence of *The Lion and the Jewel* in this anthology points out the difficulty of reading Soyinka's use of European stage and dramatic conventions. Rather than complementing the European cast of *World Mas-*

---

1. The "Shakespearean" cast of some of Soyinka's plays is sometimes traced to Soyinka's training at University College, Ibadan, and later at Leeds with the Shakespearean scholar and critic G. Wilson Knight. Ngugi wa Thiong'o provides a summary of the Western orientation of African universities in the postwar period, in which literary study was principally directed toward reading English and European classics; he also discusses the prominence of West End revivals, Shaw, and Shakespeare on postcolonial stages; see 90–91, 38–39.

terpieces, Soyinka's play may act more corrosively on the canon of European literature, assaulting the pretense that to read the literature of Europe is to gain a mastery of the world. Soyinka presents European modes of representation in *The Lion and the Jewel*—dramatic conventions, patterns of characterization, events and behavior associated with European culture—within the process of the cultural subjection of Africa, a subjection that extends the practices of colonialism into the present era. Far from writing a play in the Western tradition, Soyinka dramatizes the political implications of Western cultural production in the wider social rhetoric of postcolonial exchange.

The Lion and the Jewel is usually taken to present a conflict between the traditional values of an African village, personified by Baroka, the wily and sensual "Bale" of Ilujinle, and the impact of European culture and "progress," emblematized by the schoolmaster Lakunle. The plot is set in motion by the arrival in the village of a glossy magazine, which features appealing photographs of the "village belle," Sidi, on its cover and inside pages. The magazine alters the balance of village life by revaluing Sidi, making her an attractive prize, one more fit for the chief than for the schoolmaster. Since Baroka finally gets the girl, the play seems to militate in favor of a romanticized view of African tradition, one that disclaims the inroads of progress and that blindly discounts the ineluctable pressures of the outside world.[2] In *The Lion and the Jewel*, though, the village does not confront a generalized "progress." It faces the manifestation of Western culture in the register of representation: in the behavior of Lakunle and the image of Sidi offered by photography. To see *The Lion and the Jewel* as voicing a simple opposition between traditional and European values is to understate the intricate rhetoric of subjection that animates cross-cultural conflict and negotiation in the play and in the world at large. Village tradition meets the working of European cultural imperialism itself, the reduction of "Africa" to an image, reproduced—as photograph, as theater—for sale on the markets of the world. Unlike Chekhov's camera, which alludes to the verisimilitude urged by theatrical realism, Sidi's photo testifies to the instrumental character of images, the rhetorical labor involved in transforming a culture into a commodity.

2. See, for example, Eldred Durosimi Jones, *Writings* 39–46.

The play's critique of the invasive power of European representation first centers on the characterization of Lakunle, the schoolmaster who refuses to pay the bride-price for Sidi. Lakunle is a version of the comic *alazon*, the "deceiving or self-deceiving character in fiction, normally an object of ridicule in comedy or satire" who "most frequently takes the form of a *miles gloriosus* or a pedant" in comedy (Frye 365); as pedant, Lakunle has ties to schoolmasters from Shakespeare's Holofernes to Stoppard's George Moore. To read Lakunle simply as an instance of Western comic conventions is to miss the deeper point of his behavior: the play implicates those conventions in the wider process of representation and domination that it criticizes. In a dated and ill-fitting English suit, Lakunle personifies the depredations of "assimilation." He is a comic figure precisely because his imitation of European values can never eradicate the boundaries of his difference from and subjection to the culture he copies. Soyinka's *alazon*, that is, is not merely an impostor. The form of his imposture resonates within the dynamics of colonial social relations, in which imitation endlessly reproduces the inferior relation of subjects to the dominant culture. As Abdul R. JanMohamed observes, if the African "chooses to be faithful to the indigenous values, he remains, from the colonialist's viewpoint, a 'savage,' and the need to 'civilize' him perpetuates colonialism. If, however, he attempts to espouse Western values, then he is seen as a vacant imitator without a culture of his own" (5), for of course imitation can never break the essential boundaries dividing colonizer and colonized. Lakunle's imitation begins at the level of language itself:

LAKUNLE: A savage custom, barbaric, out-dated,
Rejected, denounced, accursed,
Excommunicated, archaic, degrading,
Humiliating, unspeakable, redundant.
Retrogressive, remarkable, unpalatable.
SIDI: Is the bag empty? Why did you stop?
LAKUNLE: I only own the Shorter Companion
Dictionary, but I have ordered
The Longer One—you wait!

(8)[3]

---

3. As Ngugi wa Thiong'o remarks, "Language as culture is thus mediating between me and my own self; between my own self and other selves;

Lakunle's idolization of the behavoir of Lagos, his desire for a European marriage, the way he slights others in his community by offering European greetings instead of local customs, and his role as schoolmaster all mark his playing with the signs of comedy. Yet although Lakunle's pretensions are laughable to the villagers, a Western audience of the play has a different relation to Lakunle's impersonation, to his adoption of Western "civilization," than an African audience, urban or otherwise. I do not mean to privilege the Western audience's access to "meaning" in *The Lion and the Jewel* but to suggest instead that different meanings will necessarily emerge when the play's dramatization of cross-cultural contact is staged on different sides of that interface. Some London audiences, for instance, would epitomize the culture that Lakunle imitates, speak his words without needing the dictionary, perhaps even hear in his speech (as the *Sunday Telegraph* reviewer of the 1966 Royal Court production did) a "bastard jargon, begotten by Roget's 'Thesaurus' on ad-man's copy, which occasionally breaks into pseudo-Auden laments." A British venue produces Western "culture" as ineffable—as the colonizer's culture always is—at the moment that Lakunle's behavior becomes (comic) imitation.[4] When the offstage audience occupies the position of cultural privilege described in the play, it becomes the inimitable object of Lakunle's acting. And the more readily Lakunle's imitation is absorbed by the classic conventions of romantic comedy, the more fully the discourse of comedy itself is involved in the discourse of colonialism.

---

between me and nature. Language is mediating in my very being" (15). Indeed, Ngugi uses this incident to epitomize the problems attendant on writing African drama in English. For although both Sidi's and Lakunle's parts are written in English, the dramatic fiction is that they are speaking in Yoruba. Yet Ngugi suggests that this fiction itself—Yoruba signified through English—presents the problem of representing Africa through European media in ways that parallel my argument here (see 43).

4. The *Sunday Telegraph* reviewer subjected Baroka to a similar reading, in which he "hymns the sweet, simian delights of being scratched and tweaked, like some debauched gorilla with the gift of tongues, in long word-encrusted arias which would not disgrace Webster or Jonson"; speaking the language of Webster or Jonson is not, finally, quite enough to humanize the simian African. In addition, *The Times* referred to Soyinka's resemblance to "The Elizabethans," while *The Scotsman* found an "almost Shakespearean turn of phrase" in the play. See Revs. of *The Lion and the Jewel*.

Reading Lakunle's imitative behavior as part of the European process for representing Africa, we begin to undo the dichotomy of tradition versus progress that sustains readings of the play's "reactionary" politics. Peter Nazareth takes the most familiar version of this position, suggesting that while "there is no conscious affirmation of *Negritude* in this play," the play's effect "is exactly that of *Negritude* after political independence has been won—it has a reactionary message":

> For what is the play really saying? That the old ways of life, with chieftainship, polygamy, etc., etc., are to be accepted because they are African and natural and that westernization is to be rejected. Yet the westernization represented by Lakunle is pseudo-westernization, and the chief's only quality is his sensual and sexual prowess. It is "unfair" of Soyinka to come down in favour of the traditional life since it has so little to recommend it in the play. (63)

Fair enough; to read the play as pitting a victorious "tradition" against an impoverished "progress" is to see the play itself as offering a kind of exoticized and romantic Africa to its audiences, a romance that maintains the status quo. Yet this reading distinguishes "tradition" and "progress," Africa and Europe, as separate spheres, where the play takes their interconnection as its point of attack. It is not merely that Lakunle emblematizes a simplistic view of Westernization; *The Lion and the Jewel* gains political urgency when we recognize the comedy of Lakunle as part of the broader rhetoric with which the play takes issue. Soyinka represents Lakunle—and Lakunle represents himself—from the perspective of European culture. As Soyinka suggests in "...And the Other Immigrant," a poem about an African student in London, this cultural cross-dressing represents the inscription of empire on the person of the colonized. In the poem, the student hides his dignity in the lining of his three-piece suit, while his stiff shirt collar shines "with the whiteness which / Out-Europes Europe."[5] Europe forces the speaker to conceal his dignity in the posture of imitation, a posture he angrily recognizes as comic, at least from the internalized perspective of his European audience. Only poor acting, Hamlet reminded his players, "out-Herods Herod."

5. Eldred Jones discusses this poem in "Progress and Civilization" 129.

I spend so much time on Lakunle here because in reading the characterization of Lakunle as an instance of Soyinka's effort to trivialize "progress," critics of the play have overlooked the more dynamic aspect of cultural exchange in the play, the extent to which "traditional" Africa is already pervaded by the West. Lakunle's behavior is in many respects paralleled by the magazine photographs of Sidi, which similarly encode an image of Africa from the dominant position of the Western voyeur:

> Oh, Sidi, he was right. You *are* beautiful. On the cover of the book is an image of you from here (*touches the top of her head.*) to here (*her stomach.*). And in the middle leaves, from the beginning of one leaf right across to the end of another, is one of you from head to toe. Do you remember it? It was the one for which he made you stretch your arms towards the sun. (*Rapturously.*) Oh, Sidi, you looked as if, at that moment, the sun himself had been your lover. (11)

Although the photo-spread of village life recalls the photographs common in travel or natural-science magazines, the eroticization of Sidi's image—"*The stranger arranges SIDI in all sorts of magazine postures and takes innumerable photographs of her*" (17)—is striking, and implies that, as a token of exchange, the image works in ways modeled on the paradigms of pornography (a stage production would, of course, have to decide this issue, choosing a particular magazine as the frame for Sidi's photograph). The object of pornography rarely if ever forms part of the audience of intended consumers, and the magazines featuring Sidi are not sold in the village. The image of the inviting other is offered to a gaze originating elsewhere, in the neocolonial city, ultimately in the once-imperial metropolis. Taken in tandem, the representations of Lakunle and Sidi—as theatrical behavior, as photographic image—duplicate colonial strategies of subjection and self-justification. Lakunle's behavior neutralizes the threat of assimilation, the threat that the other will penetrate the dominant culture, by fixing his performance as comic imitation, necessarily traced by the difference it claims to erase. Sidi's image, on the other hand, neutralizes the other by casting it as an object of willing submission to Western desire, inviting the gaze of domination.

Sidi's image occupies a field of photographs in the play, a field that contains the promised postage stamp that Baroka (truthfully or not) uses to win her affections, and also the image of Europeanized Africa so appealing to Lakunle:

> I want to walk beside you in the street,
> Side by side and arm in arm
> Just like the Lagos couples I have seen
> High-heeled shoes for the lady, red paint
> On her lips. And her hair is stretched
> Like a magazine photo.
>
> (9)

Much as magazine photos offer Lakunle an impossible image of civility, one neither actual nor achievable, so the dissemination of Sidi's image alters the reality it claims to disclose. Sidi's image not only renders her beauty more visible through reproduction, it implicitly challenges the authority embodied in the village social hierarchy, especially in that Baroka is pictured "in a little corner somewhere in the book, and even that corner he shares with one of the village latrines" (12). The image does not merely record or express Sidi's value, it constitutes it, fetishizes it. Sidi becomes valuable because she is depicted, and because her image circulates beyond the village, to Lagos, to Europe, "to the whole wide world" (12).

Although it is an item in the play's catalogue of "progress," the photograph expresses a more profound and disturbing sense of progress as exploitation. The photograph and its readers dictate the values that village culture must incorporate, while the village assumes "the passive role of *consumer*" of this enforced culture, seeing itself from the perspective of the European eye (Onoge 22). It is the arrival of the magazine, after all, that forces Baroka to devise the elaborate fiction of impotence, the deception he invents to lure Sidi to his home for her seduction. Baroka, we discover, once succeeded in diverting a railway line away from the village, but perhaps to little avail; finally, to seduce Sidi and regain his authority, Baroka employs the technology of the West, promising to use the printing press to send her image—transformed into the symbol of the village—around the world. Like colonization itself, the photograph transforms village culture forever. Moreover, the photograph's relations of visibility encode relations of power. Although the village is reordered by the image of Africa sold by the West, it also finds the means to reappropriate that image to maintain—with important changes—its own identity. If, indeed, Baroka ever does make the stamps, Sidi's image will become the image of Ilujinle, now asserting the Bale's status and the order of his society.

The play suggests that the rhetoric of photography need not have a predetermined shape, meaning, or consequence; instead, it takes part in the shifting network of social and political relations within which it is practiced. In this sense, *taking* a picture in *The Lion and the Jewel* is a much different matter than in *Three Sisters*. There is no photographer in Soyinka's play, no tripod, no flash, no act of photographing: the village girls reenact the photographer's arrival in ways that suggest the partiality (rather than the "objectivity") of the "one-eyed box" and the images it makes (11). While the village girls enact the photographer's car, Lakunle fittingly plays the role of the photographer with *"realistic miming,"* a restrained, Westernized performance surrounded by the more immediate physical exuberance of the dance. Here, the camera is not a fixed point of observation ostensibly outside the scene it discloses. Instead, there seems hardly to be a single point of privileged observation onstage, as the energetic dance-mime engulfs the photographer and his subject in a flurry of activity, activity which clearly exceeds the image that will appear in the photo. Chekhov's camera faces a field oriented frontally before it, framed by the upstage arch; Soyinka's "one-eyed box" is hardly able to demarcate a single scene of visibility before its monocular gaze. Rather than showing the camera constructing the tableau of "objectivity," Soyinka presents the camera selecting and interpreting what it will disclose from a field of activity that constantly escapes its view. Soyinka's photographer, and the instruments of Western representation he embodies—photography, comedy, theater—can never really find Africa in the lens.

The Lion and the Jewel implies a reciprocity between the rhetoric of theatrical production and the rhetorical dimension of social life. The forms of representation used in the theater—characterization, plotting, acting style, the disposition of the audience—are not inherently repressive or liberating; how those forms resemble, extend, or challenge our means of making sense outside the theater is what draws their rhetorical character into the larger arena of ideology and politics. Clearly, productions of *The Lion and the Jewel* in

Lagos, London, or New York would place the audience very differently in the spectacle of cross-cultural interaction. Onstage and off, the rhetoric of theater is never fixed, a formulaic body of strategies into which meanings are poured, a static texture of practices for realizing the ingrained meaning of the drama. Instead, we should see the rhetoric of modern theater—including the realism, poetic theater, and political theater I have discussed here—as a range of opportunities for shaping the experience of drama, opportunities that arise from, and help to create, the society of which they are a part. In *The Lion and the Jewel*, the machinery of European drama is shown to work in concert with other technologies for reproducing Western culture in the minds, on the bodies, and through the society of people it would control. Implying an affinity between photographing Africa and staging it, the play finally questions whether the necessary lies of our theater can stand apart from the fabrications of Western ideology, the coercive fictions that maintain the social order that *The Lion and the Jewel* attacks. In this sense, then, the play's allegory of postcolonial cultural exchange uses the figure of photography to embrace the process of theatrical production as well. Like Sidi's photograph, the theater provides the spectator with a partial vision, one that masks a sustaining authority in the fiction of a neutral sight. Such rhetoric marks the deepest levels of what Soyinka describes as the "social activity called theater" ("Drama" 64). The lesson of *The Lion and the Jewel*, and of the history of modern drama, is that this rhetoricity shapes our activity in the theater, and so helps to shape the world beyond the stage as well.

Works Cited

Acheson, James, and Kateryna Arthur, eds. *Beckett's Later Fiction and Drama: Texts for Company.* New York: St. Martin's, 1987.
Adorno, Theodor. "Commitment." *Aesthetics and Politics* 177–95.
Aesthetics and Politics. By Ernst Bloch, Georg Lukács, Bertolt Brecht, Walter Benjamin, Theodor Adorno. Afterword by Fredric Jameson. Translation ed. Ronald Taylor. 1977. London: Verso, 1980.
Althusser, Louis. "Ideology and Ideological State Apparatuses." *Lenin and Philosophy and Other Essays.* Trans. Ben Brewster. New York: Monthly Review Press, 1971. 127–86.
Ansorge, Peter. "Underground Explorations No. 4: War Games: Max Stafford-Clark and members of the Traverse Workshop talk to Peter Ansorge." *Plays and Players* (May 1972): 14–17, 61.
Appia, Adolphe. *The Work of Living Art. "The Work of Living Art" and "Man is the Measure of All Things."* Trans. H. D. Albright and Barnard Hewitt. Ed. Barnard Hewitt. Coral Gables: U of Miami P, 1960.
Archer, William. *About the Theatre.* London: T. Fisher Unwin, 1886.
———. *Play-Making.* New York: Dodd, Mead, 1912.
———. *The Theatrical "World" for 1893.* London: Walter Scott, n.d. [1894].
———. *The Theatrical "World" of 1894.* London: Walter Scott, 1895.
———. *The Theatrical "World" of 1897.* London: Walter Scott, 1898.
Artaud, Antonin. *Selected Writings.* Trans. Helen Weaver. Ed. Susan Sontag. New York: Farrar, Straus and Giroux, 1976.
Atkinson, Brooks. Rev. of *Dead End. New York Times* 29 October 1935.
———. Rev. of *Strange Interlude. New York Times* 31 January 1928.
Auden, W. H. *The Dance of Death. Plays.*
———. Rev. of *Modern Poetic Drama*, by Priscilla Thouless. *The Listener* 9 May 1934: 808.
———. *Plays and Other Dramatic Writings by W. H. Auden 1928–1938.* Vol. 1 of *The Complete Works of W. H. Auden.* Ed. Edward Mendelson. Princeton: Princeton UP, 1988.
Austin, Gayle. "The Madwoman in the Spotlight: Plays of Maria Irene Fornes." *Making a Spectacle: Feminist Essays on Contemporary Women's Theatre.* Ed. Lynda Hart. Ann Arbor: U of Michigan P, 1989. 76–85.
Bair, Deirdre. *Samuel Beckett: A Biography.* New York: Harcourt Brace Jovanovich, 1978.

Barker, Harley Granville. *Waste. Three Plays by Granville-Barker.* New York: Mitchell Kennedy, 1909.
Barnes, Ben. "Aspects of Directing Beckett." *Irish University Review* 14 (1984): 69–89.
Barnes, Peter. *Laughter! Collected Plays.* London: Heinemann, 1981.
———. "Still Standing Upright: Ben Jonson 350 Years Alive." *New Theatre Quarterly* 3(1987): 202–06.
Barrie, J. M. *The Plays of J. M. Barrie.* London: Hodder and Stoughton, 1928.
Barthes, Roland. *Critical Essays.* Trans. Richard Howard. Evanston: Northwestern UP, 1972.
———. *Writing Degree Zero.* Boston: Beacon, 1970.
Bathrick, David. "Brecht's Marxism and America." *Essays on Brecht: Theater and Politics.* Ed. Siegfried Mews and Herbert Knust. Chapel Hill: U of North Carolina P, 1974. 209–25.
Beckerman, Bernard. *Dynamics of Drama: Theory and Method of Analysis.* New York: Drama Book Specialists, 1979.
Beckett, Samuel. *Catastrophe. Collected Shorter Plays.*
———. *Collected Shorter Plays.* New York: Grove, 1984.
———. *Disjecta: Miscellaneous Writings and a Dramatic Fragment.* Ed. Ruby Cohn. New York: Grove, 1984.
———. *Endgame.* New York: Grove, 1958.
———. *Not I. Collected Shorter Plays.*
———. *Play. Collected Shorter Plays.*
———. *Rough for Radio II. Collected Shorter Plays.*
———. *Waiting for Godot.* New York: Grove, 1954.
———. *What Where. Collected Shorter Plays.*
Beerbohm, Max. *Around Theatres.* 1930. New York: Greenwood, 1968.
Belsey, Catherine. "Constructing the subject: deconstructing the text." *Feminist Criticism and Social Change: Sex, Class and Race in Literature and Culture.* Ed. Judith Newton, Deborah Rosenfelt. London: Methuen, 1985. 45–64.
Benjamin, Walter. "The Work of Art in the Age of Mechanical Reproduction." *Illuminations.* Ed. Hannah Arendt. New York: Schocken, 1969. 217–51.
Bennett, Benjamin. *Modern Drama and German Classicism: Renaissance from Lessing to Brecht.* Ithaca: Cornell UP, 1979.
———. *Theater as Problem: Modern Drama and Its Place in Literature.* Ithaca: Cornell UP, 1990.
Berger, Harry, Jr. "Bodies and Texts." *Representations* 17 (Winter 1987): 144–66.
Blackman, Maurice. "The shaping of a Beckett text: *Play.*" *Journal of Beckett Studies* 10 (1985): 87–107.
Blau, Herbert. "The American Dream in American Gothic: The Plays of Sam Shepard and Adrienne Kennedy." *Modern Drama* 27 (1984): 520–39.
———. *The Audience.* Baltimore: Johns Hopkins UP, 1990.
Bly, Mark, and Doug Wager. "Theater of the Extreme: An Interview with Peter Barnes." *Theater* 12: 2 (1981): 43–48.

Bogard, Travis. *Contour in Time: The Plays of Eugene O'Neill.* rev. ed. New York: Oxford UP, 1988.
Bond, Edward. "The Activists Papers." *"The Worlds" with "The Activists Papers."*
———. Appendix: First Author's Note to *Saved. Plays: One* 309–12.
———. "Author's Note: On Violence." *Plays: One* 9–17.
———. *"Bingo" and "The Sea."* New York: Hill and Wang, 1975.
———. "British Secret Playwright." *Plays and Players* (June 1985): 8–9.
———. "Drama and the Dialectics of Violence." *Theatre Quarterly* 2 (January–March 1972): 4–14.
———. "Notes on Acting *The Woman.*" *The Woman* 125–29.
———. "On Brecht: A Letter to Peter Holland." *Theatre Quarterly* 8 (Summer 1978): 34–35.
———. *Plays: One.* London: Eyre Methuen, 1977.
———. *The Pope's Wedding. Plays: One.*
———. *Saved. Plays: One.*
———. "Scenes of War and Freedom: A Short Essay." *The Woman* 133–36.
———. "Us, Our Drama and the National Theatre." *Plays and Players* (October 1978): 8–9.
———. *The Woman: Scenes of War and Freedom.* New York: Hill and Wang, 1979.
———. *The Worlds. "The Worlds" with "The Activists Papers."*
———. *"The Worlds" with "The Activists Papers."* London: Eyre Methuen, 1980.
Booth, Michael R., ed. *Dramas 1850–1900.* Oxford: Clarendon, 1969. Vol. 2 of *English Plays of the Nineteenth Century.* 5 vols. 1969–76.
———. *Pantomimes, Extravaganzas and Burlesques.* Oxford: Clarendon, 1976. Vol. 5 of *English Plays of the Nineteenth Century.* 5 vols. 1969–76.
Bornemann, Ernest. "The Real Brecht." Marowitz, et al., eds. *The Encore Reader* 136–52.
Bradford, Curtis B. *Yeats at Work.* Carbondale: Southern Illinois UP, 1965.
Brater, Enoch. *Beyond Minimalism: Beckett's Late Style in the Theater.* New York: Oxford UP, 1987.
———, ed. *Feminine Focus: The New Women Playwrights.* New York: Oxford UP, 1989.
Brecht, Bertolt. *Brecht on Theatre: The Development of an Aesthetic.* Ed. and trans. John Willett. New York: Hill and Wang, 1964; London: Methuen, 1978.
———. *The Messingkauf Dialogues.* Trans. John Willett. London: Eyre Methuen, 1978.
Brenton, Howard. *The Churchill Play.* London: Eyre Methuen, 1974.
———. *Hitler Dances.* London: Methuen, 1982.
———. "Petrol Bombs through the Proscenium Arch." *Theatre Quarterly* 5 (March–May 1975): 4–20.
———. *Plays: One.* London: Methuen, 1986.

Browne, E. Martin. *The Making of T. S. Eliot's Plays*. Cambridge: Cambridge UP, 1969.
Bruder, Melissa, Lee Michael Cohn, Madeleine Olnek, Nathaniel Pollack, Robert Previto, and Scott Zigler. *A Practical Handbook for the Actor*. Introd. David Mamet. New York: Vintage, 1986.
Brustein, Robert. *The Theatre of Revolt: An Approach to Modern Drama*. Boston: Little, Brown, 1964.
Bryden, Ronald. Rev. of *The Entertainer*. *Plays and Players* (February 1975): 22–23.
Bull, John. *New British Political Dramatists*. London: Macmillan, 1984.
Burke, Kenneth. *A Grammar of Motives*. 1945. Berkeley: U of California P, 1969.
———. *A Rhetoric of Motives*. 1950. Berkeley: U of California P, 1969.
Calder, Angus. *The People's War: Britain 1939–45*. London: Jonathan Cape, 1969.
Cargill, Oscar, N. Bryllion Fagin, and William Fisher, eds. *O'Neill and His Plays: Four Decades of Criticism*. New York: New York UP, 1961.
Rev. of *Carve Her Name with Pride*. *Variety* 18 February 1958.
Case, Sue-Ellen. *Feminism and Theatre*. New York: Methuen, 1988.
———. "From Split Subject to Split Britches." Brater, *Feminine Focus* 126–46.
Rev. of *The Caucasian Chalk Circle*. *The Times* 3 August 1956.
Cave, Richard Allen. "A Style for Yeats's Dance-Plays: 'The More Passionate the Art the More Marked is the Selection.' " *Yearbook of English Studies* 9 (1979): 135–53.
Chabert, Pierre, "The body in Beckett's theatre." *Journal of Beckett Studies* 8 (1982): 23–25.
———. "Samuel Beckett: Lieu Physique, Théâtre du Corps." *Cahiers Renaud Barrault* 106 (1983): 80–98.
Chothia, Jean. *Forging a Language: A Study of the Plays of Eugene O'Neill*. Cambridge: Cambridge UP, 1979.
Christy, Desmond. Rev. of *Poppy*. *Plays and Players* (January 1984): 40–41.
Chubb, Kenneth, and the Editors of *Theatre Quarterly*. "Metaphors, Mad Dogs and Old Time Cowboys—Interview with Sam Shepard." *American Dreams: The Imagination of Sam Shepard*. Ed. Bonnie Marranca. New York: Performing Arts Journal Publications, 1981. 187–209.
Churchill, Caryl. *Cloud Nine*. *Plays: One*.
———. *Cloud 9*. New York: Methuen, 1984.
———. Introduction to *Cloud Nine*. *Plays: One*.
———. *Plays: One*. London: Methuen, 1985.
Clurman, Harold. *The Fervent Years*. 1945. New York: Da Capo, 1983.
Coats, R. H. *John Galsworthy as a Dramatist*. London: Duckworth, 1926.
Cocteau, Jean. Préface de 1922. *Les Mariés de la Tour Eiffel*. Vol. 7 of *Oeuvres Complètes*. Geneva: Marguerat, 1948. 11 vols. 1946–50.
Cohn, Ruby. *Just Play: Beckett's Theater*. Princeton: Princeton UP, 1980.
Coveney, Michael. Rev. of *Poppy*. *Financial Times* 6 October 1982.

Craig, Edward Gordon. "The Actor and the Über-Marionette." *On the Art of the Theatre*. 1911. New York: Theatre Arts, 1957. 54–94.
Cummings, Scott. "Seeing with Clarity: The Visions of Maria Irene Fornes." *Theater* 17: 1 (1985): 51–56.
"Dame for a laugh." *Plays and Players* (December 1985): 16–17.
Rev. of *The Dance of Death* and *Sweeney Agonistes*. *The Times* 2 October 1935.
Davis, Tracy C. "The Actress in Victorian Pornography." *Theatre Journal* 41 (1989): 294–315.
Rev. of *Dead End*. *Brooklyn Citizen* 29 October 1935.
Rev. of *Dead End*. *Variety* 30 October 1935.
" 'Dead End' Cast Shuns Make-Up." *New York World-Telegram* 21 December 1935.
Diamond, Elin. "Brechtian Theory/Feminist Criticism: Toward a Gestic Feminist Criticism." *The Drama Review* 32 (T-117, Spring 1988): 82–94.
———. "(In)Visible Bodies in Churchill's Theatre." *Theatre Journal* 40 (1988): 188–204.
———. "Mimesis, Mimicry, and the 'True-Real.' " *Modern Drama* 32 (1989): 58–72.
———. "Refusing the Romanticism of Identity: Narrative Interventions in Churchill, Benmussa, Duras." *Theatre Journal* 37 (1985): 273–86.
Dolan, Jill. *The Feminist Spectator as Critic*. Ann Arbor: UMI Research P, 1988.
Donoghue, Denis. *The Third Voice: Modern British and American Verse Drama*. Princeton: Princeton UP, 1959.
Duckworth, Colin. "Beckett's New *Godot*." Acheson and Arthur 175–92.
Eagleton, Terry. "Nature and Violence: The Prefaces of Edward Bond." *Critical Quarterly* 26 (Spring and Summer 1984): 127–35.
Edgar, David. "Ten Years of Political Theatre, 1968–78." *Theatre Quarterly* 8 (Winter 1979): 25–33.
Eliot, T. S. "The Ballet." *Criterion* 3 (1925): 441–43.
———. *The Complete Plays of T. S. Eliot*. New York: Harcourt, Brace and World, 1967.
———. "Dramatis Personae." *Criterion* 1 (1923): 303–06.
———. "In Memoriam: Marie Lloyd." *Criterion* 1 (1923): 192–95.
———. Introduction. *Shakespeare and the Popular Dramatic Tradition*. By S. L. Bethell. London: Staples, 1944.
———. "London Letter." *Dial* 70 (June 1921): 686–91.
———. "London Letter." *Dial* 73 (December 1922): 659–63.
———. *Murder in the Cathedral*. *The Complete Plays of T. S. Eliot*.
———. "The Need for Poetic Drama." *Listener* 25 November 1936: 994–95.
———. Rev. of *Noh, or Accomplishment*, by Ernest Fenollosa and Ezra Pound. *Egoist* 4: 7 (August 1917): 102–03.
———. "Personality and Demonic Possession." *Virginia Quarterly Review* 10 (1934): 94–103.
———. "Poetry and Drama." *Selected Prose of T. S. Eliot*. Ed. Frank Kermode. New York: Harcourt Brace Jovanovich, 1975.

———. *The Sacred Wood.* 1920. London: Methuen, 1960.
———. *Selected Essays.* 1932. San Diego: Harcourt Brace Jovanovich, 1978.
———. *The Use of Poetry and the Use of Criticism.* Cambridge: Harvard UP, 1933.
Ellmann, Richard. *Yeats: The Man and the Masks.* 1948. New York: Norton, 1978.
Esslin, Martin. "Introduction: Approaches to Reality." *The New Theatre of Europe 4.* New York: Dell, 1970. vi–xxx.
———. Rev. of *Murder in the Cathedral. Plays and Players* (October 1972): 44–45.
———. *The Theatre of the Absurd.* 1961. New York: Anchor, 1969.
———. "Towards the Zero of Language." Acheson and Arthur 35–49.
Evans, Gareth Lloyd, and Barbara Evans, eds. *Plays in Review 1956–1980: British Drama and the Critics.* New York: Methuen, 1985.
Everett, Barbara. "The New Style of *Sweeney Agonistes.*" *Yearbook of English Studies* 14 (1984): 243–63.
Fergusson, Francis. *The Idea of a Theater.* 1949. Princeton: Princeton UP, 1972.
Fetterley, Judith. "Reading about Reading: 'A Jury of Her Peers,' 'The Murders in the Rue Morgue,' and 'The Yellow Wallpaper.' " Flynn and Schweickart 147–64.
Finney, Gail. *Women in Modern Drama: Freud, Feminism, and European Theater at the Turn of the Century.* Ithaca: Cornell UP, 1989.
Finter, Helga. "Experimental Theatre and Semiology of Theatre: The Theatricalization of Voice." Trans. E. A. Walker and Kathryn Grardal. *Modern Drama* 26 (1983): 501–17.
Fisher, Philip. "Appearing and Disappearing in Public: Social Space in Late-Nineteenth-Century Literature and Culture." *Reconstructing American Literary History.* Ed. Sacvan Bercovitch. Cambridge: Harvard UP, 1986. 155–88.
Flanagan, Hallie. *Dynamo.* New York: Duell, Sloan and Pearce, 1943.
Flannery, James. *W. B. Yeats and the Idea of a Theatre.* New Haven: Yale UP, 1976.
Floyd, Virginia, ed. *Eugene O'Neill at Work: Newly Released Ideas for Plays.* New York: Fredrick Ungar, 1981.
Flynn, Elizabeth A., and Patrocinio P. Schweickart, eds. *Gender and Reading: Essay on Readers, Texts, and Contexts.* Baltimore: Johns Hopkins UP, 1986.
Fornes, Maria Irene. *Fefu and Her Friends. Wordplays: An Anthology of New American Drama.* New York: Performing Arts Journal Publications, 1980.
———. "Interview." *Performing Arts Journal* 2 (Winter 1978): 106–11.
———. "Notes on *Fefu.*" *Soho Weekly News* 12 June 1978.
Forte, Jeanie. "Realism, Narrative, and the Feminist Playwright—A Problem of Reception." *Modern Drama* 32 (1989): 115–27.
Foucault, Michel. *Discipline and Punish: The Birth of the Prison.* Trans. Alan Sheridan. New York: Vintage, 1979.

Fried, Michael. "Realism, Writing, and Disfiguration in Thomas Eakins's *Gross Clinic,* with a Postscript on Stephen Crane's Upturned Faces." *Representations* 9 (Winter 1985): 33–104.
Friedman, Barton R. *Adventures in the Deeps of the Mind.* Princeton: Princeton UP, 1977.
Frye, Northrop. *Anatomy of Criticism: Four Essays.* 1957. Princeton: Princeton UP, 1971.
Fyfe, Hamilton. *Arthur Wing Pinero.* London: Greening, 1902.
———. *Sir Arthur Pinero's Plays and Players.* London: Ernest Benn, 1936.
Gabriel, Gilbert W. Rev. of *Dead End. New York American* 29 October 1935.
Gagnier, Regenia. *Idylls of the Marketplace: Oscar Wilde and the Victorian Public.* Stanford: Stanford UP, 1986.
Gallop, Jane. "The Father's Seduction." *The (M)other Tongue: Essays in Feminist Psychoanalytic Interpretation.* Ed. Shirley Nelson Garner, Claire Kahane, Madelon Sprengnether. Ithaca: Cornell UP, 1985. 33–50.
Galsworthy, John. *The Inn of Tranquillity.* London: William Heinemann, 1933.
———. *Letters from John Galsworthy 1900–1932.* Ed. Edward Garnett. London: Jonathan Cape; New York: Scribner, 1934.
———. *The Plays of John Galsworthy.* New York: Scribner, 1928.
———. *The Silver Box. Plays.*
———. *The Skin Game. Plays.*
Gardner, Helen. *The Art of T. S. Eliot.* 1949. London: Cresset P, 1961.
Garner, Stanton B., Jr. "Theatricality in *Mankind* and *Everyman.*" *Studies in Philology* 84 (1987): 272–85.
Glaspell, Susan. *A Jury of Her Peers.* London: Ernest Benn, 1927.
———. *Trifles.* New York: Frank Shay for the Washington Square Players, 1916.
Goldman, Michael. *The Actor's Freedom.* New York: Viking, 1975.
———. "Fear in the Way: The Design of Eliot's Drama." *Eliot in His Time.* Ed. A. Walton Litz. Princeton: Princeton UP, 1973. 155–80.
———. "The Ghost of Joy: Reflections on Romanticism and the Forms of Modern Drama." *Romantic and Modern: Revaluations of Literary Tradition.* Ed. George Bornstein. Pittsburgh: U of Pittsburgh P, 1977. 58–68.
Gray, Paul. "From Russia to America: A Critical Chronology." *Stanislavski and America.* Ed. Erika Munk. New York: Hill and Wang, 1966.
Grein, J. T. *Dramatic Criticism.* London: John Long, 1899.
———. *Dramatic Criticism 1900–1901.* London: Greening, 1902.
Gugelberger, Georg M., ed. *Marxism and African Literature.* London: James Currey, 1985.
Hall, Peter. "A Director's Approach." *A Casebook on Harold Pinter's "The Homecoming."* Ed. John Lahr. New York: Grove, 1971. 9–25.
Hare, David. "A Lecture Given at King's College, Cambridge." *Licking Hitler.* London: Faber and Faber, 1978. 57–71.
Harrop, John. "The Last Laugh: Comedy as Political Touchstone in Britain from *The Entertainer* to *Comedians.*" *Theatre Journal* 32 (1980): 5–16.

Hay, Malcolm, and Philip Roberts. *Bond: A Study of His Plays*. London: Eyre Methuen, 1980.

———, eds. *Edward Bond: A Companion to His Plays*. London: TQ Publications, 1978.

Hayman, Ronald. *British Theatre Since 1955: A Reassessment*. Oxford: Oxford UP, 1979.

Hayter, Alethea. "Tickling a rhinoceros." *Times Literary Supplement* 22 October 1982: 1161.

Heppenstall, Rayner. "Poetry." *New English Weekly* 25 July 1935: 293.

Hiley, Jim. "Liberating laughter: Peter Barnes and Peter Nichols in interview." *Plays and Players* (March 1978): 14–17.

———. "Revolution in Pantoland." *Plays and Players* (December 1977): 12–14.

———. *Theatre at Work: The Story of the National Theatre's Production of Brecht's "Galileo."* London: Routledge and Kegan Paul, 1981.

The History of Dick Whittington, Lord Mayor of London: With the Adventures of His Cat. [1814].

Hobson, Harold. Rev. of *The Recruiting Officer. George Farquhar, "The Recruiting Officer": The National Theatre Production*. Ed. Kenneth Tynan. London: Rupert Hart-Davis, 1965. 141–42.

Hoellering, George. "Filming *Murder in the Cathedral*." *T. S. Eliot: A Symposium for His Seventieth Birthday*. Ed. Neville Braybrooke. New York: Books for Libraries P, 1968. 81–84.

Hogan, Robert, and James Kilroy. *The Abbey Theatre: The Years of Synge 1905–1909*. Dublin: Dolmen; Atlantic Highlands: Humanities, 1978. Vol. 3 of *The Modern Irish Drama: A Documentary History*. 5 vols. 1975–84.

Holland, Peter. "Brecht, Bond, Gaskill, and the Practice of Political Theatre." *Theatre Quarterly* 8 (Summer 1978): 24–34.

Howard, Bronson. *Autobiography of a Play*. Papers on Playwriting 2. New York: Dramatic Museum of Columbia University, 1914.

Howard, June. *Form and History in American Literary Naturalism*. Chapel Hill: U of North Carolina P, 1985.

Hull, S. Loraine. *Strasberg's Method As Taught by Lorrie Hull*. Woodbridge: Ox Bow, 1985.

Hynes, Samuel. *The Auden Generation: Literature and Politics in England in the 1930s*. London: Bodley Head, 1976.

———. *The Edwardian Turn of Mind*. Princeton: Princeton UP, 1968.

Ibsen, Henrik. *The Wild Duck*. *The Complete Major Prose Plays*. Ed. and trans. Rolf Fjelde. New York: New American Library, 1978.

Isaacs, Edith J. R. "See America First." *Theatre Arts Monthly* (December 1935): 88–93.

Isherwood, Christopher. *Lions and Shadows*. Norfolk, Conn.: New Directions, 1947.

Jameson, Fredric. *The Political Unconscious: Narrative as a Socially Symbolic Act*. Ithaca: Cornell UP, 1981.

———. "Postmodernism and Consumer Society." *The Anti-Aesthetic: Essays on Postmodern Culture.* Ed. Hal Foster. Port Townsend: Bay Press, 1983. 111–25.

———. "Reflections in Conclusion." *Aesthetics and Politics* 196–213.

JanMohamed, Abdul R. *Manichean Aesthetics: The Politics of Literature in Colonial Africa.* Amherst: U of Massachusetts P, 1983.

Johnstone, Richard. "Television Drama and the People's War: David Hare's *Licking Hitler,* Ian McEwan's *The Imitation Game,* and Trevor Griffiths's *Country." Modern Drama* 28 (1985): 189–97.

Jones, David Richard. *Great Directors at Work: Stanislavsky, Brecht, Kazan, Brook.* Berkeley: U of California P, 1986.

Jones, Eldred. "Progress and Civilization in the Work of Wole Soyinka." *Perspectives on African Literature.* Ed. Christopher Heywood. New York: Africana, 1971. 129–37.

Jones, Eldred Durosimi. *The Writings of Wole Soyinka.* 3d ed. London: James Currey; Portsmouth, N.H.: Heinemann, 1988.

Jones, Mervyn. "Peter Nichols, the playwright who has had enough." *Drama* 148 (1983): 7–8.

Kaplan, Amy. *The Social Construction of American Realism.* Chicago: U of Chicago P, 1988.

Kauffman, Stanley. Rev. of *Fefu and Her Friends. New Republic* 25 February 1978: 38.

Kennedy, Dennis. *Granville Barker and the Dream of Theatre.* Cambridge: Cambridge UP, 1985.

Kenner, Hugh. *The Invisible Poet: T. S. Eliot.* London: W. H. Allen, 1960.

Keyssar, Helene. *Feminist Theatre.* London: Macmillan, 1984.

Kingsley, Sidney. *Dead End. Sixteen Famous Plays.* Ed. Bennett A. Cerf and Van H. Cartmell. New York: Random House, 1941.

Knowlson, James. "Extracts from an unscripted interview with Billie Whitelaw." *Journal of Beckett Studies* 3 (1978): 85–90.

———, ed. *Samuel Beckett: An Exhibition.* London: Turret, 1971.

———. "State of play: performance changes and Beckett scholarship." *Journal of Beckett Studies* 10 (1985): 108–20.

Kolodny, Annette. "A Map for Rereading: Gender and the Interpretation of Literary Texts." *The New Feminist Criticism: Essays on Women, Literature, and Theory.* Ed. Elaine Showalter. New York: Pantheon, 1985. 46–62.

Kretzmer, Herbert. Rev. of *Saved. Daily Express* 4 November 1965. Roberts, *Bond on File* 16.

Kruger, Loren. "The Dis-Play's the Thing: Gender and the Public Sphere in Contemporary British Theater." *Theatre Journal* 42 (1990): 27–47.

Lewis, Robert. *Method—or Madness?* New York: Samuel French, 1958.

Lindfors, Bernth. "Wole Soyinka, When Are You Coming Home?" *Yale French Studies* 53 (1976): 197–210.

Revs. of *The Lion and the Jewel. Cultural Events in Africa* 12 (December 1966).

Locke, Fred. *Dick Whittington and His Cat: Book of Words and Songs for Performance at Theatre Royal, Edinburgh.* 16 December 1893.

Lukács, Georg. "Realism in the Balance." *Aesthetics and Politics* 28–59.
———. "The Sociology of Modern Drama." Trans. Lee Baxandall. *The Theory of the Modern Stage*. Ed. Eric Bentley. Harmondsworth: Penguin, 1976. 421–50.
Lustig, Vera. "Howard Brenton in Profile." *Drama* 171 (1989): 15–18.
MacCarthy, Desmond. *The Court Theatre 1904–1907: A Commentary and Criticism*. London: A. H. Bullen, 1907.
McConachie, Bruce A. "Using the Concept of Cultural Hegemony to Write Theatre History." *Intrepreting the Theatrical Past: Essays in the Historiography of Performance*. Ed. Thomas Postlewait and Bruce A. McConachie. Iowa City: U of Iowa P, 1989. 37–58.
McDonald, Jan. *The "New Drama" 1900–1914*. London: Macmillan; New York: Grove, 1986.
McMillan, Dougald. "Human Reality and Dramatic Method: *Catastrophe, Not I*, and the Unpublished Plays." Acheson and Arthur 98–114.
McMillan, Dougald, and Martha Fehsenfeld, eds. *Beckett in the Theatre. Volume 1: from "Waiting for Godot" to "Krapp's Last Tape."* London: John Calder; New York: Riverrun, 1988.
Maeterlinck, Maurice. "The Tragical in Daily Life." *The Treasure of the Humble*. Trans. Alfred Sutro. New York: Dodd, Mead; London: George Allen, 1902.
Mander, Raymond, and Joe Mitchenson. *Pantomime: A Study in Pictures*. London: Peter Davies, 1973.
Marcus, Jane Connor. "Elizabeth Robins." Diss. Northwestern U, 1973.
Marker, Frederick J., and Lise-Lone Marker. *Ibsen's Lively Art: A Performance Study of the Major Plays*. Cambridge: Cambridge UP, 1989.
Marker, Lise-Lone. *David Belasco: Naturalism in the American Theatre*. Princeton: Princeton UP, 1975.
Marowitz, Charles. *The Method as Means*. London: Herbert Jenkins, 1961.
Marowitz, Charles, Tom Milne, and Owen Hale, eds. *The Encore Reader*. London: Methuen, 1965.
Matthews, Brander. *The Principles of Playmaking and Other Discussions of the Drama*. New York: Scribner, 1919.
———. *A Study of the Drama*. Boston: Houghton Mifflin, 1910.
Medley, Robert. *Drawn from the Life: A Memoir*. London: Faber and Faber, 1983.
Meisel, Martin. *Realizations: Narrative, Pictorial, and Theatrical Arts in Nineteenth-Century England*. Princeton: Princeton UP, 1983.
———. *Shaw and the Nineteenth-Century Theater*. Princeton: Princeton UP, 1963.
Meisner, Sanford, and Dennis Longwell. *Sanford Meisner on Acting*. New York: Vintage, 1987.
Mielziner, Jo. *Designing for the Theatre: A Memoir and a Portfolio*. New York: Atheneum, 1965.
Morley, Sheridan. " 'Poppy' in the wars." *The Times* 5 October 1982.
Rev. of *Mother Courage and Her Children*. *The Times* 28 August 1956.

Murphy, Brenda. *American Realism and American Drama, 1880—1940.* Cambridge: Cambridge UP, 1987.
Nazareth, Peter. *An African View of Literature.* Evanston: Northwestern UP, 1974.
Newhall, Beaumont. *The History of Photography.* Rev. ed. New York: Museum of Modern Art, 1982.
Ngugi wa Thiong'o. *Decolonising the Mind: The Politics of Language in African Literature.* London: James Currey; Nairobi: Heinemann Kenya; Portsmouth, N.H.: Heinemann, 1986.
Nichols, Peter. *Poppy.* London: Methuen, 1982.
O'Casey, Sean. *Innishfallen, Fare Thee Well.* New York: Macmillan, 1949.
Odets, Clifford. *Awake and Sing! Six Plays of Clifford Odets.* New York: Grove, 1979.
O'Neill, Eugene. *The Great God Brown. Nine Plays.*
———. *Long Day's Journey Into Night.* New Haven: Yale UP, 1956.
———. "Memoranda on Masks." Cargill 116–22.
———. *Nine Plays.* New York: Random House, 1954.
———. *Selected Letters of Eugene O'Neill.* Ed. Travis Bogard and Jackson R. Bryer. New Haven: Yale UP, 1988.
———. *Strange Interlude. Nine Plays.*
Onoge, Omafume F. "The Crisis of Consciousness in Modern African Literature: A survey (1974)." Gugelberger 21–49.
Osborne, John. *The Entertainer.* Harmondsworth: Penguin, 1983.
"Pantomime." *The Encyclopedia of World Theater.* Introd. Martin Esslin. New York: Scribner, 1977. 210–11.
Peter, John. *Vladimir's Carrot: Modern Drama and the Modern Imagination.* Chicago: U of Chicago P, 1987.
Peters, Margot. *Bernard Shaw and the Actresses.* New York: Doubleday, 1980.
Pinero, Arthur Wing. *The Collected Letters of Sir Arthur Pinero.* Ed. J. P. Wearing. Minneapolis: U of Minnesota P, 1974.
———. *The Second Mrs Tanqueray. Plays by A. W. Pinero.* Ed. George Rowell. Cambridge: Cambridge UP, 1986.
Pinter, Harold. *"The Caretaker" and "The Dumb Waiter": Two Plays by Harold Pinter.* New York: Grove, 1960.
———. *The Homecoming.* New York: Grove, 1965.
———. *Old Times.* New York: Grove, 1971.
Postlewait, Thomas. *Prophet of the New Drama: William Archer and the Ibsen Campaign.* Westport: Greenwood, 1986.
Pound, Ezra. Introduction. *The Classic Noh Theatre of Japan.* By Ernest Fenollosa and Ezra Pound. New York: New Directions, 1959. 3–15.
Quigley, Austin E. *The Modern Stage and Other Worlds.* London: Methuen, 1985.
Rabkin, Gerald. *Drama and Commitment: Politics in the American Theatre of the Thirties.* Bloomington: Indiana UP, 1964.
Rice, Elmer. *The Adding Machine. Seven Plays.*
———. *The Living Theatre.* New York: Harper and Bros., 1959.

———. *Minority Report: An Autobiography*. New York: Simon and Schuster, 1963.
———. *Seven Plays by Elmer Rice*. New York: Viking, 1950.
———. *Street Scene*. *Seven Plays*.
Riis, Jacob A. *How the Other Half Lives: Studies Among the Tenements of New York*. New York: Scribner, 1890.
Roach, Joseph R. *The Player's Passion: Studies in the Science of Acting*. Newark: U of Delaware P; London: Associated UP, 1985.
———. "Power's Body: The Inscription of Morality as Style." *Interpreting the Theatrical Past: Essays in the Historiography of Performance*. Ed. Thomas Postlewait and Bruce A. McConachie. Iowa City: U of Iowa P, 1989. 99–118.
Roberts, Philip. *Bond on File*. London: Methuen, 1985.
Robins, Elizabeth. *Ancilla's Share: An Indictment of Sex Antagonism*. 1924. Westport: Hyperion, 1976.
———. *The Convert*. 1907. London: Women's P; Old Westbury: Feminist P, 1980.
———. *Theatre and Friendship: Some Henry James Letters*. New York: Putnam, 1932.
———. *Votes for Women!* "*How the Vote Was Won*" *and Other Suffragette Plays*. Ed. Dale Spender and Carole Hayman. London: Methuen, 1985.
———. *Way Stations*. New York: Dodd, Mead, 1913.
Rev. of *Saved*. *The Times* 4 November 1965. Evans and Evans 135–36.
Sayers, Michael. "A Year in the Theatre." *Criterion* 15 (1936): 648–62.
Scarry, Elaine. *The Body in Pain: The Making and Unmaking of the World*. New York: Oxford UP, 1985.
Schweickart, Patrocinio P. "Reading Ourselves: Toward a Feminist Theory of Reading." Flynn and Schweickart 31–62.
Scrimgeour, Gary. "Naturalist Drama and Galsworthy." *Modern Drama* 7 (1964): 65–78.
Shaw, George Bernard. *Mrs Warren's Profession*. *Plays Unpleasant*.
———. *Our Theatres in the Nineties*. 3 vols. London: Constable, 1932.
———. *Plays Unpleasant*. Harmondsworth: Penguin, 1975.
———. Preface. *Mrs Warren's Profession*. *Plays Unpleasant*.
Sheaffer, Louis. *O'Neill: Son and Playwright*. Boston: Little, Brown, 1968.
Shepard, Sam. *Curse of the Starving Class*. *Seven Plays*.
———. "Note to Actors." "*Angel City*" *and Other Plays*. New York: Urizen, 1980.
———. *Tooth of Crime*. *Seven Plays*.
———. *Seven Plays*. New York: Bantam, 1974.
Shiubhlaigh, Maire Nic. *The Splendid Years: Recollections of Maire Nic Shiubhlaigh as told to Edward Kenny*. Dublin: James Duffy, 1955.
Sidnell, Michael J. *Dances of Death: The Group Theatre of London in the Thirties*. London: Faber and Faber, 1984.
Sidnell, M. J. "Auden and the Group Theatre." *Auden, Plays* 490–502.
Sinfield, Alan. *Literature, Politics, and Culture in Postwar Britain*. Berkeley: U of California P, 1989.

Smith, Susan Valeria Harris. *Masks in Modern Drama*. Berkeley: U of California P, 1984.
Sobel, Bernard. "Watching the 'Dead End' Wheels go 'Round." *New York Herald Tribune* 29 December 1935.
Soyinka, Wole. "...And the Other Immigrant." *An African Treasury*. Ed. Langston Hughes. New York: Crown, 1960. 196–98.
———. "Drama and the Revolutionary Ideal." *In Person: Achebe, Awoonor, and Soyinka at the University of Washington*. Ed. Karen L. Morell. Seattle: Institute for Comparative and Foreign Area Studies, U of Washington; Austin: African and Afro American Studies and Research Center, U of Texas, 1975. 61–88.
———. *The Lion and the Jewel*. The Collected Plays 2. Oxford: Oxford UP, 1986.
Speaight, Robert. "With Becket in *Murder in the Cathedral*." *T. S. Eliot: The Man and His Work*. Ed. Allen Tate. New York: Delacorte, 1966. 182–93.
Spender, Stephen. "The Poetic Dramas of W. H. Auden and Christopher Isherwood." *New Writing* NS 1 (Autumn 1938): 102–08.
Stanislavski, Constantin. *An Actor Prepares*. Trans. Elizabeth Reynolds Hapgood. New York: Theatre Arts, 1936.
States, Bert O. *Great Reckonings in Little Rooms: On the Phenomenology of Theater*. Berkeley: U of California P, 1985.
Stoppard, Tom. *Jumpers*. New York: Grove, 1972.
Rev. of *Street Scene*. *New York Times* 11 January 1929.
Styan, J. L. *Modern Drama in Theory and Practice*. 3 vols. Cambridge: Cambridge UP, 1981.
Symons, Arthur. *Plays, Acting and Music: A Book of Theory*. London: Constable, 1909.
———. *Studies in Seven Arts*. Vol. 9 of *The Collected Works of Arthur Symons*. London: Martin Secker, 1924. 9 vols.
Szondi, Peter. *Theory of the Modern Drama*. Ed. and trans. Michael Hays. Minneapolis: U of Minnesota P, 1987.
Taylor, John Russell. Rev. of *Poppy*. *Plays and Players* (December 1982): 22–23.
———. Rev. of *Poppy*. *Drama* 147 (1983): 26–28.
Therborn, Göran. *The Ideology of Power and the Power of Ideology*. London: Verso, 1982.
Rev. of *Trumpets and Drums*. *The Times* 30 August 1956.
Turner, Victor. *Dramas, Fields, and Metaphors*. Ithaca: Cornell UP, 1974.
———. *From Ritual to Theatre: The Human Seriousness of Play*. New York: Performing Arts Journal Publications, 1982.
Tynan, Kenneth. Rev. of *The Caretaker*. Evans and Evans 98–99.
Ubersfeld, Anne. *L'école du spectateur: lire le théâtre 2*. Paris: Éditions sociales, 1981.
———. "Notes sur la dénégation théâtrale." *La rélation théâtrale*. Ed. Régis Durand. Lille: Presses Universitaires de Lille, 1980. 11–25.
Van Laan, Thomas. "*The Dumb Waiter*: Pinter's Play with the Audience." *Modern Drama* 24 (1984): 494–502.

Vendler, Helen Hennessy. *Yeats's "Vision" and the Later Plays*. Cambridge: Harvard UP, 1963.

Walkley, A. B. *More Prejudice*. London: William Heinemann, 1923.

———. *Pastiche and Prejudice*. London: William Heinemann, 1921.

———. *Playhouse Impressions*. London: T. Fisher Unwin, 1892.

Wandor, Michelene. *Understudies: Theatre and Sexual Politics*. London: Eyre Methuen, 1981.

Wardle, Irving. Rev. of *Hitler Dances*. *The Times* 28 March 1972.

———. "Opium and old lace." *The Times* 6 October 1982.

Whitaker, Thomas R. *Fields of Play in Modern Drama*. Princeton: Princeton UP, 1977.

———. *Tom Stoppard*. New York: Grove, 1983.

Whitelaw, Billie. "From Billie Whitelaw." *As No Other Dare Fail: For Samuel Beckett on His 80th Birthday by his Friends and Admirers*. London: John Calder; New York: Riverrun, 1986.

Wilcox, Leonard. "Modernism vs. Postmodernism: Shepard's *Tooth of Crime* and the Discourses of Popular Culture." *Modern Drama* 30 (1987): 560–73.

Wilde, Oscar. *The Writings of Oscar Wilde*. Ed. Isobel Murray. New York: Oxford UP, 1989.

Wiles, Timothy J. *The Theater Event: Modern Theories of Performance*. Chicago: U of Chicago P, 1980.

Wiley, Catherine. "The matter with manners: The New Woman and the problem play." *Themes in Drama* 11 (1989): 109–27.

Wilkie, Roy, and David Bradley. *The Subsidised Theatre*. Glasgow: William MacLellan, 1970.

Williams, Raymond. *Drama from Ibsen to Brecht*. New York: Oxford UP, 1969.

———. *Marxism and Literature*. Oxford: Oxford UP, 1977.

———. *Modern Tragedy*. Stanford: Stanford UP, 1966.

———. "Social environment and theatrical environment: the case of English naturalism." *English Drama: Forms and Development. Essays in Honour of Muriel Clara Bradbrook*. Ed. Marie Axton and Raymond Williams. Cambridge: Cambridge UP, 1977. 203–23.

Worsley, T. C. Rev. of *The Entertainer*. *New Statesman* 20 April 1957. Evans and Evans 56–58.

Worth, Katharine. *The Irish Drama of Europe from Yeats to Beckett*. London: Athlone, 1978.

———. *Revolutions in Modern English Drama*. London: G. Bell, 1972.

Worthen, W. B. *The Idea of the Actor: Drama and the Ethics of Performance*. Princeton: Princeton UP, 1984.

———. "*Still playing games*: Ideology and Performance in the Theater of Maria Irene Fornes." Brater, *Feminine Focus* 167–85.

Wright, Elizabeth. *Postmodern Brecht: A Re-Presentation*. London: Routledge, 1989.

Yeats, W. B. *At the Hawk's Well*. *Collected Plays of W. B. Yeats*.

———. *Autobiographies*. London: Macmillan, 1955.
———. *Collected Plays of W. B. Yeats*. New York: Macmillan, 1952.
———. *The Death of Cuchulain*. *Collected Plays*.
———. *Essays and Introductions*. New York: Macmillan, 1961.
———. *Explorations*. New York: Macmillan, 1962.
———. *Four Plays for Dancers*. London: Macmillan, 1921.
———. *The Letters of W. B. Yeats*. Ed. Alan Wade. New York: Macmillan, 1955.
———. *Mythologies*. New York: Macmillan, 1959.
Zinman, Toby Silverman. "Sam Shepard and Super-Realism." *Modern Drama* 29 (1986): 423–30.
Zola, Émile. "Le Naturalisme au théâtre." *Oeuvres critiques 2*. Vol. 11 of *Oeuvres Complètes*. Paris: Cercle du Livre Précieux, 1968. 14 vols. 1966–70.

Index

Abbey Theatre, 108, 148
Abortion, in realistic drama, 45–46
Absurd, theater of the. *See* Theater of the absurd
Acting: pathological, 20n; as rhetoric, 2–3. *See also* Poetic theater; Political theater; Realism in theater
An Actor Prepares (Stanislavski), 56n
Actors Studio, 10
Actresses: and prostitution, 38–39; and public women, 38–39, 47. *See also* "Woman with a past"
The Adding Machine (Rice), 6, 55, 63, 71–73
Adler, Stella, 56
Adorno, Theodor, 141n
Advertising, 88
Ainley, Henry, 114n.7
Akalaitis, Joann, 137n
Aladdin (pantomime), 174, 176
Alazon, 197
Albee, Edward: *Who's Afraid of Virginia Woolf?* 81
Alexander, George, 37n
Aliénation, 82, 89, 94n
Althusser, Louis, 147, 172
American Laboratory Theater, 60
American Place Theater, 190
American realism. *See* Realism in theater: American realism
American Repertory Theater, 137n
Anderson, Lindsay, 13
Anderson, Maxwell: *Winterset*, 76
Angel City (Shepard), 87
Antoine, André, 13, 19
Appia, Adolphe, 103
Archer, William, 18, 20n, 22, 23, 24, 41, 46n, 48–49, 155, 178
Arden, John: *The Workhouse Donkey*, 153
Artaud, Antonin, 7, 106–07, 160
The Ascent of F6 (Auden and Isherwood), 120
Atkinson, Brooks, 67–68, 77–78
At the Hawk's Well (Yeats), 108, 110–19

Auden, W. H., 7, 100, 119–23, 130, 131, 198; *The Dance of Death*, 107, 108, 120, 121–23, 125; *Paid on Both Sides*, 120
Auden, W. H., and Christopher Isherwood, 102, 107, 108, 122, 128, 130; *The Ascent of F6*, 120; *The Dog Beneath the Skin*, 120, 124; *On the Frontier*, 120
Audience: and film, 9; and ideology, 3; as participant, 3–4; and readers, 49, 50–51; and semiotics, 4–5; thematic descriptions of, 4. *See also* Poetic theater: and audience; Political theater: and audience; Realism in theater: and audience
Austin, Gayle, 190
Awake and Sing! (Odets), 63, 76
Ayckbourn, Alan: *The Norman Conquests*, 190

The Babes in the Woods (pantomime), 174–75
The Bacchae of Euripides (Soyinka), 195
Bancroft, Squire, 19
Barbican Theatre, 175, 180
Barker, Harley Granville, 13, 19; *Waste*, 46n
Barnes, Ben, 138
Barnes, Peter, 8, 169–73; *The Bewitched*, 169; *Laughter!* 169–73; *Red Noses*, 169; *The Ruling Class*, 169
Barrie, J. M.: *Peter Pan*, 178; *What Every Woman Knows*, 29
Barthes, Roland, 13, 14, 154
Bathrick, David, 152n.5
Baxter, Stanley, 176n.18
Beats (in Method acting), 57, 60, 62
Beckerman, Bernard, 4n.4
Beckett, Samuel, 7, 8, 10n, 86, 100, 108, 131–42, 145; *...but the clouds...*, 133n.19, 137; *Cascando*, 132; *Catastrophe*, 82n, 132, 134, 141, 142; *Endgame*, 83, 137n; *Footfalls*, 138, 139n; *Ghost Trio*, 137; *Happy Days*, 133n.19, 138; *Not I*, 107, 138–39, 139n, 142; *Play*,

221

Beckett, Samuel (*continued*)
135–37, 138, 139–40, 141, 142; *Quad*, 137; *Rockaby*, 132; *Rough for Radio II*, 133, 134–35; *Rough for Theatre I*, 133n.19; *That Time*, 132; *Waiting for Godot*, 81, 82, 88, 90, 131, 132, 133n.19, 134, 143, 145; *What Where*, 133, 136, 142
Beerbohm, Max, 48n
Belasco, David, *The Return of Peter Grimm*, 18
Belsey, Catherine, 49, 70
Benjamin, Walter, 10–11
Bennett, Benjamin, 3, 4n.5, 9, 69n, 192n.29
Bentham, Jeremy, 21
Berger, Harry, Jr., 21n
Bergman, Ingmar, 27n
Berliner Ensemble, 152, 153
Bernhardt, Sarah, 30, 104
Betrayal (Pinter), 83, 85
The Betwitched (Barnes), 169
Bingo (Bond), 93, 94
The Birthday Party (Pinter), 81, 83
Blackman, Maurice, 140n
The Blacks (Genet), 166
Blanche, Ada, 178
Blau, Herbert, 4, 62n, 88n
Bloody Poetry (Brenton), 158
Boleslavsky, Richard, 56, 60
Bond, Edward, 8, 29, 55, 89–98, 154–55, 155n.7, 160; *Bingo*, 93, 94; and Brecht, 89–91; *The Pope's Wedding*, 91–92; *Saved*, 6, 94–98; *The Woman*, 93; *The Worlds*, 93, 94n
Booth, Michael R., 175n.15
Bornemann, Ernest, 153
Box set, 5, 17, 88, 192. *See also* Realism in theater: staging of
Bradford, Curtis, 116n
Bradley, David, 177n
Brater, Enoch, 138n
Brecht, Bertolt, 7, 10n, 13, 107, 120, 121n, 148–52, 176; *The Caucasian Chalk Circle*, 153; *Galileo*, 155n.7, 169; influence on British and American theater, 7, 152–55; *Mother Courage and Her Children*, 153; *Threepenny Opera*, 195
Brenton, Howard, 8, 155n.7, 158–69, 193; *Bloody Poetry*, 158; *Christie in Love*, 158; *The Churchill Play*, 157, 159, 164–69; *Greenland*, 158; *Hitler Dances*, 157, 159–64; *Pravda*, 158; *The Romans in Britain*, 158; *Scott of the Antarctic*, 158; *Weapons of Happiness*, 158
Broadway musicals, 179, 180

Brook, Peter, 10
Brustein, Robert, 63
Bull, John, 159n
Buried Child (Shepard), 86
Burke, Kenneth, 2, 2n.1, 26n, 113n.5
…but the clouds… (Beckett), 133n.19, 137

Calder, Angus, 167n
Campbell, Herbert, 175n.16
Campbell, Mrs. Patrick, 30, 39
Camwood on the Leaves (Soyinka), 195
Candida (Shaw), 44n
The Caretaker (Pinter), 83–84
Carve Her Name with Pride (film), 160, 162
Cascando (Beckett), 132
Case, Sue-Ellen, 182
The Cat and the Moon (Yeats), 133n.19
Catastrophe (Beckett), 82n, 132, 134, 141, 142
The Caucasian Chalk Circle (Brecht), 153
Cave, Richard Allen, 115–16
Chabert, Pierre, 132, 139
The Chairs (Ionesco), 81
Chaplin, Charles: *The Great Dictator*, 170
Character. *See* Poetic theater: "character" in . . . ; Political theater: "character" in . . . ; Realism in theater: "character" in . . .
Chekhov, Anton, 12–13, 14, 68, 69, 84, 100, 102, 120, 123, 196; *The Cherry Orchard*, 93; *Three Sisters*, 12–13, 25, 194, 202; *Uncle Vanya*, 66
Chodorow, Nancy, 192n.28
Christie in Love (Brenton), 158
Churchill, Caryl, 8, 182, 183–87, 193; *Cloud Nine*, 43, 157, 169, 183–87; *Top Girls*, 187; *Vinegar Tom*, 158
Churchill, Winston: as character in Brenton's *The Churchill Play*, 165–69
The Churchill Play (Brenton), 157, 159, 164–69
Cinderella (pantomime), 174, 176
Citizen's Theatre of Glasgow, 177n
Cloud Nine (Churchill), 43, 157, 169, 183–87
Cluchey, Rick, 131
Clurman, Harold, 56n
The Cocktail Party (Eliot), 102
Cocteau, Jean, 100
Comedians (Griffiths), 169
Comedy: and colonialism, 198; conventions of, 197; romantic, 194
Commedia dell' arte, 65, 121
The Confidential Clerk (Eliot), 102

The Convert (Robins), 47
Coquelin, Constant, 104
Costello, Kevin, 161
Coveney, Michael, 175n.16
Coward, Noël, 120
Craig, Edward Gordon, 20, 103, 104, 133
Cross-cultural representation in theater and drama, 194–204; and the canon, 196; and commodification, 200–02; and ideology, 203; and realism, 202; visibility and power relations, 198, 201–03
Cross-dressing, 175, 183–85
Curse of the Starving Class (Shepard), 86, 88, 89

Dada performance, 103
Dance. *See* Poetic theater: and dance
The Dance of Death (Auden), 107, 108, 120, 121–23, 125
Daniels, Sarah, 53, 182, 183; *Masterpieces*, 194
The Danube (Fornes), 187
Davis, Tracy C., 38
Dead End (Kingsley), 6, 55, 77–80, 81, 98
Death and the King's Horseman (Soyinka), 195
Death of a Salesman (Miller), 56, 76, 147
The Death of Cuchulain, 118
Deirdre (Yeats), 109
Devine, George, 133, 140
Diamond, Elin, 182, 183n, 184, 185
Dick Whittington (Locke), 175, 177, 179n
Dick Whittington and His Cat (pantomime), 174–77, 179n
Digges, Dudley, 72
Dionysus in 69 (Performance Group), 160
Directors, 8, 9–10
The Dog Beneath the Skin (Auden and Isherwood), 120, 124
Dolan, Jill, 182n.23
A Doll's House (Ibsen), 14, 48
Donoghue, Denis, 2n.1, 113n.5
Doone, Rupert, 107
The Dreaming of the Bones (Yeats), 116
Dulac, Edmund, 113, 117
The Dumb Waiter (Pinter), 83
Duse, Eleonora, 30, 104
The Dynasts (Hardy), 20

Eagleton, Terry, 91n
Eakins, Thomas, 28

Edgar, David, 155n.8
Edison, Thomas, 16
The Elder Statesman (Eliot), 102, 130
Eliot, T. S., 7, 99–103, 105–06, 118, 122, 123–31, 133, 141; *The Cocktail Party*, 102; *The Confidential Clerk*, 102; *The Elder Statesman*, 102, 130; *The Family Reunion*, 102; *Murder in the Cathedral*, 107, 108, 123–31, 129n; *The Rock*, 125; *Sweeney Agonistes*, 107, 124n.13
Emotion memory (in Method acting), 56n, 77, 149
The Emperor Jones (O'Neill), 150n
The Empire Builders (Vian), 81
Endgame (Beckett), 83, 137n
The Entertainer (Osborne), 153, 155–57, 169
Environment. *See* Realism in theater: environment as theme in drama; environment onstage
Environmental theater, 164, 191
Epic theater, 13, 154. *See also* Brecht, Bertolt; Political theater
Epstein, Sabin, 163
Ervine, St. John, 75
Essentialism, 186
Esslin, Martin, 81, 98, 126n, 137
Euripides: *Medea*, 14
Everett, Barbara, 123n
Evolution. *See* Realism in theater: evolution . . .
Existential drama, 145
Expressionism, 5, 6, 13, 21, 55, 63, 70, 103. *See also* Realism in theater: and expressionism
Extravaganza, 17, 175n.15

The Family Reunion (Eliot), 102
Farquhar, George: *The Recruiting Officer* (Berliner Ensemble production), 152
Farr, Florence, 112
Fay, Frank, 112
Fefu and Her Friends (Fornes), 157, 187–93
Feminist theater, 157, 181–93; audience in, 181–83; and popular theater, 183. *See also* Political theater
Fergusson, Francis, 59–60
Fetterley, Judith, 51n
Film, 8, 9, 194
Finney, Gail, 44n
The Firebugs (Frisch), 82
Fisher, Philip, 56
Flanagan, Hallie, 124nn
Flannery, James, 112
Fluid boundaries, 191

Fogerty, Elsie, 124–25, 126n
Fool for Love (Shepard), 86
Footfalls (Beckett), 138, 139n
Foreman, Richard, 7, 103
Fornes, Maria Irene, 8, 82, 187–93; *The Danube*, 187; *Fefu and Her Friends*, 157, 187–93; *Tango Palace*, 187
Foucault, Michel, 21, 97, 133
Fourth wall, 5, 17. *See also* Realism in theater: staging of
Freud, Sigmund, 120
Fried, Michael, 26, 27–28
Friedman, Barton R., 118n
Friel, Brian, 82
"Fringe," 148
Frisch, Max: *The Firebugs*, 82
Fry, Christopher, 130
Frye, Northrop, 197
Fugard, Athol, John Kani, and Winston Ntshona: *Sizwe Bansi is Dead*, 194
Fyfe, Hamilton, 29–30, 40

Gagnier, Regenia, 40
Galileo (Brecht), 155n.7, 169
Gallop, Jane, 192n.29
Galsworthy, John, 30–36, 42, 76; class in, 32n; *The Silver Box*, 30–33, 35, 47, 74, 95; *The Skin Game*, 30, 33–36
Gardner, Helen, 126n
Garner, Stanton B., Jr., 126n
Garnett, Amaryllis, 163
Garrick, David, 2, 18
Gaskill, William, 10, 154n, 160
Gay and lesbian performance, 187
Geddes, Norman Bel, 77–79
Gems, Pam, 182; *Queen Christina*, 158
Genet, Jean, 26; *The Blacks*, 166
Gest, 49, 149–51, 173
Getting Out (Norman), 147
Ghost Trio (Beckett), 137
Gilbert, W. S., 176; and Arthur Sullivan, 183
Gilligan, Carol, 192n.28
Given circumstances (in Method acting), 57, 77
Glaspell, Susan, 49–53; *A Jury of Her Peers*, 49–53; *Trifles*, 49–53, 192
Gogarty, Oliver St. John, 105n.2
Goldman, Michael, 4n.4, 65n, 80n, 102n
Granville-Barker, Harley. *See* Barker, Harley Granville
Gray, Paul, 56n
Gray, Spalding, 160
The Great Dictator (Chaplin), 170

The Great God Brown (O'Neill), 63, 64, 66–67
Greenland (Brenton), 158
Gregory, Lady Augusta, 114n.7
Grein, J. T., 41, 42–43
Griffiths, Trevor: *Comedians*, 169; *Occupations*, 158
Grotowski, Jerzy, 160, 164
Group Theater (New York), 56n, 63, 148
Group Theatre (London), 107, 120, 121

The Hairy Ape (O'Neill), 63, 65
Hall, Peter, 85n, 154n
Hallman, William, 11n
Hamlet (Shakespeare), 65n, 199
Hands, Terry, 180
Happenings, 82
Happy Days (Beckett), 133n.19, 138
Hardy, Thomas, *The Dynasts*, 20
Hare, David, 155n.7; *Plenty*, 158; *Pravda*, 158
Harris, Augustus, 178
Harrop, John, 155n.8
Hauptmann, Gerhart, 53
Hay, Malcolm, and Philip Roberts, 94n, 95–96
Hayman, Carole, 159
Hayman, Ronald, 167
Heartbreak House (Shaw), 90
Hedda Gabler (Ibsen), 14, 59
Henley, Beth, 82
Herbert, Jocelyn, 154n, 160
Hiley, Jim, 155n.7, 169, 176n.18
The History of Dick Whittington, 174n
Hitler Dances (Brenton), 157, 159–64
Hobson, Harold, 152, 153, 155n.7
Hogan's Heroes (television series), 170–71
Holland, Peter, 92n
The Homecoming (Pinter), 83, 84–85, 96, 98
The Hour-Glass (Yeats), 111
Howard, Bronson, 41
Howard, June, 24
Howe, Tina, 182
How the Other Half Lives (Riis), 24
Hull, S. Loraine, 58–59
Hwang, David Henry: *M. Butterfly*, 158
Hynes, Samuel, 46n, 121n

Ibsen, Henrik, 12, 14, 16, 47, 54, 66, 68, 69, 84, 85, 100, 103, 123, 154; *A Doll's House*, 14, 48; *Hedda Gabler*, 14, 59; *Little Eyolf*, 46n; *The Master Builder*, 80, 84; *Rosmersholm*, 66, 84; *The Wild Duck*, 25–27, 28

The Iceman Cometh (O'Neill), 63, 66, 81
An Ideal Husband (Wilde), 30, 39
Improvisational theater, 9
Indians (Kopit), 158
Ionesco, Eugène: *The Chairs*, 81; *Rhinoceros*, 81–82
Irish realists, 19
Irving, Henry, 2, 17, 104
Isaacs, Edith, 78
Isherwood, Christopher, 102, 120. *See also* Auden, W. H., and Christopher Isherwood

Jacker, Corinne, 182
James, Henry, 46
Jameson, Fredric, 90, 157n, 164
JanMohamed, Abdul R., 197
Jarry, Alfred: *Ubu Roi*, 104
Johnstone, Richard, 167n
Joint Stock Company, 183n
Jones, David Richard, 62
Jones, Eldred, 196n, 199n
Jones, Henry Arthur: *Mrs Dane's Defence*, 30, 44n
Jones, Robert Edmond, 64n.5
Jonson, Ben, 169, 198n.4
Jumpers (Stoppard), 143–46, 197
A Jury of Her Peers (Glaspell), 49–53

Kaiser, Georg, 63
Kani, John, 194
Kaplan, Amy, 27
Kauffman, Stanley, 191n.27
Kazan, Elia, 13, 63
Kennedy, Adrienne, 193; *A Movie Star Has to Star in Black and White*, 194
Kennedy, Dennis, 32n, 46n
Kenner, Hugh, 102n
King Lear (Shakespeare), 90
Kingsley, Sidney, 77–80; *Dead End*, 6, 55, 77–80, 81, 98
Knight, G. Wilson, 195n
Knowlson, James, 138n
Kolodny, Annette, 50
Kongi's Harvest (Soyinka), 195
Kopit, Arthur: *Indians*, 158
Kruger, Loren, 187
Kuhn, Thomas, 56n

Labor theater, 148
Lady Windermere's Fan (Wilde), 30
Laughter! (Barnes), 169–73
Lawson, John Howard: *Roger Bloomer*, 72
Leno, Dan, 175n.16
Lesbian and gay performance, 187

Lewis, Robert, 57
Lidoff, Joan, 191n.28
The Lion and the Jewel (Soyinka), 8, 194–204
Little Eyolf (Ibsen), 46n
Living Theater: *Paradise Now*, 160
Lloyd, Marie, 99
Locke, Fred: *Dick Whittington*, 175, 177, 179n
Long Day's Journey Into Night (O'Neill), 6, 54, 56, 63, 68–69
Look Back in Anger (Osborne), 147
Love's Labour's Lost (Shakespeare), 197
Lugné-Poe, Aurélien, 104
Lukács, Georg, 24, 89, 91

Mabou Mines, 10
Macbeth (Shakespeare), 14
MacCarthy, Desmond, 48n
Macgowan, Kenneth, 64n.5
McGuinness, Frank: *Observe the Sons of Ulster Marching to the Somme*, 158
Machinal (Treadwell), 63, 72
Maeterlinck, Maurice, 103, 104, 110, 111, 114, 130, 133
Major Barbara (Shaw), 35
Mamet, David, 82
Man and Superman (Shaw), 44
Marcus, Jane, 45n
Marionettes and puppets, 20, 103–05, 120. *See also* Poetic theater: marionettes and puppets in
Marker, Frederick J., and Lise-Lone Marker, 27n
Marowitz, Charles, 57
Marx, Karl, 121, 153
Marx Brothers, 153
Masks: in O'Neill's plays, 64–67; in poetic theater, 111–12, 113–14, 124n.13
Massine, Leonid, 105–06
The Master Builder (Ibsen), 80, 84
Masterpieces (Daniels), 194
Masterpiece Theatre, 173
Matthews, Brander, 16–17, 21, 155
M. Butterfly (Hwang), 158
Medea (Euripides), 14
Meisel, Martin, 36, 73
Meisner, Sanford, 61
Melodrama, 17
Method acting, 6, 19, 56–62, 63, 65, 70, 77, 79, 87, 93, 150. *See also* Realism in theater: "character" in . . .
Metonymy, in realistic stage production, 26, 26n, 70, 88
Meyerhold, Vsevolod, 7, 20, 56, 103
Mielziner, Jo, 73–74, 75, 76

Miller, Arthur, 69, 86, 87, 96; *Death of a Salesman*, 56, 76, 147
Mise-en-scène. *See* Poetic theater: staging of; Political theater: staging of; Realism in theater: staging of
Monstrous Regiment, 10, 183
Morley, John, 176
Morton, Carlos: *Rancho Hollywood*, 158
Moscow Art Theater, 19, 56
Mother Courage and Her Children (Brecht), 153
Mountain Language (Pinter), 82n
A Movie Star Has to Star in Black and White (Kennedy), 194
Mrs Dane's Defence (Jones), 30, 44n
Mrs Warren's Profession (Shaw), 42–44
Müller, Heiner, 103
Murder in the Cathedral (Eliot), 107, 108, 123–31, 129n
Music hall, 99–100, 102–03, 120, 122, 123, 155–57

National Theatre, 152, 155n.7
Naturalism, 12n, 16; in fiction, 24; and realism, 6, 13, 89
Nazareth, Peter, 199
Negritude, 199
New drama (of 1890s), 23
Newhall, Beaumont, 12n
New realism, 13, 82
Newsreels, 180
New woman (of 1890s), 43, 175
New York Theater Strategy, 190
Ngugi wa Thiong'o, 195n, 197n
Nichols, Peter, 8, 173–81; *Poppy*, 169, 173–81
'night, Mother (Norman), 182
Noh theater; and poetic theater, 109, 110, 112, 124n.13
Norman, Marsha, 82, 182; *Getting Out*, 147; *'night, Mother*, 182
The Norman Conquests (Ayckbourn), 190
Northern Ireland, theater of, 148
Norton Anthology of World Masterpieces, 195
Not I (Beckett), 107, 138–39, 139n, 142
Ntshona, Winston, 194

Objectives (in Method acting), 57, 59
Objectivity. *See* Realism in theater: and objectivity
Observe the Sons of Ulster Marching to the Somme (McGuinness), 158
O'Casey, Sean, 111
Occupations (Griffiths), 158

Odets, Clifford, 76; *Awake and Sing!* 63, 76
Oh, What a Lovely War (Theatre Workshop), 169
Old Times (Pinter), 83, 85
Olivier, Laurence, 2
On Baile's Strand (Yeats), 109
One for the Road (Pinter), 82n
O'Neill, Eugene, 14, 63–70, 85; *The Emperor Jones*, 150n; *The Great God Brown*, 63, 64, 66–67; *The Hairy Ape*, 63, 65; *The Iceman Cometh*, 63, 66, 81; *Long Day's Journey Into Night*, 6, 54, 56, 63, 68–69; masks in, 64–67; *Strange Interlude*, 63, 64, 67–68, 69
O'Neill, James, 64n.4
Onoge, Omafume F., 201
On the Frontier (Auden and Isherwood), 120
Open Theater: *The Serpent*, 160
Opera, 9
Opera Wonyosi (Soyinka), 195
Osborne, John, 8, 157n, 193; *The Entertainer*, 153, 155–57, 169; *Look Back in Anger*, 147
Ouspenskaya, Maria, 60

Paid on Both Sides (Auden), 120
Pankhurst, Christabel, 45
Panopticon, 21
Pantomime, 17, 121, 174–81; audience in, 175–77
Paradise Now (Living Theater), 160
Participatory theater, 9, 160–61
Pastiche, 164
Performance art, 9
Performance Group, 164; *Dionysus in 69*, 160
Perspective: in film, 190–91; in poetic theater, 117; in realistic theater, 78, 117, 190–91. *See also* Realism in theater: staging of
Peter, John, 4n.4
Peter Pan (Barrie), 178
Peters, Margot, 45n
Photography, 12–13, 27, 124n.14, 194, 196, 200; and rhetoric of theater, 202–03. *See also* Realism in theater: and photography
The Picture of Dorian Gray (Wilde), 1
Pinero, Arthur Wing, 26–42, 76; *The Second Mrs Tanqueray*, 23, 24n, 28, 29–30, 36–42, 44n, 45
Pinter, Harold, 6, 29, 55, 82, 83–86, 87, 102, 183; *Betrayal*, 83, 85; *The Birthday Party*, 81, 83; *The Caretaker*, 83–84; *The Dumb Waiter*, 83; *The Homecoming*, 5–

6, 83, 84–85, 96, 98; *Mountain Language*, 82n; *Old Times*, 83, 85; *One for the Road*, 82n; *The Room*, 83
Play (Beckett), 135–37, 138, 139–40, 141, 142
A Play of Giants (Soyinka), 195
Plenty (Hare), 158
Poetic drama, 13. *See also* Poetic theater: and poetic drama; poetry in
Poetic theater, 5, 7, 10, 99–142, 203; acting in, 101, 102, 103–06, 109, 110, 113–15, 116, 119, 126–27, 128, 133, 136–37, 138; and actorless theater, 103; antibourgeois, 107; aristocratic, 103, 107; and audience, 7, 100, 102, 103, 106–08, 111, 114, 117–19, 121–25, 128–31, 133, 140–42; authority of the text in, 7, 101, 108, 110, 119, 131, 132, 133, 136, 137, 140, 142; the body in, 103, 105, 119, 132, 133, 135, 140, 141, 142; "character" in drama, 112, 125; "character" in performance, 113, 115, 125, 127; and dada performance, 103; and dance, 105–06, 109, 110, 115–17, 119; defined, 100–01; as depersonalizing, 7, 108, 136, 138; and expressionism, 103; function of the text in production of, 100, 102, 103, 107, 109, 118, 121, 124, 126, 132, 135; ideology of, 132; marionettes and puppets in, 103–05, 106, 108, 113, 114, 124, 137; masks in, 111–12, 113–14, 124n.13; movement in, 109–10, 114–15; and music hall, 99–100, 102–03, 120, 122, 123; and Noh theater, 109, 110, 112, 124n.13; and pantomime, 121; and poetic drama, 7, 99, 100–02, 109, 118–19, 120, 124, 130–31; poetry in, 101, 109, 118, 122–23, 125, 132–33, 137; and political theater, 131; and popular theater, 99–100, 120–21, 123–24; and the postmodern, 142; power relations in, 134, 135; prose and verse in, 122, 127, 128–29; and realism, 100–01, 106–08, 109, 110, 113, 114, 117, 120, 126, 127, 128, 131; and realistic acting, 104, 113, 114; and ritual, 109, 118, 119, 123, 125n; song in, 110, 111–13, 115, 117, 119; speech in, 101, 108, 109–10, 112–13, 115, 116, 117, 119, 125, 137; staging of (mise-en-scène), 110; and surrealist theater, 103; and *symboliste* theater, 111, 133; and torture, 133–34, 138–39, 142
Political phases of theater, 148

Political theater, 5, 7–8, 10, 143–93, 203; acting in, 159–61, 184; and audience, 7–8, 146–48, 149–52, 155, 158, 166–67, 168, 170, 172–73, 178, 180, 191–93; audience and history in, 159–64, 170–81; the body in, 184; Brechtian style of, 154, 154n, 165, 169; Brecht on, 148–52; Brecht's influence on British and American theater, 7–8, 152–55; "character" in drama, 150; "character" in performance, 149–50, 160, 161, 184; and class, 156–57; comic conventions in, 170; and cross-cultural exchange, 196; cross-playing in, 183–85; defined, 146–47; and feminist theater, 157, 181–83; and film, 161, 162–63; and gendered audience of realism, 188–93; gender in, 8, 157, 181–93; genre in, 8, 157, 169–81; and historical drama, 8, 157, 158–69; history and class in, 167–68; as ideological process, 146–47, 156; and music hall, 155–57; and pantomime, 174–81; and participatory theater, 160–61; pleasure and/or instruction in, 152–55, 166, 181; and poetic theater, 131; and politics of drama, 146; and politics of performance, 180–81, 186–87; and "poor theater," 164; and popular theater, 183; and the postmodern, 164; and power relations, 165; race and performance, 184; and realism, 21, 146–51, 152, 155, 157, 161, 170, 191; and realistic visibility, 191–93; sexuality and performance, 185–86; as social process, 147, 150, 168, 184; staging of (mise-en-scène), 187; and television, 161. *See also* Brecht, Bertolt; Feminist theater
"Poor theater," 82, 164
The Pope's Wedding (Bond), 91–92
Poppy (Nichols), 169, 173–81
Pornography, 38, 142, 200
Portable Theatre, 10, 158
Porter, Cole, 122
Postlewait, Thomas, 46n
Pound, Ezra, 109, 124n.13
Pravda (Brenton and Hare), 158
Pre-Raphaelite decoration, 111
Privacy. *See* Realism in theater: privacy and power in
Private moment (in Method acting), 63n
The Producers (film), 170
Proscenium, 5, 17, 94, 98. *See also* Realism in theater: staging of

Index

Provincetown Players, 19
Public solitude (in Method acting), 58, 63n, 65
Puppets. *See* Marionettes and puppets; Poetic theater: marionettes and puppets in
Puss-in-Boots (pantomime), 175

Quad (Beckett), 137
Queen Christina (Gems), 158
Quigley, Austin E., 3, 36–37

Rabkin, Gerald, 70
Raisonneur, 23
Rancho Hollywood (Morton), 158
Realism in theater, 5–7, 10, 12–98, 203; acting in, 6, 15, 17, 19–20, 54–62, 96 (*see also* Method acting); and alienation, 82; American realism, 27, 70–81; and audience, 5, 14, 15, 17, 20–25, 32, 36, 52, 53, 55, 69–70, 76–77, 79–80, 81, 83, 84, 92, 94, 97–98, 192; "character" in drama, 6, 18, 54, 55, 62, 65, 67, 69, 76, 80, 81, 83, 84, 86, 92–93, 95; "character" in performance, 18, 57–60, 61–62, 69, 87–88, 93, 96; and class, 6, 29, 30, 31–32, 33, 47–48, 74–75, 92, 97–98; contemporary, 81–98; defined, 14; dramatic conventions of, 6, 15, 21–24; environment as theme in drama, 24, 25, 28, 70, 76, 91, 98; environment onstage, 21, 26, 51–52, 55, 73, 77, 78, 88–89; epistemology in, 29; evolution as theme in drama, 79; evolution in histories of, 17; and expressionism, 5, 6, 55, 63, 70–71, 72–73, 82; and fiction, 15, 69; and film, 49, 82; gendered audience, 188–93; gender in, 6, 29–53, 182–83; ideology of, 6, 13, 14, 24, 27, 41, 62, 90; and language, 68; masks in, 64–67; and naturalism, 5, 6, 13, 16, 89 (*see also* Naturalism); and new realism, 82; objectification in, 21, 54, 75; and objectivity, 6, 15, 16, 19, 52, 53, 71, 72, 191, 192, 202; and perspective, 78, 117, 190–91; and photography, 12–13, 16, 24, 202 (*see also* Photography); pictorial dimension of, 16–18; and poetic theater, 100–01, 106–08, 109, 110, 113, 114, 117, 120, 126, 127, 128, 131; and political theater, 21, 146–51, 152, 155, 161, 170; politics of, 24; and "poor theater," 82; privacy and power in, 17, 24–25, 28, 31–32, 33, 36, 47–48, 49, 54, 62, 71, 76, 80, 85, 92, 94, 95, 98, 191; and problem drama, 6; and public women, 39, 47; and reading, 49; and romanticism, 80; and science, 16, 91; and social critique, 53; sociological drama in, 70, 73, 91; staging of (mise-en-scène), 5, 17, 25, 55, 73–98; and symbolism, 82; technological determinism, 16–17; and television, 82; and theater of the absurd, 5, 81, 82 (*see also* Theater of the absurd); thesis play, 21–22; verisimilitude, 12, 14, 15, 55–56; visibility and power in, 6, 24, 28, 30, 31–32, 36, 41–42, 47–48, 54, 98, 193; vision in, 28, 191; "woman with a past" in, 6, 29–49 (*see also* "Woman with a past")
The Recruiting Officer (Farquhar): Berliner Ensemble production of, 152
Red Noses (Barnes), 169
The Return of Peter Grimm (Belasco), 18
Rhetoric of theater, 1–5
Rhinoceros (Ionesco), 81–82
Rice, Elmer, 11, 71–76; *The Adding Machine*, 6, 55, 63, 71–73; *Street Scene*, 6, 11, 55, 73–76, 79, 81, 83, 98; *The Subway*, 73
Riis, Jacob: *How the Other Half Lives*, 24
Roach, Joseph R., 2n.2, 56n
Roberts, Philip, and Malcolm Hay, 94n, 95–96
Robin Hood (pantomime), 175
Robins, Elizabeth, 8, 30, 44–49, 76; *The Convert*, 47; and suffrage movement, 44–45; *Votes for Women!* 44–49
The Rock (Eliot), 125
Rockaby (Beckett), 132
Roger Bloomer (Lawson), 72
The Romans in Britain (Brenton), 158
The Room (Pinter), 83
Rosmersholm (Ibsen), 66, 84
Rough for Radio II (Beckett), 133, 134–35
Rough for Theatre I (Beckett), 133n.19
Royal Court Theatre, 156, 183n, 198
Royal Shakespeare Company, 154n, 165n, 175, 180
The Ruling Class (Barnes), 169

St. James's Theatre, 38, 39
Saint Joan (Shaw), 129
Sardou, Victorien, 23
Saved (Bond), 6, 94–98
Savoyard opera, 179, 184
Sayers, Michael, 107, 130
Scarry, Elaine, 134, 138, 139n
Schneider, Alan, 10

Index

Schweickart, Patrocinio P., 51n, 192n.28
Scott, Clement, 39–40
Scott of the Antarctic (Brenton), 158
Scrimgeour, Gary, 32n
The Second Mrs Tanqueray (Pinero), 23, 24n, 28, 29–30, 36–42, 44n, 45
Semiotics of theater, 4–5, 117
The Serpent (Open Theater/Van Itallie), 160, 162
Sexuality and performance, 185–86
The Shadowy Waters (Yeats), 109
Shakespeare, William, 17, 18, 123, 181, 195n; as character in Bond's *Bingo*, 93, 94; *Hamlet*, 65n, 199; *King Lear*, 90; *Love's Labour's Lost*, 197; *Macbeth*, 14; modern staging of plays of, 10n.6; *Twelfth Night*, 65n
Shaw, George Bernard, 12, 24n, 36, 38n, 41, 46, 76, 89, 130, 195n; *Candida*, 44n; *Heartbreak House*, 90; *Major Barbara*, 35; *Man and Superman*, 44; *Mrs Warren's Profession*, 42–44; *Saint Joan*, 129
Shepard, Sam, 6, 29, 55, 82, 86–89, 93; *Angel City*, 87; *Buried Child*, 86; *Curse of the Starving Class*, 86, 88, 89; *Fool for Love*, 86; *Tooth of Crime*, 86–87, 88; *True West*, 86, 89; *La Turista*, 86
Shiubhlaigh, Maire Nic, 111
Sidnell, Michael J., 107, 121n
The Silver Box (Galsworthy), 30–33, 35, 47, 74, 95
Simon, Neil, 82
Sinfield, Alan, 157n, 167n
Sizwe Bansi is Dead (Fugard, Kani, and Ntshona), 194
The Skin Game (Galsworthy), 33–36
Socialist drama, 13
Sociological drama. *See* Realism in theater: sociological drama in
Soyinka, Wole, 8, 194–204; *The Bacchae of Euripides*, 195; *Camwood on the Leaves*, 195; *Death and the King's Horseman*, 195; *Kongi's Harvest*, 195; *The Lion and the Jewel*, 8, 194–204; *Opera Wonyosi*, 195; *A Play of Giants*, 195
Speaight, Robert, 126n, 127
Spectator. *See* Audience; Poetic theater: and audience; Political theater: and audience; Realism in theater: and audience
Spender, Stephen, 108, 122
Spine (in Method acting), 58, 59, 62, 87
Split Britches, 183
Stage Society, 42
Staging (mise-en-scène). *See* Poetic theater: staging of; Political theater: staging of; Realism in theater: staging of
Stanislavski, Constantin, 6, 10n, 13, 31, 56, 57, 58, 59, 60, 93, 124n.14, 149, 150; *An Actor Prepares*, 56n
States, Bert O., 2n.1, 3n, 4, 26n, 51, 112
Stoppard, Tom: *Jumpers*, 143–46, 197
Storey, David, 12, 14, 53, 82
Strange Interlude (O'Neill), 63, 64, 67–68, 69
Strasberg, Lee, 56, 58, 63n
A Streetcar Named Desire (Williams), 59, 63
Street Scene (Rice), 6, 11, 55, 73–76, 79, 81, 83, 98
Strindberg, August, 54, 63, 66, 68
Styan, J. L., 15n
Subtext (in Method acting), 60, 62, 65, 68, 85n
The Subway (Rice), 73
Sullivan, Arthur: and W. S. Gilbert, 183
Super-objective (in Method acting), 58, 149
Surrealist theater, 21
Sweeney Agonistes (Eliot), 107, 124n.13
Symbolism, 13
Symboliste theater, 21, 111
Symons, Arthur, 103, 104, 105, 116
Synecdoche, in realistic stage production, 26n
Szondi, Peter, 18n

Tango Palace (Fornes), 187
Teatro Campesino, 148
Television, 8, 9, 194
Terry, Ellen, 30
That Time (Beckett), 132
Theater of images, 13
Theater of the absurd, 13, 81, 91, 145. *See also* Realism in theater: and theater of the absurd
Théâtre Libre, 19. *See also* Antoine, André
Theatre Workshop: *Oh, What a Lovely War*, 169
Therborn, Göran, 146n.2
Thesis play, 21–22, 155
Thomas, Dylan: *Under Milkwood*, 195
Threepenny Opera (Brecht), 195
Three Sisters (Chekhov), 12–13, 25, 194, 202
Toller, Ernst, 63
Tooth of Crime (Shepard), 86–87, 88
Top Girls (Churchill), 187
Torture and theater, 133–34, 134n, 138–39, 142

Traverse Theatre (Edinburgh), 159
Treadwell, Sophie: *Machinal*, 63, 72
Trifles (Glaspell), 49–53, 192
True West (Shepard), 86, 89
Trumpets and Drums (Berliner Ensemble), 153
La Turista (Shepard), 86
Turner, Victor, 125n
Twelfth Night (Shakespeare), 65n
Tynan, Kenneth, 156

Ubersfeld, Anne, 2n.2, 4, 105n.2
Ubu Roi (Jarry), 104
Uncle Vanya (Chekhov), 66
Uncommon Women and Others (Wasserstein), 182
Under Milkwood (Thomas), 195

Vakhtangov, Eugene, 56
Van Itallie, Jean-Claude: *The Serpent*, 160, 162
Van Laan, Thomas, 85n
Vendler, Helen, 118n
Vian, Boris: *The Empire Builders*, 81
Vinegar Tom (Churchill), 158
Votes for Women! (Robins), 44–49
Vuillard, Édouard, 12n

Wagner, Richard, 117
Waiting for Godot (Beckett), 81, 82, 88, 90, 131, 132, 133n.19, 134, 143, 145
Walkley, A. B., 19, 20
Wardle, Irving, 163
Wasserstein, Wendy: *Uncommon Women and Others*, 182
Waste (Barker), 46n
Weapons of Happiness (Brenton), 158
Webster, John, 198n.4
Wedekind, Frank, 63
Well-made play, 23–24, 25. *See also* Realism in theater: dramatic conventions of
What Every Woman Knows (Barrie), 29
What Where (Beckett), 133, 136, 142

Whitaker, Thomas R., 3, 127n, 144–45
White, Edgar, 53
Whitelaw, Billie, 138, 139n
Whittington, Dick. See *Dick Whittington and His Cat*
Who's Afraid of Virginia Woolf? (Albee), 81
Wilcox, Leonard, 88n
The Wild Duck (Ibsen), 25–27, 28
Wilde, Oscar, 40; *An Ideal Husband*, 30, 39; *Lady Windermere's Fan*, 30; *The Picture of Dorian Gray*, 1
Wiles, Timothy J., 82n
Wiley, Catherine, 43n
Wilkie, Roy, 177n
Williams, Raymond, 17n, 72n, 73, 147n
Williams, Tennessee, 27, 69, 87, 96; *A Streetcar Named Desire*, 59, 63
Wilson, August, 53, 82
Wilson, Robert, 7, 103, 194
Winterset (Anderson), 76
The Woman (Bond), 93
"Woman with a past," 6, 29–49, 50, 83; as actress-like, 34, 37–38, 40, 47–48
Workers' theater, 148
The Workhouse Donkey (Arden), 153
The Worlds (Bond), 93, 94n
Worsley, T. C., 153
Worth, Katharine, 102n, 133n.19
Worthen, W. B., 20n, 56n, 189n
Wright, Elizabeth, 152n.4

Yeats, W. B., 7, 20, 100, 102, 103, 104, 105, 107, 108–19, 121, 122, 123, 124, 130, 131, 133, 141; *At the Hawk's Well*, 108, 110–19; *The Cat and the Moon*, 133n.19; *The Death of Cuchulain*, 118; *Deirdre*, 109; *The Dreaming of the Bones*, 116; *The Hour-Glass*, 111; *On Baile's Strand*, 109; *The Shadowy Waters*, 109

Zinman, Toby Silverman, 87n
Zola, Émile, 13, 15–16, 17, 53, 73, 91

Compositor:	Huron Valley Graphics, Inc.
Text:	10/13 Palatino
Display:	Palatino
Printer:	Braun-Brumfield, Inc.
Binder:	Braun-Brumfield, Inc.